My Life through My Dresses –

Growing Up Socialist

MARINA BERKOVICH

A Journey of a Recovering Idealist Series

Author Photograph by Jennifer Ziegelmaier, Naples, FL
Illustrations by Alla Karagodova, Estero, FL

Archway Publishing books may be ordered through booksellers or by contacting:

Archway Publishing
1663 Liberty Drive
Bloomington, IN 47403
www.archwaypublishing.com
1 (888) 242-5904

ISBN: 978-1-4808-6241-8 (sc)
ISBN: 978-1-4808-6242-5 (hc)
ISBN: 978-1-4808-6243-2 (e)

Library of Congress Control Number: 2018906841

Print information available on the last page.

Archway Publishing rev. date: 07/10/2018

Contents

Foreword

Marina Berkovich writes her memoir as an authentic, intimate, deeply courageous and moving personal account, accessible to all readers, regardless of their background. It is written in the easy-going style of a wide-eyed innocent girl relating, with an affinity for detailing, the tensions and fears of being isolated as a young Jewish child in the Soviet Union. She weaves her miniature epics of personal survival into a wise and compassionate story of historical value, adding a new dimension to our understanding of Russian history.

Marina's was a life of hardships, loneliness and misery, without any promising options. The essence of her memories are live snapshots, buildings and streets, interior colors and smells, and details of her uniform, the fabric, the threads, the fit, and what it represented in her daily life. Incredulous as some of these details might seem, this is a trailblazing portrayal of hot rage and cool analysis of multiple intersecting events. It is also a vivid picture of how emotional pain can lead to personal triumph. As she packs for her somehow miraculous escape from the USSR, little step by little step, Marina makes sense of the dark and dangerous years she spent growing up in a country drowning in turmoil.

This gripping memoir will keep you spellbound. Once you start reading this captivating story, you will be unable to stop until the end.

Hélène Gaillet de Neergaard
March 2018

From the Author

Completing this book was a process way more serious than I initially imagined.

It took decades to arrive at the manuscript the way you will be reading it. My life thus far, some of which was lived in the dresses I wrote about, has been an unpredictable journey of challenges, heartbreaks, setbacks and perseverance. A lot of it will seem foreign to you. Many of you will think it's a story of survival. At some junctures it was. I want you to understand what it was like to live under the yoke of Soviet socialist government, within the dysfunctional system that raised dysfunctional human beings. I was growing up in the country of denial and in the city of denial. Majority of westerners, fortuitously, do not need to undergo the kind of heartbreak and loss of irreplaceable years that comes from the inevitable disillusionment severely brainwashed people experience.

I wrote this for my dear family, especially my maternal grandparents, my mother and my daughter. Blood family we strive to be away from while we are young becomes preciously irreplaceable as we mature. We can either learn this truth as a family, or each on our own. With eternal gratitude to my two true teachers, Olga Porfirievna Krivoschapova, who inspired me to love and cherish my native language, and Geoffrey Summerfield, my English professor, who kept telling me I am a writer even when my English was still in a zygote stage. They have departed decades ago, but not from me. I thank all people who entered my life and left a mark – good or bad. I am not a sum of all your marks. I am the exponential result of your combined marks.

I thank everyone who has ever heard me speak about writing a book.

My readers and editors – my friend and neighbor Eva Huff for fearlessly suffering through my very first raw draft; my first editor Carole Greene for setting me on the manuscript transmutation track; the traveling Elise Sewall, my first beta reader of my own generation; and the refined Helene de Neergaard without whose insightful wisdom I'd still be stuck on reediting page thirteen.... Each of you gave me motivation and confidence to undertake the next step and thus it is a better book than the one I had then. I thank you. Accolades to my wonderful illustrator Alla Karagodova, who gave my book the look I visualized. The grand ovation is reserved for my maestro, my Renaissance man, my husband Alexander Goldstein, without whom I am not whole, with or without my dresses.

When I was a little girl and believed in fairy tales, I secretly dreamed of becoming a writer. I thank you for being in my dream.

Dress 1

My Striped Onesie

When I was a thirteen-month-old baby, I knew no fairy tales. My crib stood by the doorway of the first of our two adjacent rooms. The warm yellow light of the front room was what I saw immediately after I awoke that night. In a green-and-white-striped terry cloth onesie, I pulled myself up with both hands, leaned over the crib's banister, and saw Babushka's broad back. She was a bit shorter than Garrik; her head was blocking his face as he repeatedly hit her on the head with his fist. They were both yelling, so I screamed too. Stamping my feet on the crib floor, I let out, "Nooooooo! Nyeeeet!" Then everything went dark as the door slammed shut and, with it, the tunnel into my first memory.

Mama was working that evening, but even if she had been at home, I doubt she could have stopped them. Babushka suffered a debilitating stroke and never truly recovered. Garrik continued to live with us a couple more years, even after Mama divorced him. Grandpa was released from prison by the time Garrik finally moved on, and then we became a family of four again—this time, my maternal grandparents, Mama, and me.

Babushka could not move around much after that unforgettable night, so to keep me by her side and out of mischief, she told me countless fairy tales and stories about herself and people she knew. I soon knew all her stories and all her people. I loved hearing her talk about them over and over until I became the keeper of Babushka's stories and felt as if I knew them myself.

I understood a lot of difficult things prematurely because Babushka was straightforward and honest with me when we were alone. By the time I was about two and a half, I knew that Mama was only married to Garrik long enough to have me, but they'd known each other since their early childhood days in the center of Kiev. Born a decade before the Great Patriotic War, they lived as children in a beautiful old building that had a name in addition to its address. *Dom Moroza*, the Frost Building, was Grandpa's way of referring to it. Mama and Babushka were better educated and pronounced it properly, *Dom Morozova*, meaning the building of its prerevolutionary owner, kupetz (merchant) Morozov.

Mama; her older brother, Haim; and Garrik were all born there during the severest Ukrainian famine of the 1930s. In the late summer of 1941, both families evacuated, barely escaping the Nazis. Mama's family was able to return to Kiev after the war; Garrik's went to Riga. Then some of my maternal family settled nearby Garrik's, and my parents were reintroduced as unmarried adults. Mama was twenty-eight and Garrik thirty. They were considered over-ripened goods by the standards of their place and day, especially Mama. Garrik dreamed of returning to Kiev, so he proposed, and Mama accepted him fast, as she made all her major decisions without considering consequences. Yet she always made sure to tell me in her best maternal voice, "If I did not marry him, you would not be here."

In my early life, that did the trick, and I shut up.

Before my birth, my uncle Haim; his wife, Zina; and their four-year-old daughter, Lorachka, also lived with Babushka (Grandma) and Dedushka (Grandpa) in the pretty wooden building of my childhood. It was built before the revolution for just one family, and since, it has been home to many. It had an outhouse for a bathroom, a stone oven cut into our front-room wall, and cold water hand-pumped to our second-floor kitchen corner. The overcrowding that my imminent birth assured finally entitled Haim's bunch to a room of their own. They moved into one room in the communal apartment in the Pechersk neighborhood, had my cousin Stella four years later, and at last were entitled to a larger, independent-living apartment in a new building with an elevator. In the meantime, our nineteenth-century wooden two-story was demolished, and our family unit of four moved to a low-grade Khruchshev five-story temporary housing. That was in 1965. Khruchshev five-stories were long, poorly planned, and badly constructed. Soon, the Soviet citizens dubbed them "Khruchshev dumps," or *khruchshebas* in Russian slang. People still live in them now, some fifty years later.

Garrik held out for a room of his own, refusing to move out earlier, for if he had, he would have lost his coveted Kiev residency *propiska*, to the joy of my revenge-seeking mama. Soviet residency meant a stamp of efficient, bureaucratic, totalitarian control in every passport, an effective way to monitor and constrict Soviet citizens' movements. Garrik would not have been able to stay in Kiev without this stamp, and he was patient and persistent, coming home to sleep every night even though he would have been welcomed in many other places. He gave Mama no reason to evict him for the abandonment she wished she could have used.

While still under one roof, my parents fought constantly. Their scathing arguments often made them both violently insane. Once, while bathing me in a green enamel tub, Mama poured scalding water, direct from the steaming kettle straight off the coals in the in-the-wall oven, onto me. My two-year-old skin burned in several places, right through to the meat of my right foot. I proudly sported a huge blister, my badge of battlefield honor, showing it off to my day care playmates the next morning until I accidentally punctured it. That, I believe, was my first episode of showmanship, and brief as it was, I liked stardom immediately.

Garrik made Mama angry and violent. I was the court's witness at their divorce to confirm that.

After, Garrik took me to Riga to meet his mother. Grandma Gershanovich reprimanded me for everything, scaring me into peeing onto her couch. I cried loudly, yet she won, because she screamed even louder. We never met again. I don't even know her name. I have never seen her picture. My paternal grandfather, Michail Gershanovich, died before my birth, and I was named after him with a letter *m*. Mama would have totally hated me as a Misha, a name she hissed out with venom. I was, at a minimum, happy to be her girl.

"I named you after a song," Mama often said, and she sang "Marina" to me. Singing with Mama became my favorite together time. My adults—Mama, Grandma, and Grandpa—hated Garrik, and eventually so did I. All I had of him was my weird last name and the looks I could not relate to.

Later in my life, when I was around thirty and living in the United States, I ran into a woman Garrik used to know.

"I dated a Garrick Gershanovich," she told me dreamily as soon as she heard I was from Kiev.

I had always known that with his mother's encouragement, Garrik never stopped dating, even while he was still married to Mama, even before he beat Grandma. I waited for details.

"We had such good times together," she went on. "We just never knew what to do with the babe he schlepped everywhere in a stroller," complained my new acquaintance, solicitous for my sympathy.

"I am the baby from that stroller," I said simply. She concocted a quick, cockamamy contradiction as I sat speechless, embarrassed for her, the woman who my cheating father schlepped me to while Mama was working. I never got to know my inconsiderate, son-of-a-bitch father. Yet all those years later, this woman was still in awe of him. It made me question my interpretations of my memories.

My severe, super-gorgeous aunt Zina liked him and was not on speaking terms with Grandma. Zina never visited our *khruchsheba* on Batiy Mountain. Whenever Uncle Haim dropped by, he hid his whereabouts from his wife. My family asked me, a truthful girl of four, five, six, and older, to lie to my cousins, should they ask. I never liked lying, so I disliked my uncle Haim. I also disliked him because he always made Grandma cry. I sensed that he must have known how much I disliked him and that he disliked me even more because to him, just as to Mama, Grandpa, and Grandma, I was Garrik.

Before the war, Garrik was Haim's playmate and a known Dom Morozova abuser of the gullible. Three of them in the same class resided in that building—Garrik, Haim, and Syoma. Syoma died in Babiy Yar on the first day of the massacre. Babushka told me about it often. Not the details, I was then too young for the details, but she spoke like all the Kievans, with matter-of-fact finality. We never said "died in Babiy Yar." We said "went to Babiy Yar" because that day, Kiev Jews walked to that ravine in a long procession, streaming from every building, every yard, deceived into the hope of being resettled but instead united in the common Jewish doom behind the barbed wire in that place of horror. Daily reminders of people who went there were on the minds and tongues of people who lived through the war. Many knew of people who had perished, young and old, and mentioned names at family gatherings or when gossiping with the tattletales on the benches in front of every apartment building.

Mama never sat on these benches. "They are for gossipers and old *babas*," she'd say when I asked her why she never spent time there with our neighbors. I knew they always discussed her when she walked to the building from the streetcar stop out front. They'd even talk about her in my presence. Petite, beautiful, slim, and shorter even than my grandparents, Babushka Riva and Dedushka Abrasha, Mama was my heroine then. The more the neighbors judged her looks and lifestyle, the more I disliked them and wanted to become like her. Mama had short brown hair, lighter and not as curly and resistant to styling as mine. At first glance, she did not even look like me, but our brown eyes were exactly the same shape and shade. The moments when I caught my own reflection in Mama's eyes were the happiest of my childhood.

Dress 2

The One My Mama Made for Me

When I was so young that fairy tales were my only reality, I was proud of my mama and loved her more than anyone in the world.

Mama was a very elegant dresser then. She learned to sew well and made most of my clothes for me. A dressmaker made hers. We visited her dressmaker sometimes to order a new dress or for a fitting. Mama's dressmaker, a person much more revered than engineers and schoolteachers, had a posh, well-appointed, spacious apartment. She'd seat me on a comfortable, soft couch and surround me with pillows of all shapes and colors, so that I would not move. Then she'd hand me a huge book with marvelous animal pictures. Before I learned to read, I already new about dinosaurs, Darwin, and the orders of animals. I also learned that women are mean and cruel from hearing them compliment each other's looks and then make completely unflattering comments as soon as competition left the room, right in front of me, a gaping, naive girl. Both lessons, though somewhat mixed up in my head, were equally important. We lived in a dog-eat-dog world, and like everyone, I had to accept it.

Mama's dressmaker lived way down our Batiy Mountain, in the center of Kiev, near Krasnoarmeyskaya (Red Army) street. This was our former neighborhood, and we missed it. Mama and I would stroll past the Morozov building, as beautiful as the nearby Kiev Opera and Ballet Theater. Only a few buildings from the prerevolutionary period of great architecture, good taste, and ample resources still stood in Kiev. Soviet architecture was full of *khruchshebas*, and I wished my family was allowed to return to the Morozov building.

I felt as if I'd grown up there too. Babushka's vivid storytelling placed me there with little Mama and Haim. Mama also loved to reminisce, so it was as if I myself were seated on the low windowsill of the huge window in their second-floor communal apartment on that cold, dark winter evening in 1938 when the Black Crow, the feared Stalin-era automobile, pulled up to arrest Syoma's parents. Cheka, a precursor to the KGB, made people vanish without a trace into the Gulag, which was still known during my childhood days only through adults' whispers.

"Maybe best not to tell Mama what I'm telling you now," Grandma warned me whenever sharing some information with me prematurely.

"Why not?" I'd ask.

"Trust me this time," Grandma would say, "and I promise to explain when you get older."

Trusting Grandma implicitly did not cancel my curiosity. In fact, it piqued it. I always wanted to know more.

"What happened to Syoma when he walked to Babiy Yar?" I asked once, catching Grandma off guard, as we rested side by side in her bed during one of the many rest breaks she needed.

"His grandfather probably took care of him the way he did after his daughter was repressed," Grandma answered, choking on imminent tears. I already knew that the icky word *repressed* described the arrests made during the cult-of-Stalin times, before I was born, so by adding the bits of information together, I surmised that Syoma's grandfather, a legless World War I veteran, took care of his grandchildren—Syoma and his older sister, the beautiful Asia—after their parents were driven away in the Black Crow never to be seen again. Then the legless grandfather "walked" his grandchildren to Babiy Yar.

"Babushka," I asked, "the legless man did not actually have to walk to Babiy Yar, did he? Couldn't somebody drive him?"

"Not that day, *kitzele*, my kitten," Babushka said. "When you are older, I'll take you to see what's left of them all."

Grandma never took me anywhere after we moved up the mountain. Her immobility worsened, and she rarely left the apartment. She barely walked from room to room. We had no telephone then, and thus I became Grandma's last girlfriend. She often forgot how young I was, telling me many things before I was old enough to understand, sharing secret thoughts with me that have dominated my inner world since. She treated me as an equal woman of experience.

"I had your mother at the hospital," she told me. "She was my only child born at the hospital. When we came home, Haim said, 'You brought me a *lyalya*.' And so that's how your mama became Lyalya, a Ukrainian doll for a boy who loved playing with dolls."

"What was Mama's name before she became Lyalya?" I asked.

"We named her Fanny, after Grandpa's mom. We all had to change our names during the Great Patriotic War. But we always name after the dead," said Grandma. "You are named after Michael. Haim we named after my father, Haim-Srul, who died right after the revolution. Fanny Utka did too. It was a very terrible time." Grandma sighed and drifted off into one of the many endless Ukrainian songs of lament she loved.

Mama and Haim spoke Ukrainian when they were little. Babushka brought in a Ukrainian peasant woman, Marusia. She lived with them in their half room in the Morozov communal apartment. Women were still hiring help then, a custom from before the advent of postrevolutionary women's emancipation turned women into do-it-all-alone creatures of Soviet stealth.

Haim was fourteen months older than Mama. He survived meningitis when he was just a baby. Everything "best" was forever reserved for Haim by the family. His numerous shortcomings were always overlooked and forgiven, as if different rules applied to him.

The early 1930s were very difficult times in Ukraine. That famine was so widespread that many villages were completely wiped out. Always known as Golodomor it is now renamed Holodomor by Ukrainians in a meaningless effort to disassociate from the Russian word *golod* (starvation). As if renaming events can retroactively affect their outcome or resurrect the dead. In the 1930's Grandpa Abrasha's countless relatives moved into Kiev from their Jewish shtetlach, Yiddish settlements where they had to live by order of tsars for generations. Ukraine had always been the breadbasket of the Russian Empire, but when the USSR needed feeding, famine was harshest there. Collectivization expropriated everything for the revolution, including the seedlings for next year's planting. Farmers' children and pregnant women died first with their hunger-swollen bellies exploding.

"It was easier in large cities then, so everyone came through our room," Grandma shared with me. "Grandpa worked sorting vegetables in a store basement. It helped. He had first access to discards, and we used all of them. You know, there were so many of us, with his five siblings and their families as well as my mama and sisters." I usually insisted she'd go through everyone's names and where and when they were born, so I soon learned about all of them and thus became the only historian of my very numerous family.

When relatives moved into Kiev in the early 1930s, they slept everywhere in the Utkas' room in Dom Morozova— on the floor, under the table, on the table, even inside the only bathtub of the communal apartment. Abrasha helped them find housing in the nearby Solomenka neighborhood. Solomenka was also the name of the street leading to the top of Batiy Mountain, where we now lived and I attended preschool.

Down the mountain, where my relations settled before the war, was our district's public bathhouse. We sometimes went there to bathe with other women. Grandpa's sister Sonia lived near the bathhouse. She was diminutive, skinny, and dark. She always wore starched white lace collars that she made and stitched onto her dark dresses. She gave us tea and jam when we visited her. Grandpa always brought treats and necessities for his three war-widowed sisters. He was committed to them and his sickly older brother, Iosif. Grandpa loved all the Milihiker girls—Raya, my babushka Riva, and Polina—as he did his super diminutive mother-in-law, Haya, the only person of her generation I met who witnessed the pogroms of 1918.

When I was four or five, Babushka needed a new dress and made some trips with Mama and me in a taxi to the dressmaker. After one of those trips, when the driver had been too drunk to reason, I overheard Grandma make a stray remark about Garrik's alcoholism. "It just is not common for our men," Grandma said. "They are not Ukrainian or Russian drunks. They give us a bad name."

"Shh," Mama said, stopping Grandma's rare moment of speaking about my father's alcoholism in Russian. Whenever they realized I was listening, Mama, Grandpa and Grandma would speak a language I could not understand.

"What are you saying?" I'd interrogate them when that would happen.

They would exchange conspirators' smiles and make up lies, saying, "We are speaking French." I believed that for a while, but another time, forgetting they'd said French before, they told me they were speaking English. I then had proof they were lying. Yet they were teaching me to be truthful. The contradictions did not coexist well in my head.

By the time I could tell the languages apart, they'd say they were speaking German. I believed they knew many languages until I learned they were actually speaking Yiddish, the language of the Pale of Settlement Jewry, a language they did not want me to learn for really good reasons. I'd already begun to understand these reasons, even though they were unjust and hurtful.

It was during a tug-of-war over a toy with a preschool playmate that I first heard the horrible word *kike*. Everyone laughed when he called me that and even more when I broke into a crying fit. From the get-go it was me against them in my four-years-old group. I was immediately offended by their unity against kikes. I ran out the front gate all the way home, alone, crying and yelling.

I demanded answers as soon as I saw Grandma. "Why am I a kike? They are laughing at me. Kike is bad! I don't want to be a kike. I want to be like them."

"You are not like them," said Grandma, smoothing my unruly curls with her broad palm. "You are very special. Our very special girl. Only our special girls walk home all alone without fear."

Mama, too, happened to be at home that memorable Saturday. Our country still worked on a six-day work-week. Mama, who resumed her electrical engineering work when I was only three months old, was seldom at home during the day. I'd always been in day care. The majority of Soviet moms worked, and few grandmothers were able to leave their own work to take care of grandkids. People of working age who did not work were labeled freeloaders and taunted.

"He who does not work does not eat," exclaimed the watchful neighbors who loved to use the common Soviet slogans while monitoring everyone's business. Babushka became an invalid following Garrik's beating and so did not work. Before the war, she carried and raised babies. During the war and for some years after, she was a librarian. She told me stories of sneaking old newspapers home during the war years in the Ural Mountains so that she could line her children's shoes and they could go to school. She also cut up the newspapers for their notebooks. Haim and Mama could write between the newspaper print lines in their only wartime notebooks and were better off than many.

"We were so lucky to have newspapers then. There was such shortage of everything—food, medications, milk. People forgot the war so soon. We never forget. You'll remember it too. Promise me."

I promised, and we sang her favorite wartime and revolutionary songs until Grandpa and Mama returned home, bringing food up our mountain from the center of Kiev. We sat down to supper together.

Grandma could not wait in food lines on her feet even at our neighborhood store, directly below us, in our *khruchsheba*. The food supply in our old neighborhood and in the early 1960s was far better than when I was at last old enough to actually stand in food lines myself. In those old neighborhood days, before Garrik's beating, Babushka went to the stores when the lines first formed for milk, bread, and vegetables, early enough so she could be nearer the counter. Then she'd prep food, feed the family, clean, and take care of me. Grandpa took a lot of that load after his release, before he found a steady job.

My first ever car ride was when I was about three and Grandma hired a driver to visit Grandpa in prison. Grandpa was a stranger to me, coarse and rough, and I was not sure why I should kiss him. He was released before my parents' divorce, and after he returned, he took very good care of me and never lost his temper. I accepted him and soon after loved him unconditionally as the only man and the real father figure in my life. I was never told exactly why he was imprisoned. I learned it from dribs and drabs of the words that escaped adults' mouths at various times. I understood without having to be told that the secrets I was overhearing were to be kept within our family circle. There was danger in the air somehow. How did I understand it? I was a child of the USSR. We all had family secrets we were burdened with. Every single one of us.

Mama and Grandma often irked each other, so Grandpa's being with us was good for us all. He'd come home with special treats, like sunflower seeds, nuts, apples, and dates. He also brought home his side work—envelopes and paper bags to glue on endless winter evenings at the dining table. He let me help. Soon I loved Grandpa very much. I'd wait by the door till he came home with *avos'kas*, net shopping bags, hanging from his strong hands, exposing the food.

"*Lyuba moia*, my love," he'd greet me. "Fill the tub with cold water, quick. I got something good," he'd say, but already I would have spotted several fish, silently gasping for breath, tails sticking out above the newspaper they were wrapped in. Soon carp or catfish would be busily swimming in our bathtub, wanting to escape, and I would watch them resisting their fate.

"Let them swim until they sleep," Grandpa usually said, wanting to spare me from understanding death. I knew that the fish were destined to sleep tonight so we could eat tomorrow. That was my grandfather's life's essence. He was first and foremost a survivor, and all his stories and lessons were about survival and how a human being must prepare for it every day, just in case. I was not permitted to ask Grandpa why he'd been imprisoned. So many people in our building had been to prison. It was not a question I asked them either. It was a way of life then. It was a good thing, my grandparents agreed, that in the last prison Grandpa had learned the skill of bookbinding. He now went from one institution to another, as everyone wanted his services. He brought home accounting books and teachers' journals to be bound, or rebound, and he taught me how to make flour glue and paper strips and how to thread the thick needle and use a thimble to help push it through thick spots. I think I was a duly apprenticed bookbinder and envelope gluer at the age of five.

"Just in case, *lyuba moia*—one never knows," Grandpa would say lovingly when I finished my work at the table for the evening. "One never knows."

Mama was still studying sewing then and made me my dresses from the remnants of fabric her dressmaker scrapped. Sometimes she remade one of her old dresses for me. I thought that I looked best when in Mama's remade dresses.

"Pity you look nothing like us," Mama said one afternoon, dressing me up in a brown velveteen dress with a yellow bow for the photographer. I was five then and wanted to cry.

"But you are mine regardless," Mama added quickly as she hurried me. She changed my outfits several times throughout the session and hugged me intermittently. The photographer friend she brought to our apartment flirted with her, and she flirted back. No one had taken any photos of me since Garrik had left us, and I was disturbed by this stranger giving me orders and making Mama behave this silly. Those photos captured my state quite well.

A parade of strange men went though our home, but instead of getting used to the idea of man hanging around Mama, I protested their presence. They were taking her away from me, from us, breaking up our family of four. I learned to employ Mama's deceptive tricks, and she deservingly began calling me an actress. After a while, the only time she was compassionate was when I was actually very sick. Or so I believed.

One of my Mama-made dresses then was a short, scratchy wool dress of a pale-lapis color that flared over the stockings I wore pinned to my undergarments. It had long sleeves that I grew out of almost immediately. The back had to be buttoned by an adult. I was already very independent, but since my arms did not reach all the way back there, I tolerated help so that I could sport my favorite dress ever. The front was the dress's best part—a huge pocket spanned from one side seam to the other with an appliqué of a train, three or four cars with a locomotive. The locomotive was cut out of similarly scratchy wool scraps of other colors. I loved this dress. My mama was the best of all mothers I knew, and she was mine. Mama was the only one I loved as much as my dress that winter.

We had new Batiy Mountain neighbors two floors above us, Dora and her daughter, Nadyusha, who was just two years older than me. I was allowed to play with Nadyusha, in either her apartment or ours. We'd set up in the tiny hallway on cold winter evenings, as I had no dedicated play space. Nadyusha was my very first friend. Her mom was a gorgeous, stately former folk dancer who moved like a queen. She was married to Mikhail Borisovich Romansky, a short, ugly documentary filmmaker, formerly of Odessa Film but now at Kievnauchfilm. Mikhail's films were full of mystery and magic and explained science for people who did not yet know much about it, like Nadyusha and me. Mikhail's intelligence exponentially exceeded his miserable disposition, but everyone knew Dora did not marry him for his intelligence but for his status and connections. Babushka said so. Dora worked at the Central Kiev Pharmacy and could get anything for anyone for lots of money. At the time, in a country filled with dire poverty, no one got anything without lots of money or lots of connections. Everyone was sick or knew sick people, so everyone wanted to be connected to Dora. Our entire building called Dora, Mikhail, and Nadyusha "three rich kikes," after "The Three Little Pigs" folktale. Except for when they needed Dora. That's how things were.

Mama, who had a legendary lack of connections and the social skills that encouraged them, was nonetheless Dora's bosom building acquaintance, to whom a key could be safely entrusted or a cup of flour borrowed from. Dora never came down just to socialize, but every time she came, my entire family jumped.

Then one day Grandpa was summoned to my day care on a winter day because I was sick. We took streetcar No. 8 to the polyclinic, a large medical office, the only one, in fact, for our entire district. We waited for several hours for the dentist assigned to our building to see me. My toothache was bad, but I could not imagine the part that lay ahead. I opened my mouth as the dentist requested and heard the word *extraction*. It meant nothing to me then. The large community dental room was filled with rows of dental chairs. Other patients sat in their chairs, mouths open, waiting for their turns, spitting blood and saliva into spittoons shared by two patients, each enduring his or her own suffering, commiserating with others mostly through moaning.

Grandpa held me down as my dental visit quickly became torture. No anesthetics were used. The pain I was going through was intolerable. I kicked the dentist, and he had the nurses and Grandpa strap me to the chair. Everyone yelled at me. I cried and choked on my vomit, saliva, tears, and blood. The tooth refused to come out, and when it finally was extracted, I was covered in a slime of spit and blood that dribbled all over the front of my locomotive dress.

Grandpa and I rode the six or seven streetcar stops back home in silence. The falling snow smeared tears and blood down my chin and underneath the dress. My pain stirred extra attention at home. Grandma compassionately permitted me to play with her pillboxes, which she'd never before permitted me to touch, as long as I sat in the corner of the hallway. My head ached, and I refused to change out of my ruined locomotive dress. Grandma did not insist. When Mama returned from work, she promised to read and sing to me before bed.

Grandma's plethora of pills had long fascinated me, and I was busy remixing them as I wanted when Dora popped in to borrow something.

"Lyalya!" she exclaimed dramatically as she entered. "Where are you headed to dressed so nicely?" I lifted my head instantly and caught Mama signaling to Dora rapidly in an attempt to silence her, her image reflected in the trifold mirror in front of me.

"Maybe you have a hot date tonight?" Dora teased, oblivious to Mama's struggles to cover up something.

I let out a loud, hopeless wail like a distraught seal I'd seen at Kiev Zoo. I was bereaved with pain more severe and incurable than the devilish tooth ordeal an hour ago.

"You promised to read and sing," I sobbed as Mama continued signaling behind my back to Dora, still unaware that her reflection exposed her treachery. She was deceiving me, and there was nothing I could do. Except cry long and loud until Grandma shuffled to my rescue.

"Lyalya, enough!" she commanded. "You are her mother. Do something to quiet her down."

So Mama solved this in Mama's way—she took me along on her date in my filthy locomotive dress. She hastily rinsed my face and hands before we left but left the rest of me sticky and slimy. The movie theater was cold, and my coat stayed on. After, Mama's date invited her to a café, and when we sat down, he said to me, "It is really warm in here. Wouldn't you like to take your coat off?"

Mama rushed in with "Don't!" but I'd already shed the coat. I sat there in my stained locomotive dress for the rest of their date, happily savoring vanilla ice cream with black currant syrup and sipping down a glass of sparkling lemonade. I was completely satisfied.

We never saw Mama's date again. Mama always said it was because I'd forced her into bringing me along in that filthy dress. I thought so myself for a very long time, because I went on trusting Mama, loving her unconditionally and being proud of her, even as she kept hurting me.

Babushka and Dedushka knew Mama's deceptive mind. She swore them to secrecy and lied to me numerous times, crushing my childish love and trust. Still, they kept her secrets, just as they kept Haim's. They were really good, protective parents to their children. Neither of their children inherited that trait.

I gradually learned to accept that I was the unwanted child of Garrik, the man who had destroyed Babushka's final years and all Mama's chances of marrying someone she could be happy with. Garrik visited me on my birthdays when I turned five, six, and seven and then never again. If he remembered me, I did not know. I began to hate him, like Mama did, vehemently and venomously. When I was nine, I overheard that he had another daughter, Anna. I did not wonder why it hadn't occurred to either of my parents to let me see my half sister. I felt as unwanted as they made me feel.

December 31 rolled around soon after that. Babushka gave Mama a twenty-five-ruble note to buy me a New Year's present.

"I'll buy her new bath towels," Mama said in that certain manner I already recognized as her pretending that I needed something so that she could actually have it.

"Bring her along and buy whatever she wants," Babushka insisted firmly. "Let her spend her money just as she wishes."

That was how Mama and I entered the fairyland of the Newlyweds store in the final hours of 1970. Stores like this one were closed to regular folks like us, but at year-end when they needed to fulfill and overfill their prescribed annual Socialist plan, the formalized commitment each organization made to the country or their republic and was held accountable for under the threat of imprisonment, they gave everyone access for a few hours. I wasn't allowed back inside that store until my final week in Kiev, years later.

I saw Anjelika the moment Mama and I stepped into the central hall. With pale-brown hair, vibrantly brown eyes, and red-and-white polka-dot clothes, she sat on the top shelf, priced at twenty rubles. She became my instant friend and the sister I never had. I overlooked all her manufactured imperfections. Cowlick, one arm softer than the other, a body too short for such a big head—who cared! When she was new, her dress and hat were gorgeous. As we both aged, Anjelika's wardrobe tore and wore out. Her shoes and panties disappeared. Her body got darker, not dirtier but darker, as if she was forced to sun under the scorching rays in summertime, just like I was. Anjelika's face never changed. It is still the same beautiful, youthful, round face I loved the moment I saw her looking at me through her brown glass eyes, inviting me to take her home. *You will never regret it,* her face told me. I never did.

Babushka and I played with Anjelika every winter and spring day of 1971. I pretended to be their schoolteacher and taught my pupils everything I was learning in class. I thought this idyll would last forever. Then, suddenly, after telling me thousands more stories, Babushka died on May 25.

We were alone in the front room, anticipating a very lazy first day of my summer vacation. It was five minutes before nine o'clock in the morning, and Grandpa had just left to make a dash down to the store for fresh bread. I was belly up on the couch in my undies, the top of my head toward Grandma, who was seated in the armchair by the back wall. I was reading aloud from the first pages of my new fourth-grade history textbook when she suddenly tried to call me. "Mar ..."

Her final sounds were her screeching my name before she succumbed to her second, this time fatal, stroke. I did not jump up quickly enough. Grandpa returned a moment later, as Grandma was sliding out of the armchair onto the floor, her last breath still audibly oozing out. I stood helpless, my book clutched to my bare chest, shivering from a sudden chill of knowledge: Grandma was dead.

Mama told everyone I was too young to attend funerals, persistently refusing to honor my pleas to go. She did not allow me to even take a final look or say farewell to the woman who had raised me. Overcome with her own grief, Mama suddenly felt the weight of the responsibilities her mother had shielded her from until now, and she blamed me for not helping Grandma in her final moments, as if I or anyone else could have revived her. I pitied Mama as all of this unfolded, even as she punished me by not letting me say my goodbyes. I was suddenly wiser than my mother that day. In fact, that was the day I became a mother to my mother.

After Grandma's body was no longer on the dining room table, countless relatives and friends from near and far gathered in our front room, around that table, bringing food and reminiscing about the bygone days. We draped the mirrors and the new TV we'd just leased with bed-sheets. No one explained to me why I could not watch the TV; they just ordered me not to. They did not explain the Jewish shiva calls of mourning to me. They thought I was too young, too stupid, too ... something. I have no idea what they thought. They did not tell me anything. Mama sent me to hang out with the street kids downstairs, as if nothing had happened, as if it were any other day.

I told the neighborhood kids about Grandma's death, and they spoke words of sorrow to me. Those words felt good; I needed to hear them. Why did my family not comprehend that?

Later that day, or maybe it was the next, Grandpa shared the story of his life with a level of detail that neither our visitors nor I would ever hear again. He spoke so vividly that I lived his life with him. My grandpa, Abrasha Utka, was born on a farm in 1904. He was barely schooled in the Jewish school he was allowed to attend for two winters, the maximum education permitted to a Jewish farm boy then. The start of school coincided with World War I. His oldest brother, known in Russian as Alexander, was already serving time in the Tsar's army, as the firstborn male. Abrasha hardly focused on learning. His hands were much needed at home, especially after his brother was killed at the front. He learned to read or write in Russian only after he married my grandmother. It was important to the Jewish people of the Pale to teach their boys to read only in Hebrew so they could learn the prayers and Torah. They had no idea their unstable world was about to collapse. 1917 brought on two revolutions, famine and disease. Abrasha's father, my great-grandfather Meir, died after a pogrom. His wife, my great-grandmother Fanny, of typhoid the following year. Their six living children were forced to fend for themselves. Abrasha walked some nine hundred miles to Donbass and spent two years working in a mine, crawling on his knees, strapped to the coal-laden wagonettes, pulling them up to the mine's surface. As soon as he turned sixteen, he volunteered for the Red Army and became an artillery man, shooting at the enemies from his *tachanka* wagon. He was demobilized in 1925 and returned to his family's home near Vinnitsa. His four sisters and remaining older brother lived nearby.

He met and married Grandma, whose family was by then destitute and impoverished, and they moved to Kiev. They lived there from 1929 to 1941. The war, revolution and starvation ravaged the country. Some of his family perished in Stalin's purges. When Hitler invaded, Grandpa was captured defending Kiev in August 1941. He was imprisoned in a Nazi POW concentration camp. His unfathomable story included escape from the camp, survival for over two years in plain sight of the Nazis in occupied Ukraine, and subsequent service in the Soviet Army culminating with hand-to-hand combat in the Reichstag. He loved life with all of its trials and hardships. I knew him as the best cook in our household and as a decorated World War II veteran, a status that entitled him to special distribution in food lines.

He was sixty-seven years old and said that he would not last long without his Rivka. Grandpa was a survivor first and foremost, wasn't he? Shortly after the funeral, while watering flowers around Babushka's fresh grave, Abrasha met a woman at the well in the Jewish quarter of the Berkovzy Cemetery, clear on the other end of town, about a half hour past Babiy Yar by electric trolley. The woman, Tamara, was getting water for the flowers on her husband's fresh grave. Grandpa and Tamara married soon and lived harmoniously together for twenty-one years, dying only a month apart. Grandpa went last, outliving every one of his relatives and friends of his generation.

When Grandpa announced his intent to move out shortly after meeting Tamara, Mama became outraged and cursed him. She'd assumed he would take over Grandma's duties, but Grandpa wished to live, not to cook, clean, and Marina-sit. They eventually forgave each other. Mama even warmed up to Tamara. And so did I. She was annoying with her lessons on manners and attitude, but she was as close to a lady as I knew in my childhood, weird and different from anyone else I knew. She cared that I become a lady someday, a challenge highly improbable for a girl of my circumstance. Yes, I soon liked Tamara a lot, because she believed in me even more than my grandma did.

In the summer Grandpa and Tamara would rent a dacha on the Kiev Sea, which was actually a water reservoir near an out-of-the-way, little-known town called Chernobyl. Their dacha was a sorry-looking shack, near a sorry-looking city, nothing like the palatial dachas of the Communist Party members that Mama and I would espy on our summer travels through Crimea.

Tamara was considered weird for being a health fanatic at a time when Soviet culture carried no appreciation for healthy living. We ate whatever was sold in the stores. Tamara shopped differently, always making sure she had fresh fruits and vegetables. She would juice various fruits and vegetables and used scrapers to peel them, teaching everyone in our clan to preserve maximum vitamin content. Health was the central focus of her days. She marched Grandpa to daily walks at Central Stadium, not far from where they lived in our old neighborhood. They circled the stadium daily in all weather. Despite regular exercise, Tamara frequently went into cardiac arrest. She was brought back to life numerous times by the skilled efforts of ambulance doctors who "shocked" her out of dying. I witnessed a few of these episodes, and each time I felt as if I were in a trance, helplessly watching Grandma die all over again.

When Mama and I were leaving the USSR, Grandpa asked me what to do with the savings book he kept in my name. He'd been depositing rubles into this account every month, so that I could have a wedding and a honeymoon someday. There were about 4,000 rubles at that time, equivalent to two years' worth of Mama's salary, and I could not take a kopek with me. "Just split it evenly between my two cousins," I told him, "my gifts for their honeymoons."

Grandpa honored my request, but by the time the girls were ready to use this money, perestroika was in full bloom. The Soviet banking system had devalued the Soviet currency, and my cousins never saw a kopek of that money either. I wish I had told Grandpa to take Tamara to Crimea for the summer and live it up. I don't think he had a honeymoon either time he married.

Dress 3

The Crimean Stripes

When I was a little girl, I never understood the much-talked-about benefit of Ukrainian countryside. I never liked to be surrounded by filth, dust, and despair—essentially the life of every village I visited. The countryside was certainly not beneficial for my mind. Except Crimea, which I thought was the best thing Ukraine had to offer.

Mama and Grandpa took me to Crimea several times on our paupers' budget when Mama's other summer plans for me did not commit me to the Ukrainian countryside nearest to Kiev. In Crimea we went to places few kids I knew had ever heard of. Plane travel was rare, and we stopped flying altogether after Grandma died. Train tickets in soft sleepers were hard to come by, and Mama's infamous lack of connections didn't help, so we usually traveled in the common car, also known as the hard sleeper. It had three bunks of hard sleeping shelves and no mattresses.

The hard-sleeper cars were full of strangers who snored, belched, and stuck their noses into our faces, food, and conversations. Hairy men wearing "family underpants,"

or boxer shorts to an American, and sleeveless undershirts
that needed changing some days ago strolled through the
car at all times of day on their way to and from the bathroom or the *tambur*, the place where train cars were joined
and where men smoked and drank. The men all stank of
sweat, stale beer, vodka, and dried, salted fish, either *vobla*
or *taranka*. Throughout the entire train ride, these strangers played dominos or cards, cursed, and banged dried
fish on the flip table or any other hard surface to soften it
so it could be consumed. They ceased banging only after
some loud Russian *baba* went off on them, shaming them
for their unfathomably creative cursing by reminding them
there were children on the train. The men would offer the
baba a shot of vodka, and everyone would quiet down for
the duration of the sweltering night, interrupted by snoring
and the conductor's calls at scheduled stops.

These Russian or Ukrainian *babas* were fearless. They
were used to dealing with men who constantly drank whatever and wherever they could. The Soviet Union was a ma-
triarchal society on many levels, from workforce leadership
to excessive numbers of single mothers. Women made the
world somehow functional and sang a lot to relieve stress.
Men drank themselves into stupors, cursed, and beat their
women. Each sex handled despair in their unique way.

When Mama and I arrived at our vacation destination, we would procure an illegal summer rental via some
unappetizing local woman with rooms to rent to summer
tourists. Usually more families than they let you know
were already living within those communal premises. Some
families would find a decent place to stay and return to it
many summers in a row. Mama and I went somewhere
new each time. We were willing to pay only the very lowest
rents, so our accommodations were always uncomfortable,

rarely clean, and never equipped with a bathroom. We were outhousers. We washed our faces with stale rainwater and shampooed our hair and bathed at the beach. We were what was known as "wild vacationers." We were not registered into any of the formal vacation houses, though Mama sometimes had to surrender her passport to our landlady in order to register us with authorities. Crimea was a Soviet border outpost, and patrols were not uncommon.

Sienna shampoo was probably made in Bulgaria or Czechoslovakia and was hard to get, but it was specially made for sea washing. All *dikari,* wild vacationers without bathing facilities, bathed with Sienna at the beach. We used our bottle very sparingly to last us the duration of our stay. I could have saved us more. Why use shampoo, when seawater was plentiful? We went to the beach twice a day, to build up health reserves for the rest of the year. Such a health month was a unique treat, though. Most children I grew up with just went to their grandparents' villages nearby Kiev or to Pioneer camps. Mama was ahead of her time.

When I was just two, Mama took me to Sochi. My uncle Haim; his wife, Zina; and their daughter, Lora, were vacationing there, and Mama decided we should join them unannounced. Most likely, we were unwelcome intruders. While we were walking in a park that first Sochi evening, a humongous pine cone separated from its tree and shattered a park lamp, making passersby scream. Mama and I left the very next day.

When I was four, Mama and I spent a month in Odessa—also not exactly Crimea, but close enough. I remember being frightened by a young bull chasing us home from the outdoor movies. We went to the movies almost every evening and watched whatever, eating warm boiled shrimp with traces of newspaper ink left by the hand-rolled bags it was sold in. All the locals sold shrimp or cow milk to vacationers to make a little cash. All the vacationers peeled and ate the tiny shrimp at the movies, lining the floor with stinky shell carpeting that would stick to my sandals and follow me home. The movie theater smelled like sea salt, beer, and vodka. It was dangerous to walk home alone. Drunken predators would specifically target women. Vacationers huddled together on those late-night walks, and strangers would make sure that unescorted women made it to the relative safety of their shacks for the night. The scary stories that vacationers spooked one another with on these late-night walks were our equivalent of horror films, a genre mostly disallowed by our culture.

When I was five, we went to the cradle of the Russian navy, Sevastopol. We were legal residents at a Crimean resort—our only experience of the kind. It was a tourist tent camp for moms with kids that lay in the shadows of the naval base, nestled amid the sand dunes. At the naval base store Mama was able to buy me two ready-made summer dresses—one to wear immediately, white with blue stripes, and one to grow into, white with green stripes. They were pretty, and all USSR girls wore the same dresses that and the following years. I felt unusually stylish because I finally looked like everyone else.

On a walk from the nightly outdoor movies, a cobra crossed our path. Mama screamed as loud as all other women, and even though I never saw the darn vermin, I instantly acquired a lifelong phobia. Or maybe it was because they kept saying in our sleeping tent, which held a hundred or so cots, that a woman and child can survive torture and rape but not a snakebite. Anyhow, if that was the worst thing about Sevastopol, the best was the

Sevastopol Panorama Museum. It contaminated me with a lifelong craving for understanding history.

The summer before Babushka's death, when I was nine, we went to Kerch. First Grandpa and I stayed in a huge, wonderful, old hotel room. Then Mama took over. Beaching with Mama meant burning to scars. Besides the beach, Kerch was a fascinating ancient city with salty drinking water, museums, climbs up the King Mithridates steps, and tours of the catacombs, where resistance fighters hid, fought off Nazis, and perished during World War II.

The year of Grandma's death I went with Grandpa to the biostation atop the Kara-Dag volcanic range for several days and observed dolphin studies. We then went down the mountain to Koktebel country, where tourists rented mountainside caves. Then Mama took over and brought me to Planerskoe, a settlement on the other side of the Kara-Dag range, famous for its writers' retreats. This trip became my favorite Crimean visit of all time. This was before Kara-Dag was designated as a national park, and semiprecious stones could still be found on the beaches. Millions of vacationers would comb through these stones and pick ones to take home. On clear days, Turkey's shores were visible across the Black Sea. I thought, while being roasted at the beach under Mama's strict orders not to move until brown, that this would be the closest I'd ever get to the mysterious "abroad."

I was entering my poetry age about then and was a huge admirer of Pushkin. He, too, sailed under the Kara-Dag's Golden Gate and was, just like me, curly haired, strange, misunderstood, unwanted. All right, many women wanted him, but that's different ...

Mama and I sat down on a beach bench once next to the then very famous Soviet poet Robert Rozhdestvensky.

After some time, he asked us to watch his belongings and sprinted toward the water. Mama chased after him, as he was still wearing his wristwatch. She returned confused and embarrassed: his watch was waterproof. Who'd ever heard of such a thing?

Another time, same bench, it was Yuri Senkevich, the host of *The Kino-Travelers' Club*, the only travel hour on Soviet TV. The entire country envied him. A military medical doctor, he was the only Russian to sail on the *Ra* and *Ra II* papyrus boats with the modern-day Norwegian Viking explorer Thor Heyerdahl. Senkevich, handsome and debonair, visited many a forbidden land and took us viewers with him during his shows. Everything was censored, of course, but what footage we got to see was exotic—Cuba, India, Egypt, Nigeria, the Congo, and more.

Aleksei Kapler, host of *Kinopanorama*, the only USSR TV program about film, also came to rest on "our" bench, throwing a quick hello once he got used to us.

The Koktebel region, with its legends, truths, and struggles, became the only place Mama and I returned to the following summer. I hiked daily. It was very safe in that out-of-the-way place—except for snakes, spiders, and potential falls off the cliffs, of course. Before I left and after I returned to our summer dacha, I drank the cool, sweet well water, storing it inside me like a camel. I climbed like a monkey, swam like a fish, and was unafraid of the dark, like a bat. I was an animal of nature.

Planerskoe's most famous resident ever was Maximilian Voloshin, originally from Kiev. He died in 1932, the same year Mama was born. After the Civil War of the 1920's, he setup a free home for poets and writers at the foot of Kara-Dag volcanic range. Voloshin's wind-etched profile on the Kok-Kaya formation that is facing Planerskoe was the subject of our particular fascination on one late afternoon beachwalk, when we noticed a beautiful woman exercising with her back to us. I remember her silhouette embraced by the vanishing sun inside an orange aura. "Yoga system," Mama said. *My mama is so smart,* I thought, having never heard of yoga before. *She knows many things.* We watched intently as the young woman took increasingly complex poses, standing on one foot, sliding, sitting, bending, and raising her leg to her ear. She wore a brightly colored pantsuit, so unlike the rest of us Soviet country bumpkins in our housedresses and panama hats. On her head she wore a turban straight out of *The Arabian Nights.* When she finished her yoga, untwisting herself from the knot she'd formed with her body, she elegantly shook out her towel and folded it neatly into a beach bag made of the same fabric as the rest of her exotic attire. Although she was quite a distance from us, when she shook the towel, something seemed odd all of a sudden, as if an illusionist's smoke screen had evaporated. Perhaps, her skin shook too much for a person that fit. Then she turned toward us, and as she came closer and closer, Mama told me she felt like she was watching a witch. At that moment I saw a very old, very wrinkled, and very familiar face—Maria Kapnist. The woman and Mama exchanged hellos and were soon chatting.

We met with Maria Kapnist practically every evening. If she wanted to talk, she did. We soon knew her story, which was then still kept hidden from the masses. She was nobility. Her Russian great-grandfather was Count V. V. Kapnist, a poet and an advocate against slavery in Russia in the early nineteenth century. Her Ukrainian lineage was from Zaporozhskaya Sech, a place on the Dniepr River to which runaway serfs escaped, first from the Polish occupation in the thirteenth century or so and eventually from the Russian tsars. Those runaways were the first Cossacks, and those were the times when Cossacks did good, rescuing captured inhabitants of the Dniepr region from the Mongol and Ottoman white slave traders, who sold many a Ukrainian soul at high profits to Istanbul and other barbaric lands.

Maria was born in Saint Petersburg, where her family had a grand house. When redistribution followed the revolution, they were forced to run, hiding in Crimea, a temporary safe haven for many like them. Maria's father was executed by the Soviets in 1921 when she was just seven. Crimean Tatars continued to hide Maria and her mother. At sixteen, Maria returned to Saint Petersburg, studied acting, and was groomed for a bright future by her teachers, but in 1934, because of her noble blood, she was expelled from school and denied a Leningrad *propiska*, the coveted passport stamp of residency all Soviets had to have. She worked as a bookkeeper in Kiev, then moved to Batumi, a city on the Black Sea coast of the Georgian SSR.

Her independent behavior was watched closely, and in 1941, she was arrested for anti-Soviet propaganda and received the then-standard sentence—eight years in the Gulag hard-labor camps. She served out her first term in Kazakhstan, in the mines. In 1950, in the prison hospital, she had a daughter whose father, a fellow political prisoner from Poland, was soon killed in the camps.

Maria received a second term and was separated from her child. I think her daughter died. This time Maria served in Siberia. She was freed in 1956 and was completely rehabilitated, meaning reinstated back to being a "human being," in 1958, when she was forty-four. This new status allowed her reentry into large cities, like Kiev, where she lived out the rest of her life just down the road from us, on one of Batiy Mountain's slopes.

By the time we met her, she'd acted in over twenty films, the most recent one being *Olesya*, in which she played an ascetic medicine woman whom locals consider a witch but who actually is a gentle, wounded soul. That's why I recognized her face, and that's how I saw her, as a witch who could transform from a youth into an old baba in a flash but who was in actuality a fragile creature of courage.

"Yoga saved me in the Gulag," Maria told us. "When I was in solitary especially, I knew not to panic. I knew how to breathe and used all my techniques. You should do yoga." This last bit was for Mama. Mama promised she would and forgot about it the very next moment. She was not nobility and not anti-Soviet, so Mama felt she had no need to strain herself into physical knots or to keep her promises.

Maria Kapnist was and continues to be an inspiration to me. She was a woman who endured years of cruel, undeserved punishment yet was not afraid to openly tell it as it was in front of a mere child. In a world of fibbers, deceivers, liars, and cowards, Maria showed me how to be unafraid and trusted me not to betray her.

When Countess Maria Kapnist died at seventy-nine, her filmography list contained seventy-five films. I was blessed to have met her when I did.

Dress 4

The Beige Remake

When I was ready to start fourth grade, after we returned to our grandparent-less home, Mama started remaking her beige dress for me. She calmed herself a little by sewing. While she sewed, she muttered insults directed at her coworkers, who annoyed her every moment of the day; at me for whatever reason; or just at the unending list of unfinished chores. No matter what she did for me, Mama became agitated by it. She alternated between curses under her breath and out-loud utterings that were impossible not to hear, especially since she raised her voice whenever I moved to another room to escape. Soon Mama was angry with me all the time.

How did she imagine we would live? I wondered when she was unable to get clarity in her own head, mixing me in with her work and chores. If she better separated her burdens, maybe then she would not have yelled at me so much. Yet I knew quite clearly that I was a burden of insurmountable proportions to her and that she had no idea how to deal with me. I was a stranger to Mama when we were at home, though I was a friend when we traveled. We were happier in places where Mama did not have to search for food, cook, and clean. Depriving us of many basics was also Mama's new way of living. Garrik evaded child support payments, so Mama had to become very inventive in economizing by elimination, especially because I was growing all the time and my appetite was insatiable.

Mama made my new plain beige dress from one she'd bought for herself in Estonia three years before. It was a very pleasant shade of beige, a somewhat yellowish, warm hue. It gave my ten-year-old mind a balanced sense of wellness within, which I immediately understood to be my mental destination, and beige became my favorite color. Any dress made from one of Mama's and with Mama's own hands lent me the abundance of love I always yearned to receive from Mama and did not. Our conflicted, constantly clashing personalities blocked that. Our incompatibility was most certainly biological. I always knew it to be a chemical-biological intolerance. There is no opinion I value sufficiently enough to dissuade me from this view, unless the voice of the contradicting opinion belongs to someone who has lived my life exactly the way I have lived it and been subjected to the same treatments from an identical mama. Maybe some scientist will prove me right long after I am gone or even sooner. My first understanding of biology, the science of living organisms, is how I discovered that perhaps my mother was not supposed to mother me.

Maybe not every woman who has a child is biologically made to mother that child. Perhaps if Mama had a different child, even with my father, she could have been a mother who unconditionally loves her young and wants them to thrive. By the time I was ten, and even more so by eleven, twelve, and thirteen, Mama did not want to be my mother.

As I entered my most sensitive period of growth, Mama could not force herself to have a meaningful conversation with me about my needs, dreams, or desires. Our conversations were always about how I was not up to her par and how much I resembled my hateful father.

Mama must have made me that dress during a rare moment of postvacation tranquility. Or maybe it was a reaction to someone's remarks about how unkempt I looked after Grandma died. In the USSR everyone commented on everyone's business. Socialism respects no privacy of any sort.

Around that time I started picking up the condescending looks our neighbors threw in my direction, and so I began to spend a lot of time alone. Still, I had to venture to the store downstairs, walking half the building's length in the back and the same distance around the front before entering the store, inevitably meeting many of our neighbors on the way. Just like Mama, I never said hello to them. I looked just as they said—disheveled and unkempt. I pretended not to care what they whispered behind my back when I passed, but I did, and I soon became quite withdrawn, as if all this was not really happening to me.

I suppose that Mama decided to make me that dress to prove to herself that she still sewed well. She praised herself, as was her usual when she accomplished something. And the dress was wonderful. I loved it so much that I wore it to school in place of my uniform. That day a special dispatch photographer ended up photographing me, as I had been selected out of my entire fourth-grade cohort—four classes of over forty students each—as the exemplary student. My portrait was pinned to the honors board that entire year. I had the best grades and the best behavior, but the photographer's surprise visit to the school captured my violation of school uniform rules. No one could do anything about it after the fact, except chastise me for the remainder of the year. By then I'd learned to live with chastisement.

I hung on the honors board in my inappropriate beige dress—so different, so unlike my classmates. That year, after the daily nurturing from my grandparents stopped, I became an abrupt and tough grown-up, playing a mother to my mother too often. I knew not the difference between us nor who was supposed to be mothering whom. All I knew was that the previous year we'd been a family with dinnertimes, favorite dishes cooked by request, cleaning help twice a year to bring our home to order before and after winter, and weekend cleaning to live in an orderly house. We used to have occasional all-night-long singing when guests gathered, with long tablecloths hanging off the dinner table—the thick green tapestried one over the base, with strings I loved to braid, and the pretty lace one on top. I was always asked to help set up the tableware for guests in the same precise way Grandma had learned from her grandma before the revolution, when life was different and women took care of their homes and children. In those times, I was made to understand and remember, there was an order to everything with priorities and responsibilities. That time was gone now that I was in charge of our household and unable to deliver comfort to Mama the way Grandpa and Grandma did.

Mama used to dislike Grandma's telling me too much about her childhood before the revolution. Mama wanted Grandma to tell me stories of after the revolution, when bandits roamed the forests and villages stealing everything in sight and when Grandma and her sisters had nothing to eat and nothing to wear except clothing made from flour bags. Mama herself loved to tell me stories of Grandma, Haim, and her running away from the Nazis in 1941, surviving three harsh Ural winters. Haim and Mama shared one pair of shoes, sewn from a wool blanket, between them and went to school on alternate days. Mama's childhood, in comparison to mine or Grandma's, was the most severe. Never anything at all to eat. No clothes. No milk. Every morsel of food had to be shared, and the supply stretched thinner when their youngest brother, Valera, was born on September 3, 1941, just as they reached the Urals. Mama and Haim never ate their cookies and bread in the summer Pioneer camps Grandma was able to arrange for them these two summers. They instead saved their cookies and bread and brought the monthlong stash home to Valera. I knew I had it easy; there was no war and no sibling to share with. Still, I felt I was alone, abandoned, unwanted. *If I only had a sibling,* I dreamed, hugging Anjelika at night, *I could tolerate anything.* But never did I think of my actual sibling, Anna, and soon I forgot about her altogether. It was less painful that way.

In winters Mama and I spent our evenings knitting in front of the TV. Our mutual admiration for television kept the peace between us for an hour or two a day. There were no commercials, but in between shows, Mama would tell me things, like how much she loved her brother. Uncle Haim, it must be noted, did something important in my early life—when I was born inconveniently to Garrik's work schedule, Haim carried me home from the hospital. My father was then employed on the riverboat and was not due to return for three weeks.

Mama loved telling me the story of her sufferings while in labor for over fifty hours. There she was, a solitary woman in the labor ward during the time of making strawberry preserves, and all the nurses and doctors at the hospital were busy cooking their preserves right there, paying little or no attention to her. I knew this story so vividly that the sweet aroma of strawberries boiling in sugar would fill my nostrils as soon as Mama started the story up.

Occasionally, when Mama's cries were especially disturbing, one of the nurses would come to wipe Mama's forehead and shoo the flies. One time the nurse said to some other nurses, in Mama's hearing, "See how this kike is cringing from pain. Come watch her suffer."

Things like that were spoken aloud not because they thought Mama would not hear but because they wanted her to hear. These things were said intentionally, demonstratively, because people wanted to injure without leaving visible marks. Only words could do that—wound so deeply that eons of time would not repair, heal, remove, or lessen the pain. Mama, who always thought she did not look Jewish, was, no doubt, recognized as a Jew always, even when she thought she was not. She lived through some very harsh anti-Semitic incidents. She never learned to defend herself, and her offenders could smell her fear. Every incident was as if to underscore her lack of belonging, as if saying, *You will never be one of us.*

When I was born after fifty hours of difficult labor and they placed me in Mama's hands, Mama cried out, "Oh, no!"

"Your face was so deformed," Mama told me. "Your mouth was on the right side, and I had to massage it back into place. I did it every day for the entire three weeks we were in the hospital. That's why your mouth is now so huge."

I'd look into the mirror and see my deformed but, thanks to Mama, restored-back-into-place face with its huge mouth, and I knew that I could never be a fairy-tale princess.

"All you can ever be is the princess on the pea," Mama always said, referencing the Hans Christian Andersen fairy tale about a girl who does not know she is a true princess until she wanders into a castle, soaked by a downpour, and is placed atop many mattresses for the night. Through them she still feels the discomfort of a lump caused by a solitary dried pea the queen hid under all the mattresses, knowing that only a true-blooded princess would be able to discern the pea.

Mama called me the princess on the pea every night when I complained that our bed had sand in it when we shared it. I did feel every grain of dirt and was unable to sleep. When I was very young, I complained that I could not fall sleep until after my dirty and dusty feet were washed. I had many similar requests. Mama did not need a princess. She wanted me to be a staunch Soviet child, ready to endure everything now and forever, because nothing good was going to come my way, just as it would never come to her. She actually said "It is not for us" about most things I liked, wanted to try, wanted to buy, wanted to see … After constantly being told so and believing Mama was always right, I, too, knew these things were not for me. One such not-for-me thing was love. When Mama told me my father was not there to bring me home, I heard, "He did not love you." I heard this hundreds of times.

"Only my Haimochka came and carried you in his hands all the way home. Think of him as your father," Mama said. She also told me to love Lorachka, because Lorachka was the first child she'd taken care of and she'd thought she would never ever love anyone as much as Lorachka.

"But you love me more now?" I'd ask, naturally.

"Don't be silly," Mama would answer and return to her crossword puzzle or knitting. She rarely finished either. I took it on faith that Lorachka was the greatest and Haimochka, the kindest, but my young mind noticed inconsistencies in Mama's love and her loved ones' treatment of me. The very fact that I could never bring myself to address my uncle, neither by name nor by "Uncle," is my proof. Mama's storytelling had a different purpose than Grandma's, and it was full of gaps in logic and missing analysis.

When Grandmother told me stories of her tribulations, she was counting on my remembering them, so that someday I'd be able to pass them on, should anyone want to hear. When Grandma was alive, my aunt Zina never came to visit, but Haim and my cousins came sometimes. They were never there long enough for Grandma's stories, though. I had that privilege, and I treasured it.

In years before, Grandma and Grandpa rewarded me with praise, love, words of wisdom, and, most importantly, their respect. I never heard from them that I was too young to attempt to do something around the house, and this gave me trust to build inside me an early level of confidence, an internal reservoir from which I was able to draw energy all my life, long after they stopped teaching me.

To build me up, to make our home comfortable, and to love me were talents Mama neither possessed nor strived to develop. Instead of her doing anything herself, everything was always done for her, by either her maternal grandmother, Haya, or her parents. A lot of the day-to-day tasks were now mine to do, yet Mama fought any and all my efforts at homemaking by excessively criticizing me, calling me stupid and foolish, and having no foresight to praise any of my desperate attempts to create a home after she had failed to do so. There was so much confusion in my head. I was also exhausted by Mama's demands to admit that my lack of concern had killed Grandma. I soon began believing that I somehow was responsible for her death. True, I'd brought over a girlfriend the evening before, and we'd been very loud. "If you did not bring her," Mama reminded me often, "Grandma would still be alive." I blamed myself and tortured myself every evening with mental reenactments of what I should have done better on that fateful morning of May 25, 1971.

In the end I was tired of seeking Mama's love. I knew she did not love me after she stopped making clothes for me after that beige dress.

Dress 5

The Uniform

When I was a little girl and believed in fairy tales, I was required to wear a brown school dress, which was always made of scratchy wool. Like all girls, I wore an everyday black cotton apron over my dress, protecting it from school, cafeteria, and play dirt. The elbows of the dress wore out very quickly, and my grandmother patched them up regularly while she was still living. After her death, I did the patching myself the best I could learn at my sewing labor lessons. Otherwise, my sleeves would have had gaping holes, to the dismay and criticism of teachers, parents, and children of all grades. And often, my sleeves still did have holes.

During the first sewing labor lesson in first grade, while we were still learning our letters, all the boys and girls of my class cut and sewed oversleeves to protect the elbows of our clothing from becoming threadbare. Mine were from a coarse black fabric known as "devil's skin"—the only kind of long-wear fabric my family could procure. I made the oversleeves all by myself and proudly put them over my uniform sleeves to protect my first brown dress. This dress was to be the garment I would wear six days a week, eight or more hours a day, for nine months of the calendar year. I loved it then, happy in my new role of a student.

The uniform was prettied up by sewing a white lace collar onto its brown one. The lace was removed every Saturday after school only to be resewn on Sunday, after the dress was washed, starched, and ironed. The wrists of the dress were decorated with matching white lace cuffs, which were, of course, sewn atop the brown dress's natural coarse wool cuffs. Every girl had two or more pairs of white cuffs. They quickly and visibly dirtied and were changed twice a week, at least. In the later part of the school year, if our actual growth exceeded the growth our dresses anticipated, our white cuffs were sewn to our dresses in such a way as to extend the length of the sleeves.

September 1 was always the first day of school in the USSR, unless it fell on a Sunday. October Revolution Day was celebrated on November 7, Soviet Army Day was February 23, International Women's Day was March 8, and International Workers' Solidarity Day or May Day was May 1. These were our very special Soviet Socialist holidays. On these and other special occasions we wore white aprons over our brown dresses instead of the commonplace black ones.

Special occasions also included visits by foreigners. Everyone was prepared ahead of time for visits from foreigners or high-ranking government officials, and best behavior was expected. Problem students were instructed to stay at home sick so that there would be no incidents. Everyone loved to spiff up when we were little. The girls tied specially puffed-up white bows in their hair, while the boys put extra shine on their shoes, combed their hair, and tried to get their cowlicks to stay down by licking their palms and patting their hair. By the time we were at the end of school, the teachers picked the best students from each class to create a model classroom with model students. We were living in a world of make-believe we were all born to act out.

I spent ten years in school. This theoretically means ten dresses but fewer than twenty aprons. Countless collars. Countless cuffs. Because white aprons were worn so rarely and could be used for two years, they were purchased with growth in mind, which meant they were way too long the first year and too short the next one. They were pretty because they were white and frilly, even if most frills were as austere as our entire existence. Some of the frilly white aprons girls wore were actually pretty, because they were made to be so by caring and capable moms and grandmas, who all knew how to sew, knit, mend, crochet, needle-point, and many other admirable things a Soviet Socialist woman was expected to know in addition to her work and good housekeeping.

Our black aprons were totally grim and were truly meant to deliberately make a girl look unappealing. Sameness; plain, unattractive looks; and conformity to the masses were taught, demanded, praised, and rewarded. But girls everywhere want to stand out at one or another point in their childhood. We all tried, some more successfully than others, because despite the demands for sameness, conformity, and equality, by the age of seven, when we started school, we already knew that every family had different means and accesses, even though we were constantly told we were all equal and the same.

A pretty-looking dress was hard to find, but I knew they existed, because some of my classmates actually had them. Those usually were purchased in the capitals of the Baltic republics, Moscow, and Leningrad. Those cities were far better supplied with pretty things than Kiev.

Maybe my uniforms were so ugly because Mama never made finding me a pretty one her priority. There were few varieties of brown uniforms, and they were sold only during the summer, when I was usually away. Nonetheless, some timely options existed, but Mama was a devoted procrastinator. Even after I was old enough to shop for the uniform dress alone, I was always late. By the time I'd be back in town and sized up, the only uniforms left in the stores were the ones no one else wanted. I had to settle for whatever was available to me. Of course, when I was very young, I did not know the difference or did not care, but as I got older, I resented being dressed the entire school year in ugly and often uncomfortable dresses.

Cleaning the wool dress was a logistical nightmare. To begin with, after the first wash the dress lost several centimeters of length at both the hem and the sleeves. With shrinkage of fabric and growth of the girl in mind, a larger-than-needed dress was always purchased. Then the hem and often the sleeves were folded to the underside— the hem usually two or three times—and sewn sturdily. No hem was ever cut. It was neatly folded and neatly sewn. As the girl grew, the hem was unrolled, rerolled, and sewn until next rehemming.

Regrettably, most everyday-use cotton thread was of very deficient quality. It snapped at the slightest pull, and often the hems would unroll during school. Most girls carried a small spool of thread with a needle tucked right into it, and often one girl or another could be seen kneeling next to her friend in the long hallways, fast fixing the hem or some other wardrobe mishap during the thirty-minute lunch break. I carried needle and thread right in my book bag, and I recall frequently forgetting it was there and pricking a finger on the needle.

When the brown uniform dress was new, it was as all new garments are—new. Then it was washed, and its brown color ran wildly. Dried, the dress's off-color spots would be clearly visible, and as luck would have it, they rarely were in places the apron covered. The washing also exposed the pale thread of the dress, giving away the poor quality of the dye, the fabric, the uniform, and our very lives. We were all in different stages of poverty. But we did not know anything else. We knew to make the best of what we had.

Another reason the dress could not be laundered often was because it dried so very slowly, usually taking longer than the time between school's end on Saturday to Sunday evening, the break we had for drying it over the heating coils of our bathroom. We washed the dress maybe three to five times a year, typically during the school vacations or if a holiday fell on the day next to Sunday. As we got older, this infrequent cleaning added another problem clearly identified when in close proximity by the ever-present odor of stale wool dress mixed with fresh, strong sweat. But no one really cared, because everyone had the same problem. The entire school—in fact, the entire country—stank. There were no deodorants, and most women did not shave their armpits.

Drying the dress worked better for lucky people with balconies. They always dried their clothing on clotheslines. Mama and I had no balcony, so we dried indoors, over the radiator pipes, which were rarely consistently warm and too short to dry more than a couple of garments at the same time. No wonder my dress was normally still slightly damp on its first day back to school after washing, when it still refused to fully dry even after ironing, even before we bought an electric iron. To this day, the smell of damp or unclean wool is one of the least tolerable smells to my nostrils. Right up there with vomit and excrement.

No one I knew owned two brown dresses. Some girls had two black aprons, though. I recall that the dress cost about seventeen rubles. My mother made 150 rubles a month when I was in lower classes. This raised to 160 by my graduation. She was an electrical engineer and made more money than most people. By comparison, an average teacher made 90 rubles per month. But Mama was a single mom, a situation that always created a shortage of everything. One dress was all she could afford—plus the aprons, lace, shoes, hose, sweaters, underwear, ribbons, coats, boots. There were so many things a girl needed every year that Mama never seemed to be thinking about much else but getting something eliminated off the list, so she could buy something else.

Our winters were bitterly cold, but at school we were not allowed to wear sweaters over our uniforms. We had to invent ways to stay warm and layered from the inside, so as not to be ordered to the principal's office. Having a larger-than-your-size dress was strategic in this regard, but getting a thin enough sweater to hide under the uniform was problematic. We wore undershirts, but they were mostly sleeveless and cotton. In grade 4 or 5 we were taught to knit, so we could knit ourselves some warmth. We would make all sorts of undersweaters from wool, which we salvaged from previously owned family knits.

Salvaging a knitted garment was a normal thing to do. The entire family would partake in the fun exercise of undoing a knit back into a yarn ball. One person would pull, and the other would roll. Of course, there were obstacles in this process, like change in color. Then a third person might be called upon to roll the less significant colors into their own balls. If the yarn broke, it was tied, of course, and when one came across a row of worn-out and unusable thread, it was pulled out and discarded, and the ball continued growing from the usable place. Then the wool was unrolled again, from the ball onto the upturned arms of a family member lending them for this task. The arm stretcher would hold his or her hands out shoulder-length apart, elbows bent, hands pointing to the ceiling, thumbs out. The second person then wrapped the yarn tightly around the first person's hands. When removed, the yarn was tied together with cut-up threads, washed, dried, and rolled into clean balls for reusing. My grandfather was an expert arm stretcher and ball roller.

In the elementary school grades the girls' dresses were long, and we did not care. As we got older, we wore our dresses as short as we could get away with without being caught by the ever-watchful principal, whose ultimate duty was to constantly police the schoolkids and turn them into obedient Soviet citizens. The wool of our dresses wrinkled from daily wearing, so we ironed our dresses daily, as mandated by the school's prescribed rules of appearances.

Daily ironing of the wool made it shine. Sheening could be prevented by always using a cloth between the iron and the dress. Once in a while, I would actually remember to use this cloth, normally a remnant of an old sheet; the rest of the time I did not, so my dresses were always shiny. Sometimes the iron scorched the dress. Once I scorched mine so badly that Mama wanted to buy me a new one in the middle of the year, but no dresses were sold that late. I proudly wore the imprint the iron left on the skirt of my dress until school was out and the dress joined her sisters at the school-dress cemetery.

We were prohibited to let our fingernails grow long or to polish them. Our fearsome school principal himself would hold periodic surprise "Hands on your desks *now!*" inspections. We were also prohibited to wear jewelry or makeup and forbidden to let our hair down, if it was long. Neat braids or a short cut were a must. My stubborn curly brown mane was a big problem. I could not comb it, and neither could Mama, except on Sundays, our only full day off, so I had very short hair in my early school years. Later, when I let it grow, my braids often remained untouched for the entire school week.

Another type of labor lesson happened when we would suddenly be ordered to spend the forty-five-minute class hour cleaning brushwood outside the school building or sweeping the yard using brooms made out of dried rods, kicking up dust and dirt and merely resettling it around and onto us. Other times we were taken to the fruit gardens and given shovels to turn the soil around the trees. Our shoes, which were not part of our uniforms and were even harder to procure, would be practically destroyed by this inappropriate and often grueling work. Some girls had really fine patent leather shoes their military dads had brought them from abroad, and I remember they would wash them after dirty, grueling work over the school bathroom sink, using their bare fingers to scrape the dirt and animal dung off the unimaginably beautiful leather.

No labor was off limits. We were put to many tasks, dressed as we were, in our brown dresses and black aprons. We collected fallen leaves with toothless rakes and swept, washed, waxed, and repainted the school hallways. As far as I recall, the only thing they never asked us to do was to clean the latrines. I had to clean everything else in the school and vast grounds around it as part of this or another labor-class activity. Labor class was designed to shape our characters as Soviet citizens. By grade 7 or 8, we understood it as an involuntary draft for a lifetime of unprotested exploitation. There was nothing to complain about. It was a fact of life, and we knew no other life. But when I got home from school each afternoon, I removed the dress as soon as I crossed the threshold of our apartment. Most of us did. To our minds, the dress stood for oppression, so we shed it as quickly as possible, as if to rid ourselves of it, even for a short evening hour of comfort.

Darkness came early. In fourth grade we attended our overcrowded school in the second shift. It was even more dangerous to walk home that year, alone amid piles of snow that towered over me in places. It was dangerous to walk so late because predators were around. They were less daring during the day, but because their activities were probably not made public, parents were uninformed and did not caution their children. The authorities at the school most likely knew but also did not caution us. We were each on our own during the walks to and from school. Some, like me, made these walks alone from the earliest age. I saw some predators, but, lucky for me, they were those who only liked to exhibit their genitals to little schoolgirls.

In winter, we wore knit leggings over our knit pantyhose and were required to remove them after arriving to school. Maybe it would have been too hot to wear them indoors. Maybe they ruined the permitted uniform look. I'm not sure. We were bundled up on our walks to school in the winter: leggings, undergarments, uniforms, shawls to wrap around our bodies to protect us against the wind, felt boots with rubbers atop them to guard against rain and sleet, fur or sheepskin coats, and, if we were lucky, hare-fur hats or at least knit ones with ears that tied under the chin. The ties under the chin were problematic; if not done right, they cut into my neck or grew icicles on them. I often tied them so tightly I could not untie them at home. Each of us also wore a wool scarf or two, one around the neck inside, another over the nose and mouth or under the coat collar, and, lastly, wool mittens—not gloves, but mittens. Fingers keep warmth best when kept together inside woolen mittens. We either knitted our mittens for ourselves, like scarves and hats, from salvaged wool, of course, or our mothers or grandmothers made them, like their grandmothers before them, like we would be expected to do for our husbands and children, our labor teachers told us.

We carried our books and notes in leather backpacks to keep our hands free in case we had to balance in the piles of snow as we traversed the narrow paths adults footed earlier on their way from buildings to the streetcar stops.

In the mornings, in our class wardrobe area, we'd pile our overclothes, hanging them three or four onto a hook, never certain we'd get everything back after the last bell. Surely, some class hooligan would pull down on a few coats deliberately, ripping the handmade garment hooks out of coats and sweaters. We were thankful when the entire garment would not tear. All clothing was labeled with initials needlepointed with previously washed cotton colored *mouliné* thread, which was usually used for needlepointing and cross-stitch.

After elementary grades, the wardrobe area was in the common rooms—open coatrooms at the end of the top three floors of our four-story school. Two or more classes were assigned to each unlocked, unguarded rack. We could never wear anything we were afraid to lose, as our peers, the school staff, or even the teachers might move it deliberately or steal it. If we wanted to keep our scarves, gloves, rubbers, and other small items safe, we had to carry them around all day.

We brought in our lunches and carried them around with us too. If left unattended, they went into other hungry mouths. My lunch usually meant two slices of black bread with a thick layer of butter, because I could never smear it thin, and maybe a slice of Swiss cheese or doctor's sausage (bologna). Our lunches, wrapped in yesterday's newspaper, never took much space in our backpacks, where we also kept a change of shoes, maybe wrapped in newspaper too. We did not yet have any plastic bags, and paper bags were too small. Plastic bags were "invented" in the USSR when I was maybe in ninth grade or so, and then we washed and dried and treasured them.

My expandable red backpack carried everything. I used it from sixth grade through graduation. It started out as a backpack, with two shoulder straps and three sets of holes on its two front leather locks, but after a couple of years it lost its wings, and the only remaining handle tore off the top in my final months before graduation. Mama bought it for me in Leningrad. When it was new, it was too huge for my thin bod, and its red color was annoying. But as it dirtied and wore out, it became a personal artifact and an object of everyone's admiration. Someone even wrote my nickname on it in huge block letters with a ballpoint pen: MASHKA. It was a very well made backpack—rectangular and firm. Its red leather lost hardly any color on the inside, and it probably could have served me another five years through university, had I been able to apply.

There were some positive things about our uniforms, and I have to admit that I respect those lessons. Our uniforms equalized us in a constructive sense. No girl could outshine another while we were in our brown uniforms. We competed only with our lace collars, lace cuffs, white aprons, and all other accessories, like pen and pencil boxes, rulers, erasers, even lunch meats. In the era of have-not, we were proud of anything we had and could make ourselves. But primarily, for most of the duration of our education, we competed in character, academics, and personal achievements.

Shortly before the October Revolution holiday in first grade, we were sworn into the first stage of indoctrinated allegiance to the Soviet Union and became Oktiabriata (Little October Ones). The October Revolution, we learned early on, really happened on November 7. This calendar discrepancy and the elaborately scientific explanation that accompanied it burrowed the first tiny cavity of suspicion in my developing cranium, the crevices of which were then mostly blank, unfilled with knowledge but eager to be so fast. At that age one accepts without challenge any and all indoctrination—political, social, religious. In our case, it was the political we were sternly steered to adapt as the only purity, and we eagerly did, as our parents, and most of our grandparents, did before us. We were awarded a lapel pin—a red star with Lenin's face—at the first-floor hallway ceremony, near the large portrait of our leader, grandfather Lenin, killed by the enemies of the revolution but forever alive through us and in each of us.

Vladimir Ilyich Ulyanov, Lenin's real name, lived from April 22, 1970, to January 21, 1924. He was the leader of the Russian Social Democratic Party, later known as the Bolshevik, meaning "majority," party. After being convicted for antigovernment activities and serving out his sentence, Lenin lived in exile, mostly abroad, where he plotted to overthrow the tsar. He was sustained by foreign governments, most notably German, who strived to do the same. He was a prolific writer of ideology, initially drawn from the teachings of Karl Marx and Friedrich Engels. Under Lenin's leadership, the October Revolution of 1917 took place in Petrograd, formerly Saint Petersburg, which later became Leningrad and, presently, Saint Petersburg again. The Russian Civil War of 1917–1922 was fought, the KGB predecessor Cheka was formed, and thousands of learned, distinguished, and titled citizens were killed or otherwise persecuted. The first concentration complexes, later known as the Gulag, were established, and hundreds of millions of Soviet children were reared in admiration of Lenin's war against the rich.

What pride we felt then, standing under his famous order to students, written in gilded wooden letters on our hallway wall: "Learn, learn, and learn." Boys wore the awarded pin on their jackets, girls on the apron strap that ran over the heart. Forgetting the pin at home was a punishable offence, resulting in a grade of 2 in behavior instead of coveted excellence of 5. 1 was reserved for irredeemable hooligans. I never received any 2s. I was a proud Octiabrenok, happy to be a member of the Oktiabriata, the children of October, the youngest members of the Soviet Communist Party ranks. I had no idea that I was being indoctrinated. We all were, from early in our lives.

At the end of third grade we were accepted into the ranks of Soviet Pioneers. We had to purchase a red kerchief, to be tied daily atop our uniform, like a necktie, and maintain it in mint condition. Scout's honor! Just kidding, of course. Although the entire concept of the Soviet Pioneer

Organization was lifted from the West, we were still way too young that year to understand it. We worked for three long years in a secluded existence on the first floor, away from the cynical older kids, all toward one common goal: to be accepted into the ranks. We vied for the honor of it in a sincerely devout way I do not believe any of us could ever be persuaded to vie for any other rank since. We were the ideally prepared generation of the ideal country of the entire imperfect world we were going to make ours someday. We were the best, most honorable, most deserving, most potentially successful to reach the Soviet Union's goal: getting to be a Communist society by the year 2000. It was promised to us, the littlest Socialists. No, it was *guaranteed* to us that our generation would take our entire country into the happy life of Communism and change the world to live by the same ideals that we, the Soviet Socialist youth, held so undeniably sacred in the USSR.

Our Pioneer kerchiefs were silk and bruised easily. Also, they were not colorfast and would bleed red, exposing a yellowish base color. A new one had to be purchased several times a year. At the beginning, while we still believed, we cherished our Pioneer symbols. They were going to guarantee our admittance into Communism. All we had to do was be good little Socialists, listen to our teachers and parents, follow the rules of V. I. Lenin, and always be loyal to the Soviet Union and the Pioneers.

I can still recite my oath. "I, Marina Gershanovich, joining the ranks of the Pioneer Organization of the Soviet Union, in the presence of my comrades, do solemnly promise to passionately love my motherland, always fulfill the testaments of great Vladimir Ilyich Lenin, as the teachings of the Communist Party and the laws of the Pioneers of the Soviet Union require."

Then the teacher would ask, "Pioneers, are you ready to defend the cause of the Communist Party of the Soviet Union?"

And we would eagerly raise our right hands, bending our arms in salutation, screaming, "Always ready!"

In addition to the kerchief, a new lapel pin was required. Unlike the Oktiabriata pin, the new pin was not awarded at that juncture but had to be purchased from the store. We wore it pinned close to our hearts—on our jackets, if boys, or on our apron straps, if girls. Positioned atop its five-pointed flaming star was an image of Lenin's face, not as a young boy, like the Oktiabriata pin, but as a fierce leader of the October Revolution.

I was not yet ten in third grade. I believe my state of good Socialist preparedness began to deteriorate by the age of thirteen or so and had completely vanished by just over sixteen.

The next level of my acceptance into the ranks came in seventh grade, when I was fourteen. I had been the class praepostor (*starosta* in Russian), a supposedly elected class role that the school's Communist teachers consistently assigned to me over the many years of my dutiful and diligent class leadership in various capacities. As *starosta* I was charged with monitoring all students when there were no teachers or other adults present. During the third pledge of Communist Party allegiance, it was my duty and obligation to excite, motivate, convince, and enlist my classmates into the Komsomol, the Young Communist League. Most of them joined anyway, because by then we all knew that if we did not enlist, we were closing off the entryway to most higher education and better-paying jobs for ourselves and also most probably creating a situation for our parents that would not end well. At acceptance into the Komsomol, each of us received another pin, which the boys wore on their suit jackets and the girls wore on their black apron straps—over the heart, of course. We wore the pin every day from fourteen to seventeen, until we graduated. Not wearing your pin was a reprehensible offense, but only some of the teachers and the principal would ever notice. The rest turned a blind eye. It was a game we all played, the pretense dance, like the wink-wink in American reality. I followed the teachers' lead and only pretended to monitor my classmates, but the Komsomol was another story. Since I could never threaten anyone with anything, I begged and pleaded to get the reluctant ones in, and they joined.

Only one person dared not to be accepted. His name was Yura Odnoralov. It's okay to admit now that I was always somewhat in love with Yura from the age of just over four, when we were in preschool together. We remained good friends, and I could not understand his refusal. I kept haunting him to comply, and he stoically and successfully rejected all my appeals, never joining. Reflecting now, I realize what a lesson he was giving me and, through me, to our entire class—a lesson in defiance. Never a leader among us, he became a quiet hero, unafraid of harsh consequences.

In my final school year, when I was sixteen, I failed to procure a brown dress. Ugly as the brown dresses came, I did not get this last one in utter defiance of our unfortunate Soviet existence and circumstances. I defied the game I was being forced to play. I hated the dishonesty of it. I was not going to dance this pretense dance. Or at the very least I was going to dance it my way.

In the ninth grade, a miracle happened, and I visited Poland, a country presumably closest to the USSR in everything. There I suddenly became aware of the existence of other choices, supply, means, style, elegance, class, and beauty unknown to me—a little girl in the brown dress from Kiev School No. 187 who could never look or feel pretty inside that brown dress while her leaders and elders misled her. Without prior intent or deliberation, something inside me, some strong resistance from within, an intuition, a power, a force—call it what you will—simply stopped me from complying.

A few days before school started, I decided to make my own dress. I was never too clever of a seamstress, but I had a sudden attack of the skills that labor lessons had failed to instill in me, combined with my natural decisiveness. I bravely measured and cut the parts of the dress out of a piece of deep-blue lightweight wool I'd purchased a year before when Mama and I were in Riga. I don't really know what for. The wool was of really fine quality, and my little expertise did not ruin it much. I constructed my dress with a few flaws and wore it with plenty of pride and dignity. The dress was tight. It had a large collar and was short, as the fashion of the day and customs of my classmates dictated. Its most prominent decoration was its front white zipper. It technically could have exposed my bosom with a snatch, but the black apron atop successfully thwarted all attempts. Of course, I had the white lace collar to match. I actually crocheted it myself. My white apron was plain enough, but it was a glorious framing. I dared to be different. I had a blue dress. I did not comply. I wore what I wanted, and I wore it the entire year, despite the bad rap it earned me.

Every teacher made a comment about me sticking out, wanting to show off. They all knew Mama and I had traveled to Poland the year before, and many envied me my Polish pantyhose, some even offering to buy them from me. Early in the school year, at the very beginning of the first quarter, I was called to the principal's office—my one and only time there involuntarily. The assistant in charge of noneducation matters told me that I had to buy a uniform. I said that there were none to be found and that we had no money to buy one. By then I was a pretty cool liar, when lying was required to pacify school administrators, teachers, and other usurpers of their tiny powers over me. I was released. A few days later our fearsome principal died, and only my homeroom teacher continued the pretense dance by reminding me that I deserved a 2 for behavior, but I already knew that would have meant that one of the best students in my graduating cohort would not be able to be awarded her best marks. As the year wore on, I was left alone to wear my blue uniform. More so, I was actually treated with special respect and consideration during the final oral exams by my harshest irregular dress persecutors.

In the life of every teen there is a moment of rebellion that will define him or her for the rest of youth and through maturity. I was defying conformity, conventionality, obedience, submission, and compliance. I was rebelling against the Pioneers and the Komsomol, against the Communist Party and its leaders, those still alive or already immortalized and idolized. I was rebelling against my personal circumstances.

I wore my blue dress from September 1, 1977, through June 22, 1978, the date of my final oral exam. After that I never put it on again physically, but I have been wearing it over my soul always, as a vitally protective armor. The blue uniform dress gives me courage and strength. It keeps me idealistic. It keeps me youthful. It heals me from wounds and allows me to rise above my beginnings. It wards off numerous enemies who have no idea what it feels like to break through barriers.

When I recall my self-made blue uniform and how I looked and felt in it, I am invincible.

Dress 6

The Pioneer Uniform

When I was a little girl, I believed in the Soviet Pioneer fairy tale with all my heart and was, at least for the first three years, a proud member of their ranks, like any good Soviet girl.

The order to wear the summer Pioneer uniform came through the school in fourth grade. We had to buy blue knee-length skirts, if girls; shorts, if boys; and also headwear similar to that of World War II US soldiers, only ours was blue. The headwear was a *pilotka*, a Russian word literally meaning "belonging to a pilot." My thick hair made it difficult for my *pilotka* to stay on my head, even with hairpins.

We were on our own to purchase white knee-highs. Of course, I had only the Soviet kind, not the good-quality, pretty, German-made knee-highs some girls' folks were able to procure. We were also on our own with white shirts. Girls' white shirts were too hard to come by. Some moms remade a man's shirt for their girls. I made my first one out of some old bed linens and the next one from some very itchy fabric I found in the storage box under Grandma's mattress, as we had no man in our home.

I hated my Pioneer uniform, even though it was better than the brown dress with black apron over it. In the list of items we had to bring to camp every time, the Pioneer uniform was on top. For the duration of my Pioneer life— grades 4, 5, and 6—I obeyed commands without questioning. I obeyed the uniform order even though I looked and felt horrible when wearing it. The red kerchief, of course, was worn under the white shirt collar. Lucky for my generation that the daily wearing of the Pioneer tie, the official name of this red kerchief, was no longer mandatory in summertime. Lucky for me that the Pioneer uniform was not a daily requirement at summer camps I went to either. There were some where it was.

Wearing the Pioneer uniform was mandatory at a camp's main events, like opening and bonfire days and other days when the entire camp assembled in uniform. At these times, we stood still for long stretches of time, listening to the marching sounds of the Pioneer horns and then speeches. Whether we had our right hands up in salute or were at ease, we looked identical and were praised by the camp *otriad* (detachment) leaders as well as higher camp leadership. We were the youth ready to take over from our predecessor generation any tasks they'd entrust to us. It was excitement straight out of the great Pioneer-era works of Arkady Gaidar and Lev Kassil, the revered Soviet writers. Gaidar joined the revolution at thirteen in 1917 and then the Red Army in 1918. Every Soviet Pioneer read his stories for children. *Timur and His Squad* was an inspiration in Pioneer altruism and the unofficial code of Pioneer conduct. "The Blue Cup" was a story about anti-Jewish bullying. Although it was part of school curriculum, it was mocked and dismissed by most non-Jews. The Jewish children, on the contrary, appreciated it. It was important to know that a famous non-Jewish writer stood up for Jews, who were bullied and persecuted everywhere constantly. Teachers and society gave instructions to treat everyone equally, but most non-Jews inherited their anti-Semitism as a rite of passage. I particularly felt affinity for Gaidar because he served as a World War II correspondent and was killed in 1941 in action near Kiev, maybe somewhere in the forests I got to roam.

Kassil, who was a Jew, grew up at the time when tsarist-empire values were collapsing, and revolutionary ideas dominated his boyhood. His novels motivated and shaped the mindsets of several Soviet generations. In 1977 a small planet was named after his imaginary country Schwambrania, one of several he introduced to his readers.

My grandmother introduced these writers to me. We read them often when she was alive and raising me, like Mama, Haim, and herself, to become a devout Pioneer someday. And I surely was a devout Pioneer, for a while.

Pioneer uniforms were most needed on special school occasions, like whenever it was our school's turn for memorial duty at the Unknown Soldier's Monument on Pechersk Mountain, nearby the Central Pioneer Palace, where I had some memorable scholastic competitions. There was a District Pioneer Palace in our district, known as Kiev Railroad District. Our subdistrict was known as Batiy Mountain or Batyevo-Aleksandrovskiy Massiv (BAM, for short). We had a square before the mountain incline, named after the revolutionary hero Uritsky, an early Soviet Leader. Born not far from Kiev and educated at Kiev University, one of only eight universities of tsarist Russia, Moisei Solomonovich Uritsky is best known for his work at Cheka, a precursor to the KGB. His assassination in 1918 served as a starting point for the Red Terror period. *Red Terror* was not a term we knew when we had to serve honorary guard in Uritsky Square on May 9, the Great Patriotic War V-day. At school we were never told that the USSR celebrates victory in Europe one day later than the rest of the world. We were also never told that the rest of the world calls that war World War II. Maybe it made us more patriotic not to know that. Or maybe it was that we were the grandchildren of the Red Terror survivors, who knew not to question government, authority, and the KGB.

I remember marching with Pioneer or Soviet banners, counting steps, beating my sandaled soles on the smooth pavement stones of Uritsky Square in front of the Highest School of Soviet Militia, in the exact manner soldiers and militiamen taught us before our start. The banner was heavy; my *pilotka* glided farther down in my hair. What an embarrassment it would be to lose it. My Soviet-made knee-highs, made with no-good elastic, always slid down, but I could not pause to pull them up. They simply did not sustain the hard steps I eagerly threw down with my feet against the hard stones—one, two, three, four. I was always proud of my duty. Four, five, six—turn. Turning at corners, clicking my heels military style—I got that down right.

The side of the militia building was the most difficult duty. Flags from all fifteen republics flew there, and we were supposed to turn toward them or salute while marching and carrying our flags. Our feet and arms ached after a few rounds, but after all, we were Lenin's grandchildren, ready to carry on the banner of his revolution, weren't we?

Once I had to do memorial duty on October Revolution Day, November 7. It was already brutally cold, windy with rain and sleet. I had to wear knee-highs, but at the last moment they took pity on us and let us keep our coats on. I remember that duty well, because I was in bed for several weeks after.

I marched in many such guards at different locations in the city and my Pioneer camps but never once in the Babiy Yar. It just was not done. It was as if no one honored those who died there. That *yar* (ravine) was covered up, and everyone in Kiev and everywhere else in the USSR accepted the tragedy of the Jews of Kiev as a trivial and dismissible war casualty.

And then there were the Soviet Pioneer camps. I went to so many—let me count: after first grade, two camps; after second, three; after third, two; after fourth, one; after fifth, three; after sixth, two; after seventh, three, but really only two since I spent two months in the same camp without leaving; after eighth, two. Enough to never forget.

Most city parents worked through the summer and sent their children to camp because it was simply impossible to work and take care of your kids at the same time. A trip to camp was not free but quite affordable. Getting the trip, like every item that a Soviet citizen had to procure, was a huge deficit problem. Socialist distribution of free goods and services demanded daily under-the-table machinations. The organization where Mama worked, Souzkurortproect, Soviet Union Resort Projects, never seemed to have any good camp tickets for its workers' children. It was somewhat easier for her married coworkers, because they had two sides of supply, with the other parent having different access through another organization. Mama had to settle for whatever was available, and it was never anything really good.

Mama could not hold her own in these kinds of searches and exchanges, because there was nothing she could offer in return. She was a diligent Soviet worker; everyone knew it and took advantage of it. People who could procure and trade were gravitating on different levels, bound by their procurement shenanigans and secrets. Mama had no distribution presence and was disturbed by the absence of this presence. Nightly she suffered while knitting or stitching, muttering under her breath or cursing aloud at the TV screen, which at those times stood for her distribution enemies. They were, of course, anyone who stood higher in the workplace pecking order. With time, Mama became embittered and angered. Whenever her turn would come to receive whatever she'd signed up for and waited for months to get, many others—party members, higher administra tive ranks, and lovers of such people—claimed the best of whatever, and she was left with the remnants. Such was our Soviet reality. People like Mama spent lifetimes inputting into the system and usually could not successfully develop a net of tradeability. "I give you this; you give me that" was not their world, so they were frequently cheated, dismissed, ignored, and deceived by their bosses, coworkers, friends, and family members. Respect in the 1960s and 1970s was earned, in essence, via the network of procurement. Mama could not keep up. I blamed her for it then, but I also knew that, like Mama, I also would have been unable to keep up with this endless procurement game.

Mama always told me that she was sending me to camp to get fresh air of the Ukrainian countryside, meet new friends, play outdoors, and get good food. It was a lie, and we both knew it. Soviet public cafeterias had no good food. Fresh air and outdoor play were plentiful at camp, but they were just as fresh on our mountain. I had a miserable time making friends at camp. I was almost always a solitary, lonely Jew among staunch anti-Semites and thus a magnet for bullies. I would have loved to stay at home, but Grandma and Grandpa needed their rest from me when I first started going. Later, Mama needed some alone time too. She'd leave me all alone to fend for myself for strings of school weeks while she went off for work trips, and that was just fine. In the summers, Mama could have a stretch of no responsibility with me away. Reluctantly, I had to give it to her.

Pioneers were not fed well. In a few of these camps we were nearly starved. That was because at every juncture where food was distributed, much of it was stolen—that is, "redistributed" to the food-service personnel or sold by them to their under-the-table clientele. Yes, that was illegal and criminally punishable, but in most places, when employees colluded, theft was impossible to prove, even if anyone still dared to fight against this systematic and widespread abuse of the Socialist supply system. Tens of millions of Socialists abused the system daily.

It was easy to steal from Pioneer summer camps because children were there in an unsupervised situation, with parent visiting days only once or twice a month. Parents were never with us at camp meals.

A typical breakfast in the Pioneer camp consisted of a bowl of runny farina, a half slice of buttered brown bread, and sweetened tea. For lunch, which was called dinner, we might have a bowl of vegetable soup with two or three carrot slices, lots of cabbage, some potatoes, onions, and a pasta variety of the Soviet kind—thick, grayish, and with a mandatory center hole, so the soup could be slurped through it, like through straws. Sometimes instead of noodles, barley or millet would be added. Bowls and plates were only half-filled—the authorities liked serving us a daily helping of unfulfilled expectations.

For a second course, we might receive some kind of kasha or Russian groats as a side dish to a meat offering, such as meat *kotleta*, a Russian variation on the meatloaf theme, made from chopped meat of indiscernible origin abundantly mixed with bread crumbs. Most camps added only the minimal amount of meat, just enough to justify still calling it meat *kotleta*. Alternatives were nonmeat *kotletas*, like from carrot or cabbage. Another choice of camp "meat" was the Soviet version of a hot dog, called *sosiska*. There were so many ingredients mixed into *sosiskas* that their processed meat content was a huge point of controversy no matter which processing plant packaged them. Most *sosiskas* I ate came inside of an inedible plastic wrap, in which they were boiled. This plastic wrap, upon boiling, stuck to the *sosiskas* for good. We had to scrape some of the *sosiska* meat off the plastic with our teeth or our never-too-clean fingernails, plucking the wrap squeaky clean and licking the meat off our unclean fingers.

If we were lucky, we could get a wedge of tomato or cucumber with a sprinkle of salt. Cucumbers were little, the collective farmlands kind—maybe four or five inches long—and we had the remnants of the pickings. The better-quality vegetables were available at farmers' markets in the city for ready cash, and they were expensive. They were sold by privateering farmers. I have no clue how that was possible under the collectivization agreements. Our cukes were cut in quarters lengthwise, with each child receiving a quarter. Tomatoes were small, perhaps two inches in diameter, also sliced into four pieces, with a sliver per child. Portions of everything were minimalistic, certainly not large enough for our growing bodies, especially given the fact that at the Pioneer camp most of our time was spent outdoors. That famous fresh air kept us hungry all the time.

Daily dinner was accompanied by a glass of compote, an almost clear, yellowish liquid. It was sweetened and had a slice of apple or pear floating in it, as if to prove that fruit was actually used or maybe to distinguish it from urine, which it grossly resembled. These compotes always looked and smelled as if the cook had just boiled her table-cleaning rag in them. I could never get this liquid down and would trade it for an extra sliver of bread and butter, a half slice of which was also included with dinner. Occasionally dinner would include a boiled potato from last year's harvest, with gray, blue, and black eyes in it. Sometimes, herring was our "meat," and it was the stale, no-good-to-serve-to-anyone-decent kind. Often last year's sour cabbage was our side. It reeked of its old barrel and bore the rust marks from the barrel's hoops.

After a nap, mandatory even for the oldest campers, like eighth and ninth graders, we'd get a snack. Sometimes it was the compote, sometimes milk. Rarely we'd receive a sweet tea cookie, most often *suharik*—a slice of dried bread about one centimeter thick and six or seven centimeters wide, if a square. *Suharik* could also be round and smaller, depending on the bread. Very rarely we would get half of a *bublik*, a Russian bagel, maybe even a poppy seed one. *Bubliks* are much smaller than American bagels and much thinner but infinitely tastier.

No second helpings were ever offered in any of the camps. Ate your portion? Now scatter! Except if you had dishwashing duty, which came with extra food. This duty was strictly rotated, so that every camper would have a turn at the extra helpings once or twice a month.

The final meal of the day was supper, which was usually rice kasha. Kasha is like porridge or gruel. Buckwheat, which is commonly referred to as "kasha" in the Unites States, was virtually absent from the Soviet distribution chain. One got it only through special meal tickets. Our rice kasha was like a thinned rice pudding, sweetened and with a pat of butter on top. It was boiled with milk, and a film formed on top as it was brought to the table. This film also formed atop milk noodle soup, which was an alternative supper. To this day, my throat constricts at the memory of that boiled-milk film. But I was hungry and I fished the film out of the bowl with my spoon and dirty fingers and hoped no remnants would sneak into me, because when they did, I gagged and could vomit right in front of everyone.

The only supper we all truly craved was *syrniki*. *Syrniki* are fried patties made from cottage cheese mixed with flour, eggs, and sugar. If the cook wanted to save oil, she would roll, slice, and boil the same cottage cheese mass to make lazy dumplings, *lenivye vareniki*.

With all the abundance of fresh fruit, berries, and vegetables in Ukraine throughout the summer, we received an occasional handful of strawberries in June, cherries in July, and a slice of watermelon in August. Fruit and berries were in season only for two or three weeks each year. Sent to summer camps, we missed whatever was in season. If I were at home in June, I could eat all the strawberries I wanted from my grandfather's patch in our apartment building's front yard. The entire neighborhood used to steal his strawberries; they were the best. In August, watermelons were delivered to our neighborhood in large crates, straight from the collective farms. A long line formed immediately. Whoever was not at work dropped everything and waited until selling started. Quantities were limited, no more than two or three per person. The watermelons were round, about the size of basketballs. Grandpa would manage to balance three of them without dropping any up the steps to our second floor. Our building entryway and staircase were always slippery and poorly lit. It was permanent dusk there. The concrete floors were always filthy from animals' and people's urine. Dropping any unwrapped food item in the building meant the end of that food. It also meant cleaning that part of the floor. Yuk! I was proud to have never dropped any bread there, unlike some other kids I knew.

When I was ten, I could already eat an entire watermelon by myself, if they'd let me. And sometimes Grandpa did, accompanying the deed with "Easy, *lyuba moia*, not so fast, or your belly will burst."

"No it will not!" I would protest, finishing up quickly, as if to prove Grandpa wrong, so he could see that I could finish the entirety of whatever good and tasty treat was set in front of me. He'd laugh, and my belly would balloon, as if I had indeed swallowed the watermelon whole.

I was a hungry camper. All of us were. We foraged the grounds and the surrounding woods for extra nourishment, like nuts, wild strawberries, raspberries, grass roots, and all kinds of mushrooms, which we ate raw. The hunger we experienced at these Pioneer camps made us pretty knowledgeable about mushrooms, yet occasional tragic mistakes happened, and not only with mushrooms.

The forests were still littered with World War II partisan and Nazi bullets, some of them unspent. Boys used to love to pop them with stones, and some severe accidents happened in two or three of my camps. Infrequently we would discover a helmet or other World War II artifact. We were too young and innocent to hoard such items as our own. Everything belonged to the government. So whatever we found, we honestly gave to our camp leaders. What they did with these items afterward was never reported back to the finders.

I recall the camp propaganda rallies, marches, and concerts, of course, but the thing I recall most vividly about camps is the food, or, more exactly, the deficiency of it. When parents' day came, we all feasted on the food they brought: strawberries sliced with sugar and sour cream in one jar; new potatoes with butter, fresh dill, and garlic in another; fried chicken; candy; and cookies. Such items were my usual midsession visiting-day supplement, which Mama or Grandpa brought on that long-awaited Sunday. The liter-size glass jars were wrapped in a blanket to keep the potatoes and chicken warm and sour cream cold. They brought me just enough to eat while I was spending an hour or two with them atop that wrapping blanket, which we spread on the grass outside the camp's territory. Parents never entered the campgrounds. I would take a chicken leg or two and some cookies back to the barrack and eat them later that evening, fast. Bigger, more-aggressive girls would steal every morsel when smaller and less feisty ones, like me, fell asleep. Everyone was very hungry all the time.

Once Mama sent me to a camp on the Crimean peninsula, where we were fed even worse than anywhere I'd ever been before. Porridges were our only fare, and the village store sold only one item—condensed milk. We would puncture two holes in the top of the tin can with discarded rusted nails we found and then would suck out the thick, sweet milk while walking back to camp, occasionally swallowing a tin shaving or cutting our lips. Leaving the campgrounds was not allowed in camps near Kiev, but in this one the gate on the side of the village was always propped open, and we sneaked out often. I was thirteen, in the midst of my most prominent growth spurt, and so hungry I could have eaten those nails. I became very sick at that camp from malnutrition and vitamin deficiency and still have many boil marks to remind me of that summer.

Several times the Pioneer *otriads* (detachments) I was in went hiking for the day. The land did not really belong to anyone. Well, probably it belonged to this or that collective farm, but we all already knew the famous Soviet adage "Everything collective means everything is mine."

We ate everything along the road: berries, mushrooms, leaves, and grass roots. Once I ate some wild garlic—so much of it, in fact, that I became violently ill and had to be hospitalized. Another time, I got stuck in a swamp up to the middle of my calves and had to be pulled out. Luckily, I was still very young then, and my summer sandals buckled on the sides; otherwise I'd have been shoeless for the remainder of the camp term. Luckily, too, it was not a true fast-swallowing swamp, like those in Belarus that camp personnel and leadership told us about during long camp evenings. The camp personnel and leadership loved to share stories of the Nazi occupation, partisans, death, and starvation almost as much as they liked to tell Ukrainian ghost and monsters stories to scare us from wandering away at night.

Once we went camping overnight. I'd turned twelve the day before. We walked twelve kilometers on dirt roads through thick woods and long fields of tall Ukrainian cattle corn, which we could not eat raw, rendering it safe from theft by the ever-hungry Pioneers. In the evening we erected tents, baked potatoes, and sang, scaring the monsters away, until we fell asleep. In the morning we visited the village nearby, where the very important Ukrainian poet Pavlo Tychyna was born. His poetry was so pro-Socialist and so stupid that even children my age loathed it. "Traktor v poli—dir, dir, dir—my za myr," which translates to "Tractor in the field—diyr, diyr, diyr—we are for peace," and *"Na maidani kolo bani revoluzia ide,"* which translates to "In the church square revolution is a-happening," were just two of the many poems we had to learn by heart that still refuse to vacate my brain. This ideally perfect political propaganda was intended for immortality and dies hard. Tychyna was a poet of the Soviet revolution even at the time when Ukraine was vehemently rejecting this revolution and its population was being deliberately starved. By my childhood, he was a heralded hero. We spent lots of time listening to his poems and about his life in that village and then walked the twelve kilometers back to our Pioneer camp. As we entered and left the village, local kids our age hung by both elbows over the tall fences of their private yards, grinning wide and calling us many unflattering names. They were not at all welcoming, deliberately chewing on apples and sunflower seeds and spitting the shells and pits at us. We were likely providing the only entertainment they'd have all summer. Luckily, they no longer stoned or killed Pioneers during my time in the organization.

I remember how dry and dusty these Ukrainian roads were. The thirst was unbearable and the sun high. I thought that the roads must have been just this dry and dusty in August 1941, when Grandpa was captured with the entire army of Kiev defenders and led by roads just like these toward the prisoner of war concentration camp near Vinnitsia, a city about 280 kilometers southwest of Kiev. He miraculously survived the journey.

Did the fathers and mothers of these boys and girls hang over their fences by their Pioneer elbows on the day Grandpa was walked by them, thirsty, exhausted, traumatized by his brain contusion and by what he was living through and witnessing, scared, defenseless, hungry, doomed? I wondered silently. I walked and endured the summer heat and thirst, knowing that Grandpa had had it so much worse and it had not broken him. I did not share my thoughts with anyone. No one I knew at the summer camps or school could ever know what I knew about my family and its secrets. I assumed every family had their own war secrets.

The summer of 1975 was the only time I spent two consecutive monthlong "shifts," as they were called, in a Pioneer camp. This camp was in Bucha, a village near Kiev, and it was my favorite camp ever. Food was not stolen as much there, and I was not as starved as in other camps.

The camp director was Yuri. His patronymic was, perhaps, Mikhailovich. I got to know his daughter, who was my age but who did not dorm with the campers. I do not remember her name, but Yurievna, which means "daughter of Yuri," was surely her patronymic. Had she been a boy, it would have been Yurievich. Understand now? Their family had their own residence on the campgrounds, and I was called there once, under most unusual circumstances that caused him to remember me.

The Story of Relatives from Poland

When I was summoned, Yuri told me that my mother had just phoned from Kiev and that I was to be granted a four-day leave because of an unexpected visit from my "Polish relatives." Now, I was a super honest and naive girl, so I almost blurted out, "We have no relatives in Poland," but suddenly I understood just who these relatives were.

My mother, like most Soviets, knew how to make use of words that carried a double meaning that only those privy to the special code understood. She'd said they were *my* relatives instead of *our* relatives, and Yuri repeated it just as she said it (using the singular *your* instead of the plural *your*). "My relatives" could only imply one thing.

I am certain that most Soviet families by that time had developed their own linguistic associations to deceive the authorities, the ever-watchful neighbors, the oft-tapped phone lines, and the usual "well-wishers." Everyone had spied on everyone else for decades. Ears and eyes were everywhere all the time. Our Soviet world mandated subversive means of communication, since every family had a fearful experience or two to remember forever. Everyone's guard was up. Reading between the lines, assuming you were being watched and overheard, and never speaking openly on the telephone were only some of the wonderfully honed skills we accumulated as we grew up.

I had only one Polish contact, and "my relatives" could only mean her. Since the age of ten I had been corresponding with a Polish girl, Jadwiga Molas. She and I were pen pals under Soviet rule, meaning that at some point in each of our short lives some politically pushy educator had bullied us into writing each other, with the goal of connecting children from the USSR with children of the same age from Soviet bloc countries. I'd gotten Jadwiga, and in turn, Jadwiga had gotten me. We had marvelous correspondence, teaching each other a little bit of our languages and customs; sharing dreams; retelling books we read, films we saw, and music we heard; and so on. We exchanged photos and drawings. Very infrequently, maybe four times altogether, absolutely miraculous parcels arrived from Jadzia, short for Jadwiga. First, I'd receive a notification in the mailbox; then I'd go to the post office to pick up the parcel. No one I knew then received parcels from abroad, or at least they were not telling they did. These parcels were a marvel, down to their fine postal wrapping paper and stamps. They contained chewing gum; colorful patches, the use of which I did not understand; beaded jewelry; and handkerchiefs. The patches, as it turned out, were meant to be ironed or sewn over torn jeans, but who could afford or procure jeans back then? In the USSR, a pair of jeans with unrecognizable labels cost twice Mama's monthly salary, and one could get them only via the black market—a criminally punishable offense with a jail sentence of maybe five or six years and confiscation of property too, including the darn jeans. We wore no jeans—I'd never even touched jeans—and so my patches remained unused.

Mama's bureau was in the center of Kiev, not too far from the Puppet Theater. When I returned to Kiev from camp, Jadwiga, who like me was fourteen, waited for me there with her father. Both of them spoke only Polish. Luckily, Ukrainian is a language heavily influenced by several hundred years of Polish occupation, so we found a way to understanding.

Jadwiga's dad told me to call him Pan Zbiegniew—his first name with the proper form of address *Pan* (like *Mr.* in English) in front. Inserting *Pan* in front of a person's first name is a must even between some adults of long-standing acquaintance. Children typically use *Pan* plus last name, which in this case would be Pan Molas. Pan Zbiegniew specifically wanted me to call him by his first name, though, because, without Mama's and my knowledge, we had actually already became "related." The Molases arrived from Poland to Lvov, where they had some distant relations, who supported their idea and helped them board a train for

Kiev, with the Molases claiming us as their Kiev relatives. They could not telephone us to warn us of this plan, as this kind of information was spoken of only face-to-face, until a communication code was established, sort of like between anti-tsarist revolutionaries or between antifascist spies in wartime Berlin. It was very exciting. It was like I was playacting in a World War II spy film. Me—a girl from school 187 on Batiy Mountain!

The first thing my new relatives and I did was to visit our district Office of Visas and Registrations (OVIR), to get them formally registered as our foreign relations visiting us from abroad. We bonded quickly over that very first trolley ride, understanding one another best through emotions. Had we delayed this registration, say till the next day, all of us would be breaking a number of laws: they, foreign visitors' laws; we, harboring foreigners' laws. If unregistered for over twenty-four hours, they'd likely be arrested and never again allowed back to the USSR. We'd be arrested too, and ... who could predict the fate of Soviet citizens committing this crime? Siberia, perhaps ... Well, maybe not in 1975. But no more Kiev, for sure.

Anyway, we registered. Pan Zbiegniew was now my long-lost uncle, twice removed, separated by war and the annexation of Poland, a story he and Mama discussed while waiting for me. Jadwiga was a girl with two functional parents who never injected herself into adults' plans. Until she met me.

For the next four days I was their guide through my city. I was so eager to share with them the Kiev I loved. Pan Zbiegniew was eager to buy *zloto* (gold) of every grade. That's what the Poles did—bought gold in the USSR, then sold it in Poland at 300 or 400 percent profit. That was the dangerous buy-sell trade some of them engaged in. Poland was a capitalist country with active Catholic religion. They hated Soviet Socialist occupiers. I was surprised to discover that. None of that was ever in Jadzia's correspondence. I was always told, and believed it axiomatically, that everyone welcomed the Soviet Army and Soviet experts wherever they were stationed. It was an unfamiliar yet somehow logical perspective on life, to learn that Soviets were the occupiers and tyrants.

We visited jewelry stores, buying up rings with pink, red, and yellow stones, which Mama always called "villagers' jewelry." According to Mama's conception of fashion, city women wore green, blue, and purple stones. Diamonds and rubies, Mama always said, were for prostitutes. My mama always knew everything better than everyone else.

In the short time of my Polish relatives' visit, I became sort of an expert on jewels, settings, and grades, as well as on precious metals and many other things that would play out later. Most importantly, Jadwiga and I became real friends. I loved everything about her. Her *Język polski* (Polish language) made me love everything associated with Poland. Everything about her was so … foreign and therefore, in the truest Soviet fashion, most admirable. I was fascinated by her *polska maniera* (Polish manner) of moving, sitting, folding a napkin, eating, cleaning her hands, and peeling an orange from a bunch they bought in the foreigners-only store with American dollars, which I got to see for the very first time. Of course, I waited outside, anxious and excited that this was actually happening for real and that I'd met Jadzia. With or without the oranges, everything about her was superior to anything any girl has ever displayed in my presence. Jadzia was confident without being mean, caring without being smoochy, pretty without being beautiful, and intelligent without being arrogant. I ended up copying many of her action patterns and absorbing them into my daily doings without thinking. Jadzia just did everything better. She was better. Was a better person. I did not yet understand why. That was to become my 1976 discovery.

Jadzia had none of the broken-home, unwanted-child complexes I was so full of. Her parents loved her and her two older brothers. They lived in a place called Skierbieszów, a village in Zamość County, Lublin Voivodeship, in eastern Poland. They had a farm and tended farm animals every day, like Grandpa did before they lost everything in the winds of the revolution.

At the end of four glorious days, I took my Polish relatives to Kiev Central Railroad Station so they could return to Lvov and watched until their train faded out of my view. Then I returned to my Pioneer camp on a local train.

"Do not worry," Pan Zbiegniew assured Mama on the last evening they spent with us in our apartment. "We will soon invite you to Poland."

Mama was convinced he was just being polite and we would never see Poland or hear from them again. I held my breath and hoped to have evidence, despite knowing otherwise, that Mama understood the world better than me and that was why she kept telling me, "Things like that do not happen to us."

True, Pan Zbiegniew was in shock when he learned that Mama was an electrical engineer. "You should only see how our engineers live," he told Mama in our shabby apartment. Then there was an absolutely horrifying moment when he asked to see some "kikes," Jadzia having never seen them. I was kind of sorry and proud when Mama did not skip a beat: "You've been staying with them for four days now," she said.

"We will never hear from them again," Mama repeated over and over, regretting her impulsive admission to being a Jew. She said she probably should have held back. And I agreed.

Well, Mama turned out to be wrong about that and about many other things.

Anyway, that is how the story of relatives from Poland started.

* * *

In July 1976 Mama did not even bother to accompany me to the same Pioneer camp at the beginning of my shift. After all, I was fifteen now and nearly grown up.

In those days many children went everywhere unaccompanied, but not to camp, where registration was done with parents or grandparents present. Even though I was not an orphan, I often felt like I might as well have been one. Mama rarely bothered to accompany me throughout the city, but before this time, she'd bring me to camp on the local train. It was usually less than an hour away. I felt uneasy being alone that day, but I was about to learn to distinguish between premonition of something bad and anticipation of something good.

I was waiting in the registration queue, feeling lost and sad, when the camp director, Yuri, who remembered me from last summer, asked if I wanted to be a counselor's aide this time. I answered a vigorous yes because it meant skipping the dreaded registration. They always asked aloud for "nationality" during registration, and the non-Jews, as if by command, quieted down whenever a Jew answered. In the Soviet sense, "nationality" was equal to the concept of ethnicity in most of the modern world. "Jew" was my Soviet nationality. Since all religion was outlawed in the USSR, Jews were thus set up for institutionalized discrimination. It was an open invitation for Russians and Ukrainians to tell me, along with the rest of Soviet Jews, that we did not really belong in the country we were born in, where some of our families had lived for centuries. Whenever I'd give a reply of "Jew" to the nationality question at camp, the ostracizing began. Some other Jews maybe had thicker skins or could fight off better. I clammed up as soon as no one wanted to become my friend. Becoming a counselor's aide offered an optimistic way out this turn. It meant living with six-year-olds in their barrack, helping them brush their hair and teeth and make their beds. It meant I could actually be appreciated and loved by the uncorrupted younglings, who knew little about the stigma imprinted on my face and into my last name.

It was the first and only time I enjoyed Pioneer camp for the entire duration of my stay. For the first time I was unbruised by my peers. I remember the sadness I felt when camp was over. It was my final Pioneer camp stay. I hope I was able to teach my kids a few things, although, looking back, I see pretty clearly that I was the ultimate beneficiary of my last summer-camp arrangement.

Dress 7

The First Riga Twin

When I was a young girl, I wanted to spend my summertime daydreaming at home, doing nothing, except reading, eating, and going to the yar (ravine) across Volgogradskaya Street just opposite our apartment building. In this yar everyone I knew and did not know either used plain wooden sleds or just sat right on the packed snow on their butts to slide down the steep, oft-ridden slopes in the winter. It seemed then that those slopes were high and the rides long. Childhood sees most objects through a magnifying glass.

In the summer, we brought up the clear drinking water from the stream at the yar's bottom. We had long periods without running water to overcome in our busy neighborhood, the highest mount in Kiev. Many five- and nine-story buildings literally edged out the former residents of this previously private-homes-only land. The remaining private sector had wells but no indoor plumbing and good gardens but high fences and scary dogs. The kids from apartments, who were not sent away to their folks' villages or Pioneer camps, ran around all summer long, so anything not nailed down and unattended was their loot. I had some building girlfriends, but they were always away at their grandparents' villages. They, like most of the population of our mountain, were first-generation Kievans.

Thus our yar became my bosom friend. I knew every tree, every bush, every path, every bump, and all the best hideaways for shelter on lazy, long, sweaty summer days. Armed with books, old sheets, and a sandwich or piece of fruit, kids and the elderly spread all over the green slopes. It was heavenly to lie down on the soft or prickly grasses, suntan, stare into the clouds and guess their changing shapes, read, talk, and make friends. It was better than heavenly to sing if my friends were in town, altering our voices at random between first and second parts in the unending Ukrainian songs and enjoying life as it should be, uninterrupted by the chaos outside our yar. This was our neighborhood's best-hidden secret, our magical escape, our fairy-tale land. With the crickets, grasshoppers, bumblebees, birds, butterflies, cicadas, and an occasional elf here and there, there was no place quite as enchanted and enchanting as our yar.

Not even the streetcar's screeches at the sharp, almost forty-five-degree turn of tracks from Solomenskaya into Volgogradskaya Street could disrupt the yar's idyll. It was as if modern day did not exist. Time was spun into the armor of safety there. I put it on, sort of like the shirts Hans Christian Andersen's Elisa made for her swan brothers out of stinging nettle. It took a day or two to get the blistery wounds of my heart and soul to heal. They healed quicker when Mama was not around to pour her acidy words onto them. Here in the yar, I was safe, alive. The yar was irreplaceable, incomparable, and ever-lasting. Sometimes it felt as if Khan Batu, after whom our entire Batiy Mountain, or Batyeva Gora, took its name, was there himself. Now the yar was peace itself, unspoiled by civilization and the passage of centuries. My yar was my Kiev. Its connection to history and nature was what I loved most about my city when I was a child. When I was thirsty, I walked all the way down to the freshwater stream, where some unknown kind hand had placed a pipe, so that water could be channeled into my ready-cupped hands. Had the partisans drunk this sweet water? It was cold and sweet, the best-tasting water I ever had. With this water of the yar I washed my childhood of everything sad and mean. The water of the yar will always stay with me, my own fountain of youth.

After the 1986 Chernobyl nuclear meltdown or shortly before it, some thoughtless politicians signed off on a plan to pave my yar and killed its spring, turning the entire bottom into a swamp-like, unusable, stinky mess. Progress is not always progressive, just as adults are not always grown up and children are not always innocent and inexperienced.

I witnessed so many things in that yar, while I was staring at the clouds in the sky. It was as if I absorbed the entire life of my city by lingering all the long days on a patch of its soil. The yar's green spirits wove me into the fabric of the city, to forever meander among them.

When I returned home after a month of counselor's aide work, I was looking forward to spending August at home just as I wanted, in my yar, when Uncle Leon came to visit us from Riga. Leon was truly not my uncle in the purest sense of this word. He was my maternal grandma's sister's son, whom the family adored and idolized as their golden boy. In reality Leon was a spoiled *boychik*, an overgrown mama's boy. He was despotic, arrogant, and quite often cruel to those who loved him most. Many years later, his extreme laziness killed him when, disappointed in his modest US success, he ate, drank, and smoked too much and died from heart failure on his birthday. He'd cut most relations off by that point, and we all assumed he was still celebrating when he did not respond to our happy-birthday messages, so his body lay unclaimed at the Westchester County hospital for days.

Leon was only thirty years old in 1976. He thought he was hot. He earned substantially more than anyone we knew and had a show-offy lifestyle, always bragging about his superior this or that circumstance and never spreading any of his extra glory to his family, who opened their hearts, arms, and homes for him when he had times of lesser fortune. That summer, however, Leon rented an old resort home in the suburb of Riga in the Jūrmala region on the Baltic Sea. I was surprised to hear that he invited Mama and me to spend some time there. That was so uncharacteristic of him. Leon was against spending money on anyone but himself. There was probably some other motive behind it, but no one told me. Instead, my mama was only too happy to ship me off by myself almost immediately.

In Riga I stayed with my aunt Polina, Babushka's younger sister and Leon's mom. Her family lived in a communal city apartment on Henri Barbusse Street with multiple toilet covers on the walls of the only bathroom—one to each family with no privacy there. The about-to-be-demolished rental was in Bulduri, Jūrmala—an hour by local train. It was, by the end of that summer, leveled into one of the many spots of the new Bulduri Hotel's parking lot. I think Leon got that rental at little or no cost, but he never refrained from adding extra value to himself by underscoring that he was now a benefactor to his poor teenage niece from the utterly uncivilized Kiev.

Leon was actually a talented engineer, an inventor with more than fifty patents to his name. He taught descriptive geometry and put titanium to use way before the ordinary folk knew of its practical applications. His knowledge and proficiency in titanium's use was a slight hint to the secret direction of his work. Only those with special access clearances used titanium in the Soviet Union then and only for strategic military projects. His colleagues and bosses respected him for his scientific advancement, but Leon loved to behave badly. Round and bold from an early age, he thought himself irresistible to women and grinned at every passing skirt in the manner of a man who never thinks "no" is a word directed at him. Leon was then seeing a girl named Galina, about eighteen, just three years my senior. I never met her, but boy, did I get to hear a lot about her. She was a daughter of some Latvian Communist Party top-echelon official, and her father was against her dating a Jew. Leon loved sneaking into Galina's apartment when her father was away or working. He bragged to me about the various beers her apartment was stacked with and went into great detail about Galina's hair, shoes, underwear, and many dresses, each lovelier than the last. He occupied himself with storytelling on those evenings her father was at home. I imagined all these beautiful things and secretly drew sketches so when I returned to Kiev I could design and color paper dresses for my paper doll.

Unlike Galina, I had no father, no beer, no beautiful dresses, and no way of making any for myself. All my clothes were then Soviet made. Their fabrics were coarse cottons, and their prints were what Mama called "village milkmaid attire"—tiny forget-me-nots or daisies.

Leon pretended it did not matter to him if Galina's dad did not consider him a quality suitor because he was

a Jew. It was odd. Leon always talked about the importance of being a Jew. He was the only one of my relatives I
remember ever saying that. As one of the relations closest
to me in age, in many regards, he was my role model, the
only one who was not afraid to discuss the Jewish question with me. He told me stories about his closest circle of
friends, who were all arrested for a plane-hijacking attempt
when they wanted to fly out of the USSR to Israel from
Riga Airport—a daring yet unsuccessful feat. Leon said he
would have been with them had his mother not gotten sick
that day and held him back. Yes, Leon was much more a
Jew than anyone else I knew, more so than any of the rest
of my grandma's clan. They were all too battered by their
own adversities.

I knew of no such thing as practicing Jews. It was
somehow okay for Christians to talk about their baptisms,
even though formally there was no religion permitted in the
Soviet Union, but I never heard a Jew say "bar mitzvah"
or "bris." Even if they said it, I would not be able to recognize these words. They and the acts they refer to were
completely foreign to me, a good Soviet Socialist girl. All
Jews were overpowered by their persecutors—the men,
women, and children always trying to solve that unsolvable
European Jewish question by punishing the Jews for all the
bad things in history since time immemorial and adding a
little extra for everyday life.

The Jewish struggle for acceptance has preoccupied me
nightly and daily from the age of twelve. I was bullied and
abused and suffered self-torture by reliving the offenses I
was not capable of fighting off on the spot. I cursed the
fact that I was a Jew and plotted how to not be one. I lay
awake nights thinking up strategies for how to handle
things differently the next time. Alas, I was just as limp

and defenseless at each slur thrown in my face. Mama, Grandpa, and everyone else said, "Endure it." Leon was the only person I knew who said, "Fight back," but he could not teach me how without actually fistfighting, as he did. The more I suffered, the more I was incapacitated and dumb. Words stuck in my throat. Sleepless nights never led to a different tomorrow. Like Mama and many others, I was learning to absorb offenses and imagining how different things could have been if I were not born a Jew.

When Leon was not serious, he loved to tease me. He made fun of my deficient intellect, my homemade clothes, and my Ukrainian pronunciation of Russian words. Once on a roll, he did not know when to stop, always bordering on cruelty. He also loved to grab me by my nose with his fat boxer's fingers and squeeze until it hurt and I cried and screamed and gasped for air. He'd laugh, unperturbed by my crying. As a youngster, he'd been a competitive boxer and had studied judo. He was a stout man, with great physical power, which he never learned to curb. He used his fists frequently to hit his own mother. Aunt Polina was thus the most abused Jewish woman I knew during my childhood. The only abused Jewish woman I knew. Not counting Mama and Grandma. Leon was loaded with foolish pride and acted cruelly to all of us who loved him till the very day he died, leaving no heirs that he acknowledged, no will, no instructions on disposition of his personal belongings. Even photos of his parents were not possible to dig out from his hoarder's den of a house. Everything was thrown away. It is now as if he never was.

To an average Soviet citizen, Latvia, like all Baltic Soviet republics, was the closest thing to being abroad. I have never been to Estonia and Lithuania, but Latvia I knew to be a wondrous land of plenty. Although stifled and constricted during the Soviet regime, Latvia, in comparison to Ukraine, was a universe above us. The drawback of being in Latvia as a Russian speaker was the hostility of its natives toward all Soviets. For example, Latvian store clerks demonstratively refused to understand the invaders' language. Often at a counter or cafeteria line, Latvian speakers would be served first, even as there were many Russians in front of them. Objections from the Russian speakers were verbally shut down with "We did not invite you" and "Learn our language" comments. The Letts were not afraid to speak out against the occupiers and used excellent practical Russian to make sure these comments were understood. Leon loved to watch these fights escalate and then throw a few sentences in his perfect Latvian to scare the salesgirls. I think he would tell them he was KGB or something to that effect.

The first time I visited Riga, when only two years of age, I stayed at my paternal grandmother's and met my uncle Mark, Garrik's brother. None of that side of the family ever knew I was in Riga again.

When Mama sent me off to Riga, she told me I'd be staying mostly in Jūrmala, the area linking many small towns nearby Riga. It was the most exclusive Baltic seaside resort of the Soviet Union. Mama gave me a lot of cash in case there would be things to buy. Mama earned maybe a quarter of Leon's pay, but with minimal rent and electric bills and the absence of many basic necessities, she was somehow able to save money every month for summer vacations and special purchases. For the first time in my life I had a bank of about 200 rubles to use.

We were so poor then, Mama and I. I owned only one pair of nylon pantyhose. They cost 7 rubles and 70 kopecks—a small fortune representing more than one-tenth of Mama's monthly salary. By then over a year old, my pantyhose had many runs, which I repaired with different colors of *mouliné* thread. I think they had around forty such "fixes." I could not wear these hose anyplace other than my own school, where everyone knew of our poverty. Besides, most of the students in my school lived in similar conditions. Also, my grade knew that I was using different-colored threads to make a statement of my poverty, to show it off, not to hide it, as was commonplace then, by using threads carefully pulled out of an already retired pair of hose in order to repair another. Well, the things we did then ...

Leon made tons of money and spent it flamboyantly. He was always going to bars and restaurants with his friends. If he was in the city, he drove Aunt Polina mad with his comings and goings. She was a sick, immobile woman whose life was now reduced to sitting in front of the TV set or chatting in rare long-distance telephone conversations with her older sister Raya, who lived in Kiev. Polina's early life was complex. Her first family was lost to Stalin, and her misfortunes were magnified by her complete unwillingness and inability to stand up for herself to her second family, who abused her. When I was spending my month in Riga, she showed me some bewitching photos of herself as a young woman. I'd heard family tales of Polina's incredible beauty, but I'd never imagined her to be so cinematically gorgeous.

Polina's marriage to Leon's despotic, though superintelligent, father and her miserly in-laws in that communal apartment on Henri Barbusse Street made her sick. She tried to run away to Kiev several times but always chose to return when her husband, Naum, followed her. Naum's parents and his own disease-like stinginess ultimately resulted in the unhappiness of them all. Not one of them was ever able to enjoy life. Later I learned they had a stash of hidden gold they'd discovered when they moved a picture on the wall of their newly occupied rooms after the war, revealing a safe filled with prerevolutionary gold. Maybe it had belonged to the Jews killed in the Riga ghetto, maybe to some Russians who had fled to Riga, seeking refuge after the revolution but ending up killed or shipped to Siberia in 1940. At any rate, I think that gold was tainted. Leon offered to gift us a five-ruble coin once but never followed through.

Aunt Polina sat like a sack of flour in her armchair, fat and bloated at only sixty-five years of age, no more able to defend herself than to take care of herself or her rooms. Mama had deceived me into thinking that I was going to Riga to spend a month by the sea, but I figured out after a few days that she'd really made an agreement to send me there to help Polina. Polina did not want me going to Bulduri at all. I sometimes did, but then I did not want to remain there for long, knowing she'd be worried. She would have preferred me staying in the city, cleaning out Leon's recently departed paternal grandpa's belongings. They were gathered together in one of the three rooms their family occupied in the communal apartment, where several other families also resided, using the same bathroom, toilet, bathtub, kitchen, and so on.

Aunt Polina wanted to tie me to her side, but no one, not even I, respected her wishes. To get away, I'd rummage through Leon's grandpa's stockpile of garbage. His furniture and clothing had already been removed. All other belongings sat in a large pile in the center of what used to be his room. No one gave me an assignment. I had no idea how to approach this pile. But it was a good escape room.

If I found a book, I'd read it. I'd sift a little and throw away anything I recognized as certain garbage, not that there were any plastic bags or anything to cart it away in. I had to use their unwashed garbage bucket. It smelled worse than the room. I'd open a huge window and let some air in.

The famous old Laima chocolate factory adjoined the backyard of this once-wonderful old building, and on days the factory made chocolate, everything was permeated with its sweet scent. I'd be inspired then to leave and explore the streets of Riga. In Latvia one could and should buy things not available in Ukraine, so I was hunting for them and used my bankroll to buy them. I bought myself a shoe tote bag to carry my school shoes to school. I'd been dreaming of such a bag for many years, since I first saw it in a film about Riga schoolkids. Emerald-green, sapphire-blue, and black squares were printed on its weatherproof fabric. I bought a couple of records of Rigas Doms, the famed Riga Cathedral of Saint Mary, known for its pipe organ, because no one wanted to go there with me for a concert and I was too afraid to go to any concert hall alone. I also bought a Riga leather piggy bank with some fierce Lett deity on it. I still have it.

But most importantly, one day I bought a very pretty dress. Actually, I bought two of the same dress—the Riga twins. That, I'd learned, was the thing to do when the opportunity presented itself: buy two—one to wear, one to sell or trade. Anyway, my new dress was a pattern reminiscent of paisley in faded shades of blue and gray over an off-white background with black contouring. It had a V-neck. Even though I have understood for years that my neck is long, very unlike the rest of the women in my family, I now saw myself with this long neck sticking out. I remember thinking it was a pretty sight I was not expecting, so I looked every time I passed a mirror. The dress was very elegant but too simple in Mama's view, because of the similarities of its colors. Mama would have preferred something many shades louder, like purples, oranges, and reds. I was so happy to have found it before she arrived. I much preferred the pale blues and grays. The sleeves were short, just over the shoulder. The skirt flared a little from the hips. Its soft fabric fell just below my knees, but as I was still growing, the hem eventually ended up above them.

For some years before this purchase, my only dresses were uniforms or those I made myself. I do not recall having a single well-made garment between the ages of twelve and fifteen. All my clothes were Soviet-made fashion and fabric disasters, which made even a pretty girl look like she was an outright tractor driver from anywhere but Kiev. And I was not a pretty girl by any description. I was nerdy, sloppy, with feverishly freckled skin and thick, curly dark hair that was perpetually tangled. My pantyhose, always hanging too loose around my knees, matched the remainder of my unkempt look, but none of that would have mattered if my mama liked me. During our very rare moments of peace, Mama kept calling me her "ugly duckling," and though perhaps her intention was to remind me of the story of the beautiful swan the duckling becomes at the end, the word *ugly* became imprinted on my brain. I saw ugliness each time I saw myself in the mirror, so I stopped looking and did not care to take better care of myself, because there was no way to fix this ugliness.

I developed without receiving any explanations or support from Mama or school. As my body changed, the ugly clothing I wore for weeks at a time belonged on me, because I was made to believe I deserved no better. On family visits to my first cousins, I saw the pretty foreign clothing

and cosmetics their mama was able to get for them, and I
envied them for it. Their mama, my aunt Zina, had had a
falling-out with my mama many years before. Aunt Zina,
even though she could have, never helped my mother get
any of the wonderful things she was able to get for her
girls. She worked as a bookkeeper at the foreign currency
store Kashtan and had access to the plentitude of resources
unavailable to Mama. Yet Mama could not humble herself
to fix her once-excellent relationship with Zina.

Before the end of preceding school year, the boys from
my class had a "looks review" of girls while we were all
working on a collective farm for two weeks, harvesting
radishes and strawberries for the city population in long
ten-hour shifts in the sweltering June heat. I clearly heard
what they said about me—"That stinking Jew? No way."

Ella Gladshtein, a Jewish girl I knew, had taught me a
response to comments like these, but I was always afraid
to use it, afraid to be beaten, slapped, hurt. The heat and
dust of that harvesting summer blocked my usual fears,
though, allowing my newly emerging desire to fight back
to seep out. Without looking or unbending from my vegetable labor, I threw back at the boys gathering radishes in
the next row over just what Ella had told me to say: "It's
better to be a stinking Jew like me than a shallow Russian
like you." I said it loud and clear for everyone working
nearby to hear. Laughter followed, and my offenders were
temporarily silenced. But still I was left on that field ugly
and undesired by the very same boys who used to turn their
heads toward me up through fourth grade, before the older
ones told them to stop admiring me. That was when they'd
learned that Jews were "inferior" people and turned into
my bullies and abusers.

Rejection was something I had from every possible direction, and before I bought the Riga twins, I was resigned to my awkward ugliness and general undesirability. The Riga dress almost immediately transformed me from a child into a young woman, from unwanted and undesired to a whole new set of hopes and expectations. I could be, as far as I was concerned, just as desirable now as Uncle Leon's Communist Galina with all her pretty dresses.

It is amazing how my memory responds now to the recollection of that new fabric's smell and feel between my fingers. When I first put the Riga dress on and Aunt Polina saw me, she wanted to tie me to herself with an even stronger string. Leon's reaction was weird. He gave me his broad, happy smile and, calling me a wonderful diminutive from Maria, told me as only he would, "Man'ka, you look awesome!" A day or two later, he took me to a restaurant where his friends were celebrating their whatever. It was my first ever evening at a restaurant. I was growing up by the minute, even though Leon did not allow me to sip anything except lemonade.

After two weeks of all this Riga and Jūrmala fun, Mama arrived. Proclaiming that she was there for her aunt and would stay only with her aunt, she immediately went to spend some time in Bulduri, taking me with her. We'd leave our untidy, stale-smelling rented house early in the mornings to have a delicious breakfast of buns and coffee at the inexpensive self-service café. Mama would head straight to the beach to lie down after breakfast, but I'd go to a strip of pines that grew right out of the sandy soil along the beach, a pine park really, where I could sit and read in shade. At lunch in the same café I had my favorite beet soup, smoked chicken entrée, and berry dessert every day. The temperature of the Baltic Sea in August was high at 18 degrees Celsius but still too cold for me. I could put my feet into it after the sun had warmed it for a few hours, but I could never swim in water that cold. I loved wading, though, and did a lot of it, enjoying my solitude. Mama lay on a beach towel, getting a suntan and sand all over herself. Then Mama swam in that cold water, loving it and demonstratively ridiculing me to all our beach neighbors for not wanting to join her. By then I knew very well that Mama never passed up an opportunity to belittle me to strangers. I just did not understand why she thought that would make her seem better to them.

About a week later, we received an urgent telegram from my grandfather in Kiev. "Approved to go," it said. Pan Zbiegniew had not lied after all. He'd sent us an invitation to visit our "relatives in Poland." Mama had registered the visit at the OVIR while I was at the collective farm earlier that summer, and now we had to return to Kiev immediately, so that I would not miss many school days.

At that time very few people traveled to Poland. It was, indeed, a foreign country. Ironically, after we left the USSR in 1979, going there would become commonplace. But in 1976 Poland was more exotic to us than Tahiti or Japan are now. Mama's coworker Mara had recently gone there, and she instructed Mama what to buy for sale, how to sell it there, and at what price. It was Mara who made sure Mama bought two electric irons and some Soviet-made battery-operated stuffed toys. Mara also supplied Mama with an address in Warsaw, where we were to stay for a few days before heading out to the Molases'. Our purchases took longer than expected, and we actually left after school had already started. My teachers said they would mark me as present in exchange for lipstick. I guess I did not inherit Mama's bargaining handicap.

On the day of our departure, Mara arrived at our apartment early and asked Mama to take a huge stuffed dog and some battery-operated small appliances to her Warsaw people. I specifically remember a coffee grinder. Mara, to her credit, immediately revealed to us what we were about to take with us and sort of gave my mother an option to decline. Seated at our kitchen table, Mara carefully opened up the coffee grinder and removed one of its two large carbon batteries. Next, with surgical meticulousness, she opened the battery, after first lining our tabletop with an old newspaper. We always had plenty of newspaper in the bathroom, as we used it in place of toilet paper, which was never to be found in stores. Incidentally, most propaganda newspapers were purchased only because they were in demand for bathrooms.

The Soviet carbon battery was a green-white-and-black cardboard cylinder, D size. Under its cardboard top, it was half-filled with dry carbon; the bottom half was filled with anthracite-colored gook that looked like tar but was almost solid. I had never before opened up a battery, and I was mesmerized. Mara carefully removed the top layer of carbon to reveal to us that she had strung several gold rings with large center stones around the metal rod in the center of the battery. The stones were of the "for hookers only" kind: rubies and diamonds.

"You can hide your ring here too," Mara offered, and Mama, as if in some sort of a trance, removed her only gold ring off her finger and handed it to Mara. Mara slipped Mama's slim wedding band onto the center rod, replaced the carbon, and carefully resealed the battery, wiping it clean and reinserting it into the grinder. Mama's eyes were wide with disbelief, mostly at Mara's ability to purchase such expensive jewels. But she said nothing.

About an hour later, still under Mara's supervision, we took the taxi she ordered and paid for to the Central Railroad Station, boarded the train, and waved goodbye to the very happily chattering Mara.

There were two other passengers in our train compartment, so we could not discuss Mara's visit nor open up the second coffee grinder battery to examine its contents. Perhaps it would have been dangerous to open it right there anyway. The train compartment could have had listening devices or peeping holes for all we knew. When we reached the border town of Brest, our train was transferred to the narrow set of train wheels. Russian railroad tracks were wider than the European ones, so at the border the train cars were slightly lifted one by one, with passengers still inside, and the wheels reset. With contraband inside our suitcases, I was too scared to notice any specifics of this fascinating process. It took a couple of painfully long hours. In the meantime, the USSR border control and customs police (*tamozennaya milizia*) canvassed the train, opening compartments and passengers' luggage. They were getting near us from both ends of the train, as we were somewhere in the middle. Mama sat pale as a ghost. By then it was just the two of us left in our compartment; the others had gotten off in Brest or maybe even earlier, in Minsk.

Periodically, Mama whispered to me, "I cannot lie. They will arrest me. What have I done? You will be left all alone. How stupid was I? Mara is a total bitch. She probably has gold in every battery of that fuckin' dog!"

I must have been very naive indeed, because up until then I never thought that Mara could have hidden gold in all the other batteries. I probably could not comprehend that much money then. Or that sort of deception.

I sat still, afraid to stir and disturb the very air around me, lest I break the shield of safety I was creating by believing everything would be okay. The men knocked and entered our compartment. There were three or four of them, in different uniforms. It was clear that they immediately understood my mother's guilty composure. She was always such a terrible liar, yet she lied all the time. It's a shame she never learned to lie better. The men were speaking Russian and Polish; some of them were customs and some border control. The border people left rather quickly, but one customs man hung around, questioning Mama about gold. "Do you have any? Why are you not bringing jewelry to Poland? Everyone brings jewelry to Poland. You can sell two pieces there legally and bring other things back. Didn't you know?" It became evident that the very absence of any rings on Mama's fingers was a conspicuous detail that she and Mara had not bothered to consider all those hours ago. He left and returned several times, finally saying as he left our compartment, "*Wiem że pani zloto zahovala*" ("I know you hid the gold, lady"). The wheels turned, and we were soon out of the USSR.

Mama recovered fast, happily whispering, "Ha ha, how I fooled them. Mara is a bitch. I could have been arrested," and similar bull.

I sat pretty much in the same position, wearing my Riga twin dress, smoothing its soft fabric on my shaking knees, still afraid to disturb the air around me. I did not notice it at first, but soon I realized that my left eye was twitching violently. If I knew what praying was, I probably could have acknowledged that was what I'd done for the past few hours. For all I knew, Mama's bad acting and her carelessness could have landed her in Siberia. We were, indeed, very lucky the customs officer decided not to open our suitcases and examine all our batteries. He could have done that, no doubt. Yet he did not. It was a really scary situation, one of the scariest ever in my life. Now, for Mama, the danger was all over, but she did not care about what I felt or even that I got that horrible eye tic that I still get whenever in very disturbing situations. It was never over for me. To this day, I jump every time I am questioned by people in uniform. Mama soon fell asleep, and when she awoke, it was morning, and we were in Warsaw.

Poland

The couple Mara sent us to intercepted us at our sleeper compartment and drove us to their apartment. The car ride was the first of many new experiences for me, but I could hardly enjoy it. I barely remember the ride and the striking look of Warsaw, filled with all the colors from my box of colored pencils. So different from the grays of Kiev and the absolute dinginess of Minsk, which we'd passed by just yesterday. Forever after, I would describe arriving to Warsaw like going from a black-and-white film into a colorized one.

After closing all the window shades of their apartment tightly, our hosts began to unload. The stuffed dog alone had eight batteries, and there were many more batteries in the appliances. Out of these batteries came rings, earrings, chains, cufflinks—all containing rubies, diamonds, emeralds, sapphires. There was a small mound of thick gold wedding rings, with Mama's the tiniest. But she never claimed it back anyway, perhaps sending me the first signal of uncharacteristic things to expect.

Our hosts took everything out of our suitcases except our meager personal belongings and the gifts we carried for Jadwiga and her family. Everything was for sale. Mama and this couple made plans for the goods—what to sell, how much to get, and what to buy with it for the trip back. I do not think they understood she was only a carrier. My head spun. The woman told me I could go take a bubble bath in their bathtub.

The bathroom was really pretty and clean. It had mirror tiles on the wall, and for the first time in my life, I saw myself fully naked in a mirror. I am a natural prude and did not like looking at myself, but I was thrilled knowing that was how it could be done on the other side of the border—full view, not a tiny chip of a mirror, like everywhere back home. They had fragrant bath soaps and shampoos, thick towels, white bath slippers, loofahs and scrubs, and many other things I had no idea why or how to use. Everything was scented and spick-and-span. I had the first enjoyable bath of my life there and repeated it daily. Indeed, I mused, if we had clean baths like that back home, we would all be so much cleaner.

Poland stormed into my life with a whirlwind of experiences, and I loved every discovery. Rynek Starego Miasta (Old Town Market Square) in Warsaw will forever remain the most beautiful place on this planet to my mind's eye. With no space between buildings, these expensive residences were constructed and destroyed several times in Warsaw's history. Completely renovated after the total destruction in World War II, each building had its own color and design. The cobblestoned sides of the square were seeded with artists selling their works. This was the happiest place I had seen by then. The sellers were busy selling, not chastising or pushing their items onto prospective customers, as in the Ukrainian and Latvian markets and stores. They also praised their prospects—"Pretty lady, give me your pretty smile!" That could not have possibly been addressed to me, and I could not have possibly understood it! But I did. I understood everything everyone was saying. I understood everyday Polish just like that. It sounded nice and kind and made me want to buy the world. Happy people made all the difference. What wouldn't I give to live in a happy land!

Mama and I had to choose one of many cafés. It was a real café, and we ate September strawberries. Who'd ever heard of strawberries this late in the season? They were sold clean and in individual tissue paper. The dusty, sandy strawberries I'd grazed on in the hungry days of June at the collective farm seemed insane now, as did the vegetable-and-fruit store in the side alley of our apartment building, where nasty female store workers forcefully shoved their metal shovels into mounds of mud and angrily dispensed the soil-wrapped fruit or vegetable of the day in limited quantities into customers' bags, verbally fighting off complaints from the back of the endless queue that there would not be enough for all. In the USSR, I noted in my head, we paid for the dirt mixed with rudeness. Not in Poland. Poland had shown me with one clean, beautiful, delicious strawberry that there could be culture in service and respect for consumers.

In a movie house in the center of Warsaw, Mama and I watched *The Godfather*, a film that was banned in the USSR. The movie ran in English, which I did not understand, with Polish subtitles, which I could not follow fast enough, but I still understood everything and explained to Mama in Russian what was taking place on-screen. The only thing I could not understand was why the movie was banned. There was nothing anti-Soviet in it. Maybe they just did not want us to see how pretty life was for Americans. It sure was also very pretty for the Poles.

We went to shops, markets, and department stores and were shocked by the availability of clothing, footwear, undergarments, cosmetics, and every possible household and life necessity, all of which were impossible to procure in the Soviet Union, even if one had a fortune to offer for each item.

In a Polish bookstore I bought Russian books that I could not possibly buy in the USSR. They were printed in the USSR but were sold only abroad, as if to show everyone "Yes, we allow everything."

I bought boots on Aleje Jerozolimskie (Jerusalem Avenue) in a very pretty shoe store, where my feet were measured for length and width. An elegantly dressed salesman assisted me—the very first such help in my life. To top it all off, I bought my very first pair of jeans at one of several markets where Polish citizens, quite legally, sold clothing they were able to buy abroad in Germany or beyond. The Poles lived in a different kind of Socialist reality, where so many USSR taboos were not taboos at all. The pocket and label of my first jeans bore the name Monsieur, a word I could neither read nor pronounce then. They were the best pair of jeans I ever had, because they were my first and very much desired. I wore them for a couple of years, even after arriving to the United States, converting them into shorts at the end of their wonderful life.

Jadwiga and her family gave us a king's welcome. The Molases lived in the largest house in Skierbieszów, save for that of the *ksiądz*, their priest. They gathered everyone to welcome us. Pani (Mrs.) Irena made a feast. They even killed a hog, for we were dear guests in their home and at their table. I had very few social graces. I'd only read about them. The only practical experience I had was the little I'd learned from spending four days in Jadwiga's presence the previous year. I followed her lead now, copying her in everything. She was the only real young lady I'd met thus far. Pani Irena had only one hand, having lost one in an accident, so Jadzia helped wherever and whenever possible. There was no screaming or bullying at their home. I wished I could stay there longer, but Mama made new plans all of a sudden, and they didn't include spending more than three days in Skierbieszów. Altogether, combining both years, I spent just one week of my life with Jadzia, but what eye-opening days they turned out to be. There were many different people who came into my life for short spans of time, but none of them had the influence of Jadzia.

I questioned then, in Poland, why all these Poles came to welcome us. The answer was in front of me, but I was too young to pay proper attention: there were almost no Jews left in Poland by then, and they just wanted to see Jews. Jews were numerous in Poland before the war, but not after. Many Jews they'd known since they were children could no longer feast with them, and so these Poles brought their own prehistory and perhaps some guilt to that evening's feast. Without realizing, I took over for those Jews for that one very special evening.

The next day was a Sunday. We went to church with Jadzia's entire family, and I witnessed religion for the first time in my life. Their church was not like a nonworking Kiev church, where only very old, black-garbed women prayed and crossed themselves. Theirs was a magnificent cathedral where everyone—old, young, male, female— seemed happy to be and happy to pray together aloud or silently, like Jadzia, who was seated next to me on the balcony. I questioned, for the very first time, the rationale of removing religion from the people and replacing it with ... whatever the doctrines we were being served were. These doctrines did not fill our hearts with passion any more than the Soviet economy filled our stomachs with everyday delicacies I now knew were sold everywhere in Poland. I could almost feel my mind expanding as my heart shrank with the realization that soon this experience would all be over for me. I was changing and very rapidly.

My appearance was still the same. Anything new I bought was being saved for home. I kept wearing my Riga twin dress, and I wore it on the day we went to Lublin. I liked myself in it more and more. I was becoming something other than the girl I was used to. It was as if I was brighter and better by association with Jadzia and being in her country. I was walking less uncertainly. I was looking at myself in the mirror without disgust or shame for my inadequacy. I was cleaner, prettier, softer, stronger. I even wore my dress differently. I remember that when that Lublin day began, I liked looking at my own Jewish face in the mirror of Jadzia's pretty bathroom. Everything was so likable in Poland. The world was still full of anti-Semites, but I knew I could learn to deal with them better than Mama, because I had a good friend in Poland.

Poland could do no wrong to me.

Majdanek

Mama and I were on a streetcar to visit a furrier Pan Zbiegniew had recommended to make a *gesheft* (deal). We were going to buy mink pelts, of which we were legally permitted only four, so that Mama could have a fur hat and collar made in Kiev for her winter coat. The recommended furrier was going to sell us the finest-quality pelts *z pod lódu* (under the counter; literally, "from under the ice") and provide us with a document saying they were the

exact lower quality allowed to be brought out of Poland
and into the USSR.

I loathed governments and the authority they exerted
over the regular people. Why could we not buy what we
wanted and take it where we were going? Governments
always made things so difficult for good and honest people. They made us lie, steal, and transport contraband,
and who could predict what else governments could force
people to do?

I was deep in this analysis when the conductor announced the next stop. Mama jumped up and insisted we
get off to see something important. That was the first time
in my life I'd heard the word *Majdanek*.

I was raised with a very strong sense of Soviet patriotism and of the great losses the USSR suffered during the
Great Patriotic War of 1941–1945. My grandma made
sure I remembered the horrific fate of the Jews in Babiy
Yar, where, as I later learned, 33,771 Jews were shot in
two days in a tragic massacre, a statistic then unknown to
her. Like most Soviet citizens, I was never told about and
did not understood the historic catastrophe of the Jewish
Holocaust, until that day, in mid-September 1976, when
Mama decided to get off the streetcar upon hearing a simple word—*Majdanek*. What was so special about a place
called The Little Field? It was about two or three in the
afternoon, and I was hot, tired, and hungry. What was the
attraction of this stop?

We walked under the gate, which was the exact same
gate the people sent to the Majdanek concentration camp
some thirty years earlier had walked under. No other explanation was needed. What took place here was still in
the air.

What is thirty years to history? A blink of an eye. More than forty years has passed since that day in September 1976, when I walked under that sign, and it is still as if I went there yesterday to "meet" those Jews' unfathomable story for the very first time.

Slowly, as I traveled from exhibit to exhibit, from barrack to barrack, I learned the sad truth about humans—how they were, in their large mass, so easily deceived. The Germans thought themselves so superior and intellectually progressive to the rest of humankind and were so admired for their progressive thinking, science, art, and literature before the Great War. Yet somehow they were duped into believing that it was all right to annihilate all Jews for just being Jews, all right to starve and torture them, kill their children, and burn them alive. My mind was so used to various sorts of abuse over being a Jew. But nothing I'd experienced or learned from listening to my grandparents, from reading a vast number of novels, or from watching hundreds of films about World War II and the Nazi atrocities toward the people of the USSR in Ukraine, Belarus, and the Baltics could compare. I suddenly comprehended the vastness of Nazism.

It was there in the items left behind.

The lampshade and pillow made from human skin and filled with human hair.

Gold teeth of various shapes and sizes, pulled out of the mouths of ordinary people upon their arrival to this concentration camp.

Piles of combs, eyeglasses, glass eyes, teddy bears, dolls, suitcases, and shoes.

Thousands of children's shoes.

Those shoes were once brown, black, green, and red and worn on many feet. Now they were gray and faded, together in immense heaps within chicken wire bins. All that was left of some of these humans were their shoes.

Nothing ever shocked me as much as the sight of those many shoes.

Those shoes were what the greatest evil left behind.

The mountain of ashes and the monuments that the concentration camp prisoners erected, the smell in the barracks, the crematoriums, the close proximity of the Polish homes on the outside, the vast expanse so visible from the neighborhood atop the hill ... impossible not to hear, see, and smell ...

Millions of Jews died. One and a half million Jewish children died. So many of them right here.

It has since become important to many people to reduce the numbers of victims. These people—some of whom are bona fide, respected historians and scientists—argue about the exact death toll and methods of correctly estimating it. Some contemporary historians often rely on Internet-era information and legitimize many illegitimate sources planted by Holocaust deniers. There is an ongoing effort to change the trail of history until new troops are ready to eradicate the entire Jewish population off the face of the planet once again. For as long as there are Jewish people, there are anti-Semites, plotting, conspiring, codifying, and implementing new methods of killing Jews for just being Jews. That will never change.

Modern Holocaust deniers are now doing it with the same sophistication and charm bequeathed to them by some of their Nazi predecessors. Once again they are fooling decent people and discrediting their opponents using the newfound means of easy propaganda on social networks that refuse to take down their hate pages in the name of free speech. Haters play many games of deception through revisionism while acting nice and finding ways to larger forums of young followers by becoming professors, historians, historical writers, and politicians. I have encountered some, and the damage their efforts cause is visible. Many decent people now claim "Holocaust fatigue," even many Jews. *Will the death of the last survivor of the Nazi Holocaust be the beginning of the next Holocaust?* I often wonder. And then I try to do the little I can personally do, because I saw the worst of humanity in Majdanek when I was only fifteen.

In Majdanek, inside the chicken wire bins, I saw the pencils that had once belonged to the children of this concentration camp—children who did not live to maturity; did not write love letters; did not have weddings; did not have children of their own; did not have fights with their friends, teachers, husbands, mothers, and mothers-in-law; and did not do so many other ordinary things humanity expects of people. Even if the people who had walked in the very shoes piled before me at Majdanek were the only ones killed in such an organized manner, it was still plenty of proof of hatred to me. The shoes of Majdanek were the most convincing statistical sample of despicable atrocities committed against me and my kind.

I was a child visiting these departed souls in 1976, walking where they'd taken their last steps, said their last words, breathed their last breaths. I, a girl from school 187 on Batyeva Gora in Kiev, was now walking among these dead. I knew I would forever carry them with me to the outside. It was as if I was suddenly aware of them having lived so short a life and still wanting to live when specially trained, cruel executioners of small children took their lives to serve someone's agenda of world domination. I could not have not known about this before, even if I did know so many other things about the war. In reality, I knew nothing of war until I saw Majdanek and walked among those who never left it.

Years later I met a Jewish man who had escaped from Majdanek and later on from Auschwitz. He said, "God was not there." I also met a Jewish woman whose family lived in the vicinity of Majdanek on false Polish papers during the peak of the camp's crematorium activity, when they could smell the burning human flesh often. "Everyone knew," she said to me. "We all knew." In 1976, I did not question whether they knew; I knew they all knew. The camp was inside the city. The city always knows what happens within it.

Still, I was only fifteen. A group of teens my age in torn jeans, chewing gum, stereotypically American, walked toward me, having just left the walls of the crematorium, giggling and pinching each other, as if they did not just see the same things I saw. "Americans," said someone nearby in Polish, "always stupid wherever they go. They have no clue about anything."

I turned around to take a final look at the bunch of them. *Americans,* I thought, *have everything everyone else wants, but we, the Europeans, have better hearts, because we understand the inevitability and tragedy of war.*

I was only fifteen. We make so many quick judgments when we are young. Mama and I left through that same gate, and life resumed, as did the whirlwind of purchases. We were quickly as carefree and careless as the torn-jeans Americans. We packed up to leave Poland, taking back different stuffed animals, for a different transport.

On our final night in Warsaw, Mama had a really good idea. She woke me up, showing me the largest of the stuffed animals our Warsaw hosts were sending back to Mara.

This dog had no batteries. Mama and I examined it very carefully and slightly opened the hidden seam on the dog's bottom. Inside, the dog was suffused with brown mink pelts, the same color as the its fake fur.

We said nothing to our hosts and took another risk. This time, deliberately. We thus returned to Kiev much better off than we left.

Mama had a talk with Mara and returned to her only half of the pelts. I was very proud of her, demonstrating she was not willing to be duped or uncompensated for her risks. Mama, too, matured in Poland. Mara and Mama remained lifetime friends.

After Poland, we had good clothing and many things to sell. Mama was very happy with this venture. My friend Yura Odnoralov was by then involved with some black marketers (*farzovshiki*) who bought things from foreigners and took the risk of covertly selling them to citizens. That was a criminal activity, with jail terms for everyone along the chain if caught. Yura helped us quite a lot selling these and other goods from Mama's next trip the following year. We finally had money.

A couple of days after I rejoined my class upon my return from Poland, in late September 1976, my homeroom teacher, Valentina Lazarevna Shilo, who was a Jew and with whom I'd shared my impressions from my visit to Majdanek, asked me to speak to the class at our obligatory Saturday-afternoon political meeting. We did not discuss it then, but now I'm certain she knew it was the eve of the thirty-fifth anniversary of the Babiy Yar massacre, a fact I did not know at the time. I think she took a risk in inviting me to share my visit with my entire class.

I stood in front of the girls and boys I had known from the age of seven and said, "When I was in Poland, I went to the concentration camp in Lublin—"

Someone called from the back, "You should have stayed there!" The shout was quickly drowned in supporting, admiring laughter.

As I stood in front of them in my brown uniform, I realized suddenly how lucky I was not to live in 1941. Then, I would have had to wonder which one of my classmates would have the most joy in personally beating and killing me in Babiy Yar. I realized, bitterly, that many of them would have fought one another for this thrill. Many, but not all. Yet it is the crowd that rules in times of despair, and I was too weak to take on a crowd. It was a surprise to me that I did not cry. I always did as soon as I was bullied for being a Jew. But not that day. I stared at their laughing faces and contemplated *me*. Before that afternoon, I would be offended by their laughter and cry. Before that afternoon, I was so frequently reminded of my inferiority that I believed myself unequal to them. But was I really inferior to those who laughed at the mention of an extermination camp? Or was I at least an equal? I pondered over this thought momentarily.

Then I sat down silently, a different Jew than when I arose.

I was now a proud Jew—a feeling I experienced at that moment for the very first time in my life.

Dress 8

The Scarlet

When I was a young girl and believed in fairy tales, I had to survive graduation. Graduation from the tenth grade of Soviet school was no simple affair. After making it through the monthlong written and oral exams, with the enormous stress they created and pressure they represented, the day before graduation, I still had no dress and no way of getting one.

I was doomed to sit out. At least it seemed that way. Here's what led to the situation. Mama had brought home two very different cuts of fabric from Poland earlier that year, when she'd gone there again without me. One fabric Mama bought especially for me. She said she wanted me to have my graduation dress made out of this very fine pale-pink-and-silver brocade. She even purchased shoes in Warsaw to match: silvery open-toe high heels with straps. I loved her so much for this. I would finally have a chance to look pretty and ladylike and maybe be admired. For some months, at least, I truly believed my mother wanted me to look and feel my very best at my graduation. I also believed that she planned to attend it.

Graduation took place on the same Saturday for the entire country. My year, graduation fell on June 24, 1978. Can you imagine, the entire graduating class of my country celebrating the end of ten arduous years together on the same day, though maybe not the same hour, as the country spread over several time zones?

All the girls I knew were busy having their dresses made at their moms' seamstresses all over town. My mother was delaying hiring a seamstress, using many different reasons to justify this delay. Mama often procrastinated, so this alone was no cause for concern.

The other piece of fabric she'd brought from Poland was a scarlet polyester. Soft to the touch, it had neither the dignity nor the purity of the pink-and-silver brocade.

For many weeks—three months, actually—my mother, who repeatedly said things like "You choose" and "It is your day," had been plotting to deprive me of my graduation. I should have seen it clearly, but I was only sixteen then and still believed my mother wanted me to be, look, and do my very best.

Mother always stressed how she constantly sacrificed everything for me. And I believed her. Believed her and did not recognize the warning signs when she hinted daily that I always looked my very best in red. I hated the color red, and Mama could not have missed knowing it. Periodically, she assured me that red was my color, and I vehemently protested. The older I got, the more I resented the color red.

Red stood for Lenin and his successor, Stalin, born Iosif Vissarionovich Dzhugashvili. Stalin was the Soviet dictator known for his reign of Red Terror. By the time of my birth his leadership was denounced as the "Stalin cult" and compared to that of other great dictators of the period—Hitler, Perón, Mao Zedong, Mussolini. He was the mastermind of purges, famine, annexations, collectivization, deportations, and pacts with Hitler and China. Mama's generation was told to worship him; mine was never told a word about him. All mentions of him—in portraits, books, and songs—were removed or rewritten, as if he never was. Removing mention of him did not lessen the grief he'd caused to millions of families, including ours. Removal of statues does not eliminate the painful past; it compounds the memory of its legacy.

The color red also stood in my mind for endless and senseless hours of Young Pioneer and Komsomol meetings. It was at these countless mandatory gatherings that the decisions of the Communist Party congresses would be read, promulgated, shoved down our red throats, and lauded by the people whose only intentions were to brainwash us into their likeness, so that we, too, would brainwash the innocents younger than ourselves.

Every citizen of Soviet Socialist Republics had a responsibility to know the exact number of congresses the Soviet Union's Communist Party had as well as the gist of their declarations and promulgations. Students graduating or entering higher-learning institutions were expected to recite many of them, and much time was spent memorizing only to forget them the morning after the exams. By the time I left the Soviet Union, there had been twenty-five such congresses, with the last one occurring in February 1976. I remember watching some of it on TV, immediately after the XII Olympic Games, and innocently wishing that there would be no more political meetings on TV.

Red also meant my red Pioneer kerchief and all the humiliation and discrimination I had to endure as a Jew in my apartment building, in red Pioneer camps, and at my very own school, despite equality slogans and nondiscrimination laws.

Red also meant only reading about and never ever tasting pineapple, banana, asparagus, mango, and many other delicacies that only Communist Party members were permitted to buy in their special stores, where only card-carrying Comparty (Communist Party) members shopped and where everything unavailable to the general public was available only to these elitists. Access to those stores was more unattainable than to the Newlyweds store. They never opened to the ordinaries to fulfill the Socialist plan. The Comparty stores carried delicacies and goods at prices several times lower than they would be if and when, once in a blue moon, they hit the common people's stores. The Comparty members did not want us to see what these items were or how much—rather, how little—they cost. Comparty members had special cafeterias that offered dinner for eleven kopeks, while ordinary citizens were charged one and a half to two rubles for a dinner of lower quality at open-access cafeterias. The Communists' salaries and affordability levels were disproportionately higher than those who had not enlisted into the card-carrying membership, so for the same job—you guessed it—they'd be paid significantly more.

The entire country engaged in this Socialist cover-up. By the time I am describing, there were no naive adults willing to sacrifice their lives for the cause of the revolution, like in the preceding decades, when they collectivized, expropriated, fought against counterrevolutionaries, redistributed wealth, rebuilt after wars, and settled the barren lands. Such heroes were for the history books and films. Now, in times of longtime peace, everyone was climbing up, as humankind is programmed to by Mother Nature. Despite prevalent oppression and tyranny by the Socialist leaders, glimpses of freedom seeped through the Iron Curtain in the way of foreign goods that members of Communist families wore. They bought such goods in their Comparty stores or from the black marketers at Odessa's markets and consignment shops. Another whiff drifted in with foreign music that foreign children brought into the Pioneer elite summer camps on the Black Sea. This music's energy and sound spread quickly and uncontrollably on illegally recorded audio tapes. These tapes were like the very capitalist disease we were conditioned to keep away from lest it contaminate us—too good to refrain from, treasured and revered as anything that is forbidden.

The entitled offspring of Communist parents were the first I knew to use plastic bags, Lancôme mascara, and Japanese-made folding umbrellas, while the rest of us admired, envied, and devised plots to somehow come in possession of these exotic goods.

People like us never even got to see the items that were designated for Communists only. People like us never tasted bananas. People like us had few privileges in our supposedly classless system. Life existed as if on two parallel platforms, and I was resigned to my deprived existence, like anyone who knows no other life firsthand. Then Mama and I went to Poland, and our world began to include gorgeous things like that silver-and-pink brocade for my graduation dress.

But Mama did not let me have the brocade, after all. Sometime during my monthlong exams, when she could delay no longer, she let me know that her coworker's daughter was getting married in late June. My mother had sold her my fabric. I would have to wear something else.

"How about a dress from the scarlet fabric? Red really is your color. It looks best with your brown hair and brown eyes," she insisted in her sweet-sweet, my-mama-the-traitor voice. And just like that, my graduation dream became my nightmare. Had she had the courage to tell me earlier, I could have asked Grandfather for some money to let me keep my dress. Even when I learned of this, we still could have gone to the dressmaker, except Mama did not seem to care how I'd be dressed or what I felt.

Now, not only did someone else have a dress made from my graduation fabric, which Mama had quietly removed from the apartment so that I would not even notice, but I learned that Mama had presold my shoes as well, for the bride to have on her honeymoon. The bride was to be married on my graduation day and was leaving for her Black Sea honeymoon the morning after. Dressy shoes were nowhere to be purchased in the USSR, so I was reduced to one night's right to wear my own graduation shoes before they would depart for this bride's honeymoon.

The next blow hit when I learned that Mama was not even planning to attend my graduation. She acted shocked when I became upset that she would have to work that Saturday. By 1978 people in her field no longer worked six-day weeks. She would have had to ask her boss for overtime or forget to ask to be excluded from mandatory overtime, which she easily could have had off with the good reason of attending her only child's graduation.

In truth, no one was coming to celebrate the occasion with me. I would be alone. Technically, of course, I'd be among classmates I'd known all my school life. But none of them loved me. And, I realized, none of my family loved me enough to share this day with me.

I was lucky to at least have Darina. It was only during the final two grades that I was friendliest with her. She was a short girl of no God-given beauty, so she worked very hard on her hair, skin, nails, and clothes. She also had no God-given talents and, as it would become evident to me only many years later, stored up plenty of envy toward me, which she learned to camouflage like one of her visible blackheads.

Darina shadowed me in grades 9 and 10, sharing my desk whenever she could, pretending we were real friends, studying with me—all, as it turned out, to earn my trust and disengage my protective shield. By sitting next to me, she copied my answers. I always let her do it, even when I caught her. I was always a good student and never minded sharing my knowledge or answers, whereas she never was studious and shared nothing. Besides, it was commonplace to help your friends pass tests, whisper answers to them from your seat when they were grilled at the chalkboard, and throw tiny notes to them when they did not have their own cheat notes—all means were employed in times of need, and it was dishonorable not to rescue a sinking classmate.

Surprisingly, as we got our diplomas that Saturday at graduation, Darina's marks were very good, almost as good as mine. Her mom quickly yanked her diploma from my hands. The USSR high school diplomas contained all subjects and final grades earned in the final two years of school, and everyone in that room was learning their final grades right at that moment, I presumed. I had no idea that every so-so student's grades were being pulled up, not only Darina's. Grades, as I later learned, were traded for favors and money. Teachers were undercompensated and overworked, and many were willing to trade a few better grades to the parents who paid.

In the chaos of the final stretch, many of our teachers helped students cheat during the orals exams and even during the two written ones—Russian literature and mathematics, which our cohort took simultaneously in the long school hallways. Desks were pulled from the nearest classrooms and arranged in endless rows in the vast open space, where we all struggled together, monitored by exam proctors. Darina's sister volunteered to be such a proctor, and she monitored her sister's row. She was there to "help." Cheating was nearly impossible in that setting, yet the majority of students invested in all kinds of cheating methods. Notes hidden in shoes, socks, bras, undies. Formulas written in black, blue, and red ink on wrists, ankles, bellies, socks, thighs. While preparing their elaborate cheat notes, such students memorized most of the material anyhow. People privy to the "help" arrangements received information very discreetly from the supposed proctors. Had they been caught, punishment, like loss of work and future education, could be levied for both the cheating students and their helpers. Yet many still tried to work out help arrangements, because the exams were actually quite deathly, especially the orals in physics and astronomy; chemistry; foreign language; mathematics, which included years of algebra, trigonometry, and geometry; and, especially for me, USSR social studies, which I defied by refusing to study in protest of a specific teacher. We studied and restudied the topics for our final orals. Who knew that the teachers were not interested in failing the students? Darina knew it from her sister but never told me. Year after year teachers networked to develop a foolproof system to help the tenth grade pass.

All of that I learned, bit by bit, as we took the exams and after graduation. Darina's family knew of all the scheming and secured Darina's grades way ahead of time and during our written exams. The topics of the final essay and all the math problems were delivered on the exam mornings from the regional office of education. There was no such surprise element during the seven oral exams. Each of the orals had one hundred tickets with three questions on each. Students had to be lucky and hopefully draw a ticket with questions they could answer well. To be safe, you had to learn at least a little about all three hundred topics. Each member of the examining committee had the right to ask any questions within the three topics on a student's ticket. Some teachers were especially brutal when they did not like a particular student. They wanted to know too many specifics about the topic, explore it in depth outside of school curriculum and asked follow-up questions until the student was sunk. As each of us entered the examination room and greeted our examiners, we drew a ticket from the bunch spread out like a deck of cards, facedown, on the teacher's desk, then sat down in the prep area to gather our thoughts while the students who entered the room earlier were questioned. Every one of us was raised an atheist, and still all of us failed the godless Socialist system by praying for a miracle. Some even did so out loud while crossing themselves secretly.

I must have done my share of praying, and I had one or two miracles during the orals, having not studied all the tickets. I was lucky to squeak through with last-minute, completely unexpected assists from two teachers, one of them the school Communist Party leader, whose orders I'd so defiantly ignored with my noncompliant blue uniform and who taught the very USSR social studies I refused to study.

The day before graduation, when I still had no graduation dress, I pleaded with Darina to help me sew my dress out of that awful scarlet fabric, the color of whores and Communists, not of young, innocent, idealistic girls who so wished to become ladies. I had no other fabric, no other choice, and no time to delay. I would be wearing a scarlet dress and, now, completely mismatched silver shoes. I had to have a dress, any dress. When I asked Darina two or three weeks in advance, she promised to sew it when she was not busy. She was not too busy to let me help her study for the finals during the entire month of June, but here we were on the eve before graduation, still no dress.

On Friday, June 23, after Darina's family ate and the table was cleared and thoroughly cleaned, we spread my fabric over it and began cutting. I never could have made that dress without her. The fabric needed a more experienced hand. Darina, who knew that her shaky knowledge and grades were not going to place or keep her into college, had been taking sewing classes to be employable at a factory after graduation. She measured and outlined. I cut and loosely stitched. She sewed with a special clip on her sewing machine, exactly what was needed to keep this fabric from fraying. The dress was going to be a tunic-like garment and was not very appealing at all. It just sort of hung loosely on me. But I did not dare to suggest anything regarding its style; Darina was in charge here and would have thrown me out if I'd done that.

Mine was not the only last-minute dress Darina was making. There was a third girl with us, from a different school, whose mother had been instrumental to Darina during our written mathematics final three weeks earlier,

passing Darina's sister the answers to the long algebra problems while the exams were on. So while Darina worked on
the algebra dress, I was sad and ready to sob. I was so often
sad in my childhood and youth that I floated in and out of
these states many times an hour.

While I waited, maybe because of the sadness I felt,
I started humming Nino Rota's theme from *Romeo and
Juliet*. Singing always cheered me up. I drifted off into en-
visioning myself as sort of an Olivia Hussey. Olivia was a
beautiful, sexy British actress, Juliet in Franco Zeffirelli's
1968 film. This film was not released to Soviet screens until
1976 or so; it was then very fresh to us, and I absolutely
loved Olivia as Juliet. I loved the way she moved and spoke,
the way she pouted; she was so feminine, so rounded, so
appealing. She carried herself with none of the awkward
angles found in the bag of bones and skin I was.

With Rota's tune and Olivia's pretty face in my brain,
my idle hands rolled a long, thin string out of a scrapped
piece of scarlet polyester, which almost rolled into this
string on its own. To cheer myself as I waited for them
to finish the algebra dress, I tied together all the scrapped
strings. I then rolled and wrapped that long string around
my torso many times, five or six at least, cinching the
scarlet bag, and suddenly, I was Juliet. As I twirled in front
of the large mirror, Darina, her family, the algebra-dress
girl, and her algebra-teacher mom froze, agape with envious stares once I at last stopped. I knew instantly and for
the very first time in my life that I was beautiful. Their
stunned faces spoke of it, and their closed lips denied me
the compliments.

Ten minutes before, I'd been a nothing girl in a
bad-fitting, unflattering dress made out of an ungodly un-
becoming fabric, not good enough to stand beside these

two girls, who, though far less attractive than me, enjoyed the glow of their families' love and beamed with pride in their elaborate and properly pastel-colored dresses. Now, here I was, transformed by a sheer twist of fate and rolling fabric into a radiant seventeen-year-old. Yes, my birthday had been only three days before, and the next day I would walk to school alone and proud in my very becoming scarlet dress.

I grabbed the dress and ran almost the entire way home. It was way past the ten o'clock curfew, and I was always afraid to walk alone that late; way too many drunks and hooligans lurked around, waiting for innocents like me. Safe inside my apartment, I spent half the night putting finishing stitches on the dress: the hem, the sleeves, the neckline—all needed to be hand sewn. I do not recall whether Mama was already sleeping when I got home. She usually was at that hour, asleep in front of the still-on TV, with a book or newspaper under her chin, snoring lightly, worn out after her workday and the all-evening-long conversations about it with her girlfriends.

She was gone before I awoke that Saturday morning.

I needed to iron my dress and the pink slip Mama had also bought for me in Poland. Of course, that pink slip had been intended for under the pink-and-silver brocade, but now it would have to do, since I owned no other.

I was too nervous to eat anything, so a cup or two or three of instant coffee was all I had that day. I put on my street clothes and traveled to the market and back by streetcar to purchase a bouquet for my class's headroom teacher. It was a must to bring one.

Then came the very difficult task of taking a bath. Our bathroom was as dysfunctional as the rest of our life. Hot water was rarely available. In June there was no regularly running water at all. But somehow I heated the water we had saved in buckets in the bathtub and managed to bring the large pots and kettles of water around through the L-shaped hallway from the kitchen to half fill the tub without burning myself. I bathed, and then I flattened my clean hair with a black-market curling iron converted from a factory-made welding tool. Listening to my favorite music—the Dutch band Teach-In, Soviet singers Sergey and Tatiana Nikitins, and that unforgettable French songbird Édith Piaf—I put on my makeup and perfume. I decided that I'd skip pantyhose, because of my open-toe shoes.

I was just getting in the mood for my very first dressy evening of dancing and partying and was slipping on my pink slip when the phone rang. It must have been around five o'clock. The evening was to start at six, and the school was a mere five-minute walk away.

I picked up the receiver. An unfamiliar man's voice asked, "Is your mother at home?"

There was nothing unusual thus far. Men I did not know always called to ask for my mother.

"She is not at home," I replied. "Who should I say called?"

And with the next sentence, just like that, my life changed.

"Tell her it was your ex-father," said the unfamiliar voice.

I don't remember what happened next. I know I hung up almost immediately. I do not recall if he was still trying to say anything.

I remember realizing for the hundredth, no, for the thousandth time of my life how stupid adults are and how cruel they could be to children. Especially their own. I knew it very well.

This man, who had just told me he was my "ex-father," who the devil was he? He'd never cared about me, my age, my birthday just four days ago, or my graduation tonight, which families from Minsk to Vladivostok celebrated in our one-sixth of the world, as if this night were New Year's Eve.

I was all alone. I stood clean, scented, in my pink slip, hair done, and I sobbed, trying to choke myself with my own hands, because my tears of despair were all I understood now. After a few initial moments, I fell into the maroon armchair, the same one Grandma had died in, in the most excruciating pain of my once-again-breaking child's heart.

I do not know how long I sat there like that. Twenty minutes maybe, no more. The sun shone brightly through the waving branches of the birch tree my grandfather had planted for me when we'd moved here. My birch tree was my devoted friend. Always a good listener, it once again gave me the wisest advice: *Wash your face, redo your makeup, and get dressed. It's nearly showtime.*

I did just that and for the very last time walked the five-minute walk to the school. That ten-year-long era was ending now, and I felt nothing.

I crossed the schoolyard, a paved square in front of the four-story building I loved and hated at the same time. The new principal, a woman who had replaced the feared principal following his death, was waiting by the doorway, also oddly alone. I realized that I might be a little late. I did not notice anyone else walking as I approached the school, carrying my flowers in my arms, looking oddly magical in my scarlet dress and silvery shoes.

Just then, a teacher I did not know took her place next to the principal, opening the door from the inside so that

I could get in. The principal, who had spoken to me only once before, said to the teacher, turning away from me, "And here walks the best dress of the evening." The door closed behind me, leaving me again without any courage, comfort, or dignity to face what may come. Alone.

All I remember of that principal is that she was stupid to say "Here walks the best dress" and not "You look so lovely in this dress" or "Your dress is so beautiful." Yes, she was mean and maybe deliberately intolerant of my Jewish face, unwilling to disengage her intolerance and behave as a school principal should have—welcoming and inclusive.

But none of that truly mattered, ever. It was purely incidental, tangential specifics. The straight line of that evening was "I have an ex-father." That was my real tragedy, with which I had to cope right there and then and which I was not going to handle well. Maybe I could have, had it not been for that best-dress comment, as if I were a nonperson. *Ex-father ... Here walks the dress ...*

Adults were cruel, obtuse, and abusive. They were never there to stand by me.

Garrik was even stupider than that principal. Life was unfair, and I was victimized by many uncaring adults throughout my childhood. They were killing the "I" inside me. However, I must have been born with a very strong will to live and to rise above my bad beginnings. After all, I had been taught by Grandma and Grandpa to survive.

My schoolmates were celebrating all around, seated in the school hall, wearing their best, holding their bouquets. Not a single one of them was alone. Just me.

There were so many versions of dysfunctional families in my childhood long ago. About half of my schoolmates came from broken homes. If a father was present, he often drank a lot. Some mothers drank too. Despondent drinking was all around us. Everything was a problem in the city of my childhood. The entire country was despondent, down to its very best citizens.

I find it ironic now, as I am writing these words in twenty-first century, that some of USSR's former citizens yearn for the return of those lackluster days. One never understands when appealing for change just where such change may steer them. There are so few leaders willing to honestly guide their flocks to better times. Most leaders are there only to have a good time for themselves. A deeper state of misery can always follow a promise of hope and change, as it did again to the city of my childhood with the Russian-Ukrainian conflict over Crimea in 2014.

Despite everything, once-upon-a-time ideology helped the princess on the pea in me. My name was called out on June 24, 1978, and no audible applause followed. I walked onstage to receive my diploma in silence, my scarlet dress symbolic of some impending revolt and a certain humiliation.

No one else's fathers ever referred to themselves as "ex." Broken-home kids I knew actually got together with their fathers once in while or even regularly. Since Garrik had last formally visited me on my sixth birthday, I'd caught only a glimpse of him, when I was twelve. I was humiliated by his last name, his patronymic I had to carry through my lifetime, his permanent absence, the vile legacy he left behind for my folks—that is, my mother's side of the family. I was humiliated that Garrik's mother, my other grandmother, never bothered about me. My uncle Mark, Garrik's brother, I knew from a photo taken of us in Riga when I was two and he was twenty. I looked at the photo once in a while to recall those good times in Riga, so memorable that I could actually feel the fun and laughter whenever I held the photo in my hand.

Boy, I wished I had that photo now. The graduation part of my evening was over in a flash, and, surrounded by all sorts of families, I sat back down—a solitary scarlet ostrich. Then the party started, and it became even lonelier. Everyone ate, laughed, and danced, but not me. I sat hidden most of the evening, recalling over and over the sound of Garrik's voice as he pronounced these hateful words: "your ex-father." I was imprinting them onto my brain to never forget the pain. And I completely succeeded.

There was a long-standing tradition in Kiev for the graduating students to take a streetcar to the river and then a cruise down the old, wide Dniepr River, with Kiev spread along its high right and low left banks. (Some dictionaries now use Dnieper instead of the Russian spelling Dniepr or the Ukrainian spelling Dnipro. I prefer the Russian Dniepr—that is what I always called it.)

Our school, like every other, had a streetcar—actually I think there were three—reserved for us at the circle end stop of Line No. 8. We loaded on in the near darkness with most streetlamps not working. The streetcars ignored their regular paths from atop Batiy Mountain to Saksaganskogo Street and went down, down, down to the Central Railroad Station, descending all the way to Podol. This was the lowest part of the city, where a river cruise ship was reserved especially for our school. A band of musicians played, and food and dance continued, and everyone got drunker and louder as the night progressed.

It was customary to travel just far enough down the river and time the turnaround to arrive back to Kiev at dawn, when the city was at its most glorious, its shining gold cupolas visible from afar. Night hid the tired yellowness of the Dniepr's waters. The river looked stately and contented in its blacks, violets, and deepest of blues. I sat somewhere in the corner, unwilling to partake in any of the activities. The word *ex-father* was stuck in my throat and mind, choking me, eliminating me. The tears ran from my eyes, faster than the tired Dniepr's waters, and everyone who even attempted to sit next to me got to hear about it. I just could not stop myself. I was completely distraught. The blacks and blues of the river matched the colors of my soul.

People came by and left. I ate nothing. I drank nothing. I had no fun, but I was there. I remember being there.

Sudden splashing and screams halted my tears. It was Oleg Zhuk, a boy I'd known since kindergarten. He'd jumped overboard, stirring instant gossip as to the reasons. Darina, who periodically came to check on me, whispered the exciting news: Oleg had jumped over because Tania, a girl from a lower grade, who was not even supposed to be there with us, had rejected him in favor of our Yura Odnoralov. I knew Tania. She was slim, pretty, and not Jewish. None of the three of them were. Not that Yura ever made this a requirement; our entire social system did by making Jews a ranking or several lower than non-Jews, so not even secretly could I entertain for a moment that Yura would ever like me as more than a friend.

"They always jump overboard for the non-Jewish girls," I said to Darina. We sighed, she left, and I resumed my weeping.

After fishing Oleg out, the boat turned around. Our long-anticipated excursion down the river was now over.

Kiev, My Kiev

Kiev from the river was as glorious as I had always imagined it would be on the dawn of my maturity. We were sailing upstream. This brought the ancient part of Kiev into view to the left. Twice before, during the fifth- and sixth-grade educational trips down the Dniepr River to Kanev or Pereyaslav-Khmelnitsky, we'd left Kiev very early in the morning and retuned when it was dark. Never before or since had I seen Kiev from down the middle of the river. I'd seen it from the train, entering the city from the left bank over the railroad bridge. But that morning was my first and only chance to see it the "authentic" way, the way it was when the Rus' people came to rule it and the way its children carry it away through the ages wherever destiny lands them after they leave it forever.

The timid first sunrays reached down to the high Kiev hills to awaken them, gently washing them into the luscious hues of late-spring and early-summer greens. White bursts of chestnut flowers—chestnut candles, we called them—and late lilac clusters of deep and pale purples, rich creams, and modest whites were reluctantly revealed. The Vydubytsky Monastery, with its dirty onion–like green domes and the sky-blue cupola seeded with gold stars, was my favorite in this part of town, which I visited too infrequently. The monastery was built in 1070 and, according to the lore, exactly on the resurrection spot after Prince Vladimir, known as Saint Vladimir, forcibly converted the aggrieved Kievans to Christianity from paganism, and perhaps from Judaism, in 990. This conversion took place in Podol and included sinking their wooden objects of worship in the River Dniepr. The forcibly converted followed their idols downstream, screaming, *"Vydubai!"* ("Surface! Resurrect!") Hence, Vydubytsky stands where the wooden idols surfaced.

Vydubytsky has always been a favorite. Its cupola is visible from afar and graces many Kiev postcards. When the sunrays touched its stars that morning, we were back home. The surroundings all went by too fast from the river. Too fast, but as I stared, I snapped mental pictures with my eyes, as I always do to keepsake a memory. The botanical garden followed its neighbor, Pecherskaya Lavra, up on their hill. Lavra is the most mystical of Kiev's religious sites. It was there that the anti-Semites were said to be always devising plots, like the one in which they accused the Jews of killing a Christian child to supposedly use his blood for matzo bread in the early 1900s a false allegation that the Jews of Kiev were never able to live down. Mendel Beilis was accused of this crime in 1913 during a round of particularly severe institutionalized anti-Semitism in tsarist Russia. His trial resonated with Jewry everywhere. After his acquittal, he settled in New York, where he died in 1934. Neighborhood children and their parents often reminded me of Beilis's crimes, ready to unearth the entire ordeal without cause or warning. I wish at those times some wise Jewish adult would have known and shared with me the words inscribed on Beilis's Saratoga Springs tombstone in Hebrew:

> Here lies a holy person, a chosen man.
> The people of Kiev made him a victim,
> And upon all Israel spread the travail
> Falsely accused him and his community of taking the blood of a Christian child as demanded by him and his faith for the festival of Passover
> They bound him in chains and lowered him into a pit
> Many years he did not see the light of day
> On behalf of all Israel he was harshly tortured...

Between Beilis and Babiy Yar, my Kiev did not revel in its rich Jewish history with the same pride it did in the Christian and Socialist. It saddened me and did not dispel any of my gloom.

The receding morning dew was just then rising from the wide river span, the sun turning it once again from black and blue to murky yellowish green. To our right was the left bank, the one we mostly ignored in our right-bank residents' superiority. Kiev Metro Bridge had our own version of Soviet sculptor Vera Mukhina's *Rabochiy i Kolkhoznitza (Worker and Kolkhoz Woman)*, the celebrated sculpture erected in 1937 at the Russian Exhibition Center in Moscow. The collective farm woman was a definite child of the Soviet Union. Kiev Metro statues were infinitely prettier and represented intellectual pursuits, no doubt by design of their Soviet architect, a Kiev-born Jew, Georgiy Borisovich Fuchs. Kiev had been an intellectual city for quite some time. I knew some of its hidden heroes, but for the most part I was too wrapped up in my own struggles to genuinely appreciate the grandeur my city carried. I was only stringing the memories but unable to enjoy the reality.

Askold's Grave, the eleventh-century burial site of Prince Askold from the ruling family of Kievan Rus' was nestled before the Pedestrian Bridge to the beaches of Truhanov Island. The island is named after Kievan Rus' conqueror Tugor-khan, who forced the Rus' prince Svyatopolk II to marry his daughter to legitimize Tatar-Mongolian rule over Kiev. A stone Saint Vladimir stood tall that morning blessing the Kievan Rus' to Christianity, just as he did in 990, forcibly and irrevocably. The Andreevsky and Sofievskaya cupolas were gleaming high and far. Then we came to the funicular incline, and briskly we were at our journey's end—the river port of Podol, still the most Jewish of the neighborhoods, predating the Kievan Rus'.

I loved my city with its not-too-ancient but exciting history. I wished I could see it when all four gates into Old Kiev, including the Jewish Gate, still stood and every fresco on the now-destroyed church walls was still intact. I wanted to see every bridge as it stood before being blown up by wars and revolutions. I wanted to see Kreschatik as it was before the Nazis blew it up in September 1941, when every prewar building still stood along the street. Mama and my grandparents remembered the prewar Kreschatik, but such was the destiny of Kiev that some of it was periodically leveled by its enemies as the city itself periodically expelled its friends to make room for something completely unanticipated.

* * *

We were tired and quiet on the streetcar ride back. I came home as my mother was rising. I made it past her with an "I'm tired" and sank into the safety of my grandparents' bedbug-ridden bed.

It was all over … Childhood, school, life …

Garrik called Mama again and arranged to meet with her on the coming Tuesday. He wanted her to sign a document to allow him to leave the country for good. He was going to pay her the remaining year of child support in one lump payment. Mama wanted me to go too, and I agreed without thinking. Swept by the anticlimactic mood of the day, I slept and wept intermittently. "It's only a word" was the only consolation Mama managed to offer after I told her what Garrik had said. She had always thrown words at me, never understanding the damage her frequent outbursts of cruelty would have on me for decades.

Mama wanted me to go with her to meet Garrik so that I could show off the scarlet dress, even though the silver shoes were now on the unknown bride's Black Sea honeymoon. "Wear it with any shoes; he should just see you,"

Mama said over and over. Grandpa, too, called to say that I must go meet Garrik. I gave in several times, promising to go, but in the end, I did not. On Tuesday morning, with Mama at work, I put the red dress on again for the second and last time, and I heard my own clear voice inside my head: *He did not earn it. Don't give him this satisfaction.*

I will not give either of them this satisfaction, I resolved.

I sat in the same armchair I'd crumpled into on Saturday after his call, and I listened to the phone ringing again and again. It must have been Mama, the traitor, and Garrik, the ex-father, together for the only time I could ever remember, calling their child. And the child was not to be found. She was not present. There was a grown woman sitting in the chair now. And she was not theirs.

After an eternity, I took the red dress off, neatly and tightly formed its scarlet polyester folds into the smallest square I could manage and tied it with the long string of the belt I'd rolled for it.

Juliet was dead.

Mama and me at a year and a half in front of the wood house

Mama made me this brown jacket and made me pose for the photograph.

The locomotive dress

Babushka Riva and Dedushka Avrum, 1929

Grandma Riva and Grandpa Avrum, 1958

Great-Grandma Haya

First Pioneer camp
parents' day

Our khrusheba on Volgogradskaya Street, Kiev, 2011

Final school photo, Kiev,   *USSR exit visa photo, 1979*
spring 1978

Dress 9

The Second Riga Twin

When I was a little girl and did not need proof to believe in the goodness of people, I also knew that if I was good, I would someday meet my intended match. There were no princely possibilities in our Soviet homeland, but I was convinced I'd get one. I foresaw no other options, and I mentally prepared myself only for the best possible scenario once I became grown up enough. There was not a twitch of doubt in me that I might be way too deep into my fairy tale and that in reality people were not as good as I imagined them to be. Oddly enough, my reality had many really bad people in it, displaying varying shades of badness toward me as well as others I knew. But still, I insisted on believing in the underlying goodness of humanity.

After Poland, my wardrobe swelled to a collection of several very fashionable garments, the most important of them being a navy velour jacket I wore to all occasions. I had a matching midi-length skirt with tiny white dots that did not spoil the luxurious blue look. My new, also very fashionable, demi-season overcoat was a deep shade of blue, close to navy but not quite. I had denim shoes, also blue. Mama made me buy red turtlenecks, because they would "elongate" my neck, and some bright-red knit tops. In the ninth grade, if I'd been permitted to wear any of my new clothes to school, I think I would have been the best-dressed girl in my class. Everyone knew we'd been to Poland, and the admiration and envy for my new coat was evident daily. I had to carry it with me everywhere so it would not be stolen or damaged at the coatracks. I could not flaunt my other new things for a variety of reasons, the least important to me at the time being modesty. I was so happy inside my new clothes and wanted to show them off but only rarely could. My only chance to do so was at the seldom get-together in someone's apartment when I was certain none of my bullies would pop in.

We did that sometimes—crowd the front room of someone's two-room apartment, listen to music, sing, slow dance. Girls mostly. These rooms could not have held more than eight or ten of us. Boys were rarely at any of the get-togethers I was told about. It was okay to dance girl with girl, hugging tight. None of us knew that homosexuality even existed. None of us understood what sex meant. We used the English word *sex*, but to us it meant something very benign. For instance, when a girl unbuttoned the top button of her uniform when she was hot, she'd say, "I'll show you some sex," before exposing just a tiny bit of her neckline. Even the most immodest among us, as far as we all knew, were virginally innocent. There was a nasty rumor, though, that two girls, one from my class, one from a parallel one, were raped either right before or at the beginning of tenth grade somewhere on the far school grounds, in the apple orchard. These girls were the least modest ones among the rest, but so many things have changed since. I think they'd be considered saintly in today's world. Besides, it was a vicious rumor that likely was not even true.

The absolute ignorance about the reality of sex caused many early marriages, of the shotgun variety. There was a girl in our district who gave birth to twins at fourteen, with the father being a classmate. A court hearing followed, with a decision to split the twins between their parents' homes and let each family raise one as a sibling to his or her parent. Everyone in Kiev was gossiping about this case. Few parents enlightened their children on the basics of the post-1960s sexual revolution, and the school was silent altogether. What we knew we learned through the backyard grapevine. Soviet-made contraceptives, like most Soviet-made products, were stupid but sturdy. Actually, I knew of only one contraceptive: a thick red rubber thingy that was reminiscent of a long red rubber finger. It was barely bendable, but with Soviet ingenuity, we used it for something besides its intended purpose, something precious—little girls cut it up to use as elastic ties, like rubber bands, for their ponytails and braids. There were no hair ties sold, but the unusable Soviet preservatives, or condoms, were abundant at local pharmacies, so parents purchased them for their daughters. These rubber bands would catch hair and pull and tear it on removal, but they were our only hair ties for those years, when we made our own clothes, hunted for Western-made anything, and did not realize how fast we were maturing.

During my final school year, tenth grade, I wore my Riga twin dress whenever I went to after-school or weekend get-togethers. I was saving my Polish clothes for my college life, if I should be lucky enough to get in. I even wore the Riga dress during winter, despite its short sleeves. It looked great over my blue Polish turtleneck and blue

Polish pantyhose. But because of that, by the spring, it was stretched and nearly worn out, so I moved on to wearing the second of the Riga twins soon after high school graduation.

The dress was even more becoming when it was still unfaded from washings. If paisleys were not among my favorite patterns before, the Riga dresses certainly brought to me a love of paisleys. I used to trace the pattern of the dress with my fingers anytime I daydreamed. I would even doodle paisleys in class when I was bored in that final year and color them in the same pale-blue and green hues of the Riga twins for my paper doll fashions.

I remember how wonderful I felt in the second Riga twin on that certain summer day in July 1978, about a month after my high school graduation. The dress exposed my knees by this point. I must have grown taller. Its short sleeves and V-neckline made me feel summery, slick, and cool. Because it was very becoming, I wore it almost every day, including that summer day, the day that two of my newly former classmates came to rape me.

I believe it was a Thursday. The sun was setting, and I was sitting in the armchair reading, as usual, when the doorbell rang. We rarely had visitors, but our neighbor from the fifth floor was pregnant and often asked to use our bathroom, so that she would not need to climb all the way up when she was out for her late-afternoon walks with her mom. We lived on the second floor right over the supermarket, so there was no one below us. Our building, like most buildings in Kiev, had no elevators. None of the five-story buildings on Batyeva Gora had elevators. The newer, nine-storied ones did, though.

Igor Gadina lived in the five-story building immediately behind mine. Although I visited almost all my classmates during the ten years we studied together for this or that get-together, I had never been to Igor's apartment. In fact, I'd been afraid of him for quite some time. He was okay until about fifth grade or so, but after that, he became a bully.

Aleksei Koziavka had been in love with me in the fourth grade and had not hidden it, giving me gifts of dolls, stuffed animals, and flowers. That love had been knocked out of him as he was taught that I was a Jew and, therefore, not deserving of his attention. But he was never my adversary. In fact, during the last winter of school, he'd asked me to knit him a hat with a large pom-pom, and I'd done so. Then his new best friend, Igor Gadina, had asked for one too, and I'd also crafted one for him. The head measurements and the transfers of wool and hats had happened at school. They had never visited my home. Well, Aleksei had come once, in fourth grade.

I have to admit that even if school exams were bad, sitting at home alone all day long was worse. Books were fine, but I was bored. So I was initially happy to see them when they came. We went into our far room and played piano for a little while, banging the keys of the black Ukraina upright without much sense and generally acting giddy.

Then suddenly, without warning, I found myself sitting on a chair with my hands tied and the V-neck of my dress exposing some skin it was not intended to reveal. One of the boys, I think Igor, who was much stronger, began tying my feet as I tried in vain to free myself.

A wave of absolute calm suddenly came upon me. The quickly disappearing sunlight was all I could see when I looked at their faces. I saw no faces. They were blurred by the sun and now by the time that has passed since that long-ago day.

Igor and Aleksei were two boys who'd grown up near me, with me, who'd listened to me in class, their mouths agape, when I read poetry better than anyone else in school, applauding me when I finished. They were the boys who'd witnessed my activities as the leader of the class and whose rights I'd defended many times when certain trouble headed in their direction from the teachers' room. Now they had come to my apartment with one thing on their minds, one plan. They were there to rape me. Igor very calmly informed me of their intent.

Some years before, Mama had told and retold to all her girlfriends during their many evening-long conversations a story about an incident during one of her vacations to Soviet Georgia. A man had approached her when she was returning to her rental after a movie. It had been dark, with no one around. I remember my mother saying, "The only thing that saved me was that I was being very nice to him." I'd been very young when I heard this, way before I was able to grasp the full meaning, but I remembered it now.

I spoke only to Aleksei, asking him to reconsider. I was speaking as I imagined "nice" should be in this circumstance. It was all too surreal to feel the weight of its realism. If they did it, I would tell, I promised. They would be punished and would not be able to go on to whatever universities they were headed for. Igor was already aiming for a military career, like his father. Aleksei's father was also in the military. Did they really need all that trouble? Did he, Aleksei, need this trouble?

After a while, Aleksei sided with me and untied me, against Igor's protests. I followed them to the door, as calmly as I could pretend, wanting to quickly lock the door behind them but exercising self-control I'd never known I was capable of.

In the darkness of our narrow apartment hallway, Igor grabbed me and kissed me on the mouth. I wanted to spit. Still, I calmly said goodbye and closed and locked the door behind them. Once alone, I wiped my lips with my bare right arm and ran into the far room, where my bed stood next to the chair to which I'd been so recently strapped, helpless. Only then, sprawled facedown across my bed, did I begin to weep. More than anything that had transpired, the idea of my forced first kiss haunted me for decades.

I did not wear that dress for a while but then changed my mind. It was such a good dress; it made me calm. When I am calm, I win.

* * *

Soon it was time to begin my first semester of college. I was too afraid of the anti-Jew oral entrance exams to Kiev University and the other colleges—institutes, they were called—that I did not even try to apply. I knew I would not withstand the barrage of questions designed to sink Jews, or at least those of us without bribe money. My exceptional grades in math and Russian allowed me admittance without examinations to the Kiev Pedagogical College. It was a two-year school, and I could go on to further higher education after, if I so decided and stopped being afraid. I already knew that a teacher's job was guaranteed me, having served at our regional department of education the summer before as a secretarial assistant while everyone else was repainting our school. They all knew me there and thought well of me, especially after my school's assistant principal, Alexandra Nikolaevna, visited there one day and told them that I could have a job in her new school on Solomenka, near the new bazaar, when I was ready.

Teaching was my career dream since I first learned to read and write. I knew I had a gift for it. Besides teaching being my favorite game to play with my dolls, I practiced it regularly since I was about thirteen, substituting in the lower grades during many unexpected teacher absences. I had some really wonderful teachers too, among whom Alexandra Nikolaevna, who taught chemistry, was one of the best.

In actuality, the number of indifferent and incompetent teachers largely outweighed the good ones. No wonder so many girls and boys in my class who had excellent potential became statistical write-offs. Little wonder still that kids like Darina were able to negotiate and even pay for improved grades. One of my teachers, for example, handed out 5s in exchange for Lancôme lipstick. I actually brought her a couple from Poland. Tatiana Andrianovna was her name. She taught English. English, she once admitted in class, was not the primary foreign language she'd studied, and she did not know it well. French was her true love. We suffered through her limited knowledge of English and learned little, yet most of us still had 5s or 4s, even if we learned zero or close to it from Tatiana. In our five-level grade system, a 5 meant "excellent," and 4 meant "good." I think most of my grades were truly earned through my ability; however, some of them, like English, were also stretched to cover my lazy attitude and immense number of illnesses. Others spoke to my anti-Semitism-related absences, like my 4 in Ukrainian literature. The greater the Ukrainian writer, the more times he berated the Jews in his works. There were no Ukrainian writers before mid 19th century. When they emerged they realistically transferred the widespread anti-Semitism of Ukrainian culture and daily life into their writings. I could not sit through lessons condemning Jews, for instance, for money lending or saloon-keeping, the two occupations they were free to pursue in the mostly restricted Jewish life of Ukraine's countryside. 19th century Ukrainian writers hated Russians and their tsars. But they hated Ukrainian Jews even more. Ukrainians owed money to their Jewish booze-purveyors and moneylenders. They willingly took part in the pogroms to escape paying debts, but Ukrainian writers never mentioned that. As a child I never understood why Soviet education system permitted institutionalized hatred through literature while demanding all Soviet citizens be friends. I was never taught about the Pale of Settlement. I just skipped Ukrainian lit classes during anti-Semitic writers as a way of coping with everyday anti-Semitism of my surroundings.

On September 1, the school year started. Wearing, the second Riga twin, which I thought made me look just like my favorite teachers, I was proud to be embarking on the first step of my pedagogical career. I walked from the No. 8 end stop at Kiev University through the Old Botanical Garden to my next house of learning, grinning too wide, as Mama would have undoubtedly observed had she been there with me. Mama often cautioned me not to be too happy or optimistic and not to laugh, since "laughing always leads to crying." I looked forward to my new adult life. Soon I would start receiving the monthly stipend of fifty-five rubles, which I was entitled to as an "excellence" entrant. Having my own money meant freedom from Mama's inept kitchen. I could eat in some cafeteria. Bad food though it was, it was still better than my usual—uncooked hot dogs, frozen pelmeni, fried potatoes, boiled eggs, bread and butter, lard with black bread, stale Swiss cheese, and even the gourmet dish of pan-fried cabbage with breadcrumbs, which I'd learned to make at my friend's home. Eating in a cafeteria beat even the meal of just-baked Ukrainian *palianiza* bread with a half-liter bottle of *slivki*, our version of heavy cream, the best tasting of milks.

Pelmeni is a dish of supposedly Siberian origin that we bought frozen in our downstairs Gastronom, a multidepartment food store, with separate lines to each counter and department cash register. The small pelmeni balls sold at our Gastronom were made of ground meat of an unidentifiable animal slaughtered around the Mesozoic era. The balls were bound into a thick gray dough wrap, pinched to seal the wrap, then kept frozen since about that prehistoric period. About fifty pelmeni were stuffed into a thin cardboard box, sticking to the box's walls and to one another. They were never kept in proper refrigeration. No one in my home ever questioned the source of the meat and the defrosting/refreezing factor except me, since I was the one left to cook and eat them—and was often sick afterward.

Get a pot of water boiling fast, and add a pinch or two of salt. Drop and boil the square brick of pelmeni balls. Before they start sticking to the pot, stir to separate. Careful not to peel the dough off the meat—well, at least try hard not to do it. When they're fully cooked, after about fifteen minutes, pull them out of the soup. Dress with a dollop of sour cream, butter, or vinegar, or use all three if you so like. Or leave them in the watery soup, and add the sour cream to flavor. That was actually my mother's favorite soup for me—quick to make and very filling. If any cardboard was stuck to the pelmeni, not to worry; it was sure to detach during boiling, leaving a residue of the blues and greens from the box inside the pot and on the former pelmeni hostages.

I knew there were other kinds of pelmeni, made with thin, tasty dough, yellowish, not gray, and stuffed with finely ground and seasoned chicken breast or veal. These pelmeni were eaten in the homes where families made them together from scratch, like we used to do when Grandma was alive. But never in Mama's kitchen. I spent many of my after-school afternoons visiting my friends' homes, secretly hoping to be fed at their tables. I often did eat there, but more often, I was asked to leave before dinnertime. Everyone had problems. No one wanted to constantly feed extras.

Mama was hardly ever home at dinnertime; in fact, there was no set dinnertime at our home after Grandma died. We ate whenever, whatever, and wherever. For years we had no table to eat at. Then its surface was occupied by filthy items unrelated to the current meal, such as bottles of souring milk with flies hovering over them and yesterday's or even week-old dirty dishes and pots—whatever. That was our world or disorder, and I knew no other at home. I only espied other mothers' kitchens and wished that someday I could have a small world of my own to keep clean and safe and orderly.

College was certainly a step toward that dream.

In very late August 1978, before school began, the mailwoman left a note in our mailbox with the evil word *Israel* on it. After cautiously examining it, Mama summoned just enough courage to walk into the tiny post office to receive a thin blue paper, which upon careful opening turned out to be both envelope and letter. It contained a "par avion" seal and had tethered edges, because Soviet censors had read and resealed it. A stamp imprinted directly onto the blue paper above that evil word *Israel* for a return address said "registered mail." Even I, who could not tolerate the thought of Israel, had to admit that it was the finest and prettiest blue paper I'd ever held in my hands. Hmmm!

Our entire motherland was at arms against the evils Israel represented, and the country did not report about Israel except to illustrate the point of it being the Israeli aggressors' homeland. During classes and school foreign news updates, news bits were read in the same disapproving manner the national newscasters used to deliver them on air during the nightly news program *Vremya* (*Time*), which aired at 9:00 p.m. The entire country watched it. Revered reporters rolled the *r* in *Israel* with deliberate hatred, sending subliminal messages of Jewish inferiority through things like Russian pronunciation. Most Jews born in Ukraine, Belarus, and Moldavia, whose parents' primary language was Yiddish, burred and also pronounced certain softening sounds where they were not needed. In short, some Jews were identified by their speech, and these TV reporters insinuated and provoked their faithful audience to follow suit. And the people did.

When Jews from large cities began leaving for Israel, the country began to condemn them, using the terms "Israeli aggressors," "traitors of the motherland," and "ungrateful people" on the TV news, in the press, in the government, and everywhere—on buses, in schools, within offices. The more Jews who left, the more repercussions were used against the remaining Jews—like depriving them of promotions or college admission—and the more the remaining Jews wanted to prepare for their own imminent departures. It was a very scary period of Soviet history. The Gulag was still very active, and people were sent there daily to labor, perish, or suffer, often without proper trial. One was assumed guilty, especially so in Jewish cases.

It must be stated here that the very arrival of an envelope from Israel was equivalent to an admission of intent to commit a potentially punishable act against our motherland. Mama, I clearly know now, was by then a completely broken-down Soviet soul. A neighbor had headed to Israel in the winter of 1978 and as such had become a persona non grata in all remaining Jewish and non-Jewish households, for fear of repercussions. I wonder where Mama got enough courage to ask him to deliver our address, names, and exact birthdays to the Israeli consulate in Vienna. Vienna was the first free-country stop after Jewish expulsion from the USSR. Perhaps Mama got this courage in the whirlwind of our post-Poland new money. She regretted also that Garrik was not the right sort of a former husband and would not do this for her. But this neighbor came through, with great expediency, to Mama's complete surprise.

I write this for those readers who have little familiarity with the Cold War and its effects on Soviet citizens. In brief, the Iron Curtain was always closed. We knew nothing and had nothing to compare our lives with. Mama and I had a little preview in Poland, but most Soviet citizens, by means of totalitarian control, repression, and other acts of complete deprivation of personal freedoms, in fact believed that life in the USSR was far superior to that outside of it. It was an odd paradox that military and high-powered executives and Communist Party officials, who were allowed to travel and sometimes served abroad, brought back with them into the USSR many Western-made goods that plainly demonstrated the opposite. They, of course, claimed these goods were the products of decaying capitalism, as they'd been taught. "Made in USA" was a most desired label, even if we read it then as "Maadei in Oosa" and daily condemned all actions by the United States everywhere in the world. We signed multiple protest petitions against the advent of the United States' imperialist hold, obsession with money culture, banks and Wall Street capitalist sharks; and resistance to income equality. What a pact of deception Communists had with the Soviet Union. The Communists were the direct result of the redistribution of postrevolutionary everything. Now they occupied the positions of wealth and power, and it was easy for them to lecture the ordinary have-not Socialists on the evils of wealth and power. Regardless of the sixty years of lecturing, the masses still desired plenty of unattainable goods they saw less and less of since the October Revolution of 1917.

At the time I'm writing about, everyday items like sneakers, T-shirts, plastic shopping bags, makeup, toilet paper, toothpaste, deodorant, shampoo, and so many other commonplace things considered by most people as sheer necessities were rare or impossible to come by in the USSR. It was hailed as the country of all countries, the gleaming empire of the Red Banners, soaked in the blood of its heroes for the promised land and times of Communism. These years were touted as the cherished times when one could work only as much as one wished but still have everything and anything one desired and in abundance.

Since very early childhood I remember hearing voices questioning this idea, among them my own: *How is this going to be possible?* The answers always lay somewhere between Lenin, Marx, Engels, and the many contemporary proclamations of the 1970s Soviet leader Leonid Brezhnev. He was a man with thick, bushy eyebrows, a Ukrainian accent, and very bad dental prosthetics, which caused him to turn *s*'s into many an unworthy sound.

Once, during an important televised speech Brezhnev made the Russian words s *systematicheskimi* (with systematic) sound like *sosiski-masiski* (teeny hot dogs). This mishaps was instantly interpreted by the seeking laughter at the expense of Comparty while deprived of much else Soviet masses of that decade as inadvertent admission of Soviet truth. The entire country reveled in that hot dog incident and our hot dogs were getting even littler and less edible. Rumors of toilet paper being processed into hot dog and bologna meat prevailed.

Since very early childhood, I noticed that our schools, our parents, our doctors, our leaders, our entertainers, and our academics instilled in us the double standard of the Soviet system. Nothing was sacred. Tyranny and spies were everywhere. There was no escape. Or was there? A tiny loophole was forming in my universe. I was getting a glimpse into the other side of the Jewish question.

I, a Jew, an inferior Soviet citizen, could now leave the USSR forever. That thought gave me, for the very first time in my life, a sense of infinite superiority over almost all my now-former classmates. They were not Jews. I was. They could not leave. I could. Mama and I could register this blue envelope from Israel with authorities at our district Otdel Viz i Registraziy (Office of Visas and Registrations), or OVIR, and we, too, could be on our way, like our former neighbor, to Vienna and then the US, Canada, Australia, or Israel.

"Not so fast" was Mama's position. I could read in her face the spectrum of emotions in favor of registration, and then the what-if shadow would overtake her completely. She talked to everyone she knew—her family, her Jewish friends, her Jewish coworkers. In person, not over the tele-phone lines. Telephones were as unsafe as always. By that

time so many people were leaving, and we knew many people who were contemplating departure. Many left; more
were just thinking of leaving. Scant news reached us via
story swapping at birthdays and other infrequent gatherings. Random letters made it through to their addressees,
after being held hostage by censors for weeks or months.
Our few Jewish neighbors were contemplating leaving,
but no one in our family was, except Garrik, who was, of
course, not really family. He told Mama he was going to
Toledo, which was very confusing to me, because I thought
Toledo was in Spain. Mama laughed and lectured me on
my ever-unstable knowledge of the atlas. Toledo was in
Canada, she said, near Ohio, which was one of the fifty
states of the United States of America. Neither of us could
have conceived then how many American cities and towns
reflected nostalgia of their founders.

Mama was crazy with plans and with her never-ending
conversations. She thrived on telling the same story differently to each of her listeners. Her planning was premature
and her quick changes of mind and mood insane. I was
glad to find out when classes began on September 1, 1978,
that for the first thirty days of the first semester we were being shipped off to a collective farm to assist with this year's
harvest. It would be my second time at a collective farm.

Socialist Collectivization

In early September 1978, 250 girls and 1 boy, who had
begun their teacher's degree matriculation studies just a
couple of days prior, were sent to the barracks of a collective farm's agricultural school. The entire local class
was away harvesting somewhere else and could not attend
classes until that was done. Our metal cots were covered
with soiled mattresses and worn-out, threadbare sheets.

The cots were pushed together tightly so that a girl needed to climb over everyone else's beds to get into her own. Our only boy was sleeping in one of the bathrooms. There were no showers, only an army-style chain of faucets with sometimes-running water, ice cold, of course. There was no heat anywhere in the building. I was cold and miserable for the duration, and so was everyone, except for a couple of students who were fresh from the periphery. Country girls had much higher thresholds of doing without. Out in the fields it was not as damp as indoors, unless it rained. The food was awful. They fed us coarse oats, mush, and gray macaroni, with infrequent *kotletas* from the relatively newer Paleozoic era and mandatorily souring, stale butter. A glass of tea and an occasional plain teatime cookie was our dessert. We picked tomatoes, potatoes, cabbage, and corn. Our reward for this monthlong labor was one day of apple picking. Since we illegally supplemented our diet with whatever we picked that day, the apple-picking day was the best, by far.

We picked everything by hand and then carried it and loaded it onto trucks that took what we harvested to the city. There was little automation in our mother of all nations. We were never given proper tools to do our jobs. One day we had to tear cabbage heads off their stalks with our bare fingers while standing knee-deep in a field of mud that was even muddier after the recent rain. *How could this be the best country in the world?* I thought. *Even Poland is better.* No respectable Polish farmer, like Pan Zbiegniew, would send his daughter, like my friend Jadwiga, to tear off cabbage heads with her bare hands. At least if he did, he'd give her rubber boots to wear and a shower afterward to wash off the mud that was stuck to her entire body.

Filthy, dirty, tired, with ripped fingernails, torn city clothes, smelling like the manure used to fertilize the cabbage fields, we returned to our barracks on foot in pouring rain. Such a start to my education was unsatisfactory. I wanted more. I wanted respect. I was tired of the lies the entire country lived by. I wanted to be a teacher, but my faith in the validity of all Soviet assertions was evaporating quicker than September rainwater. We were stuck in the barracks. Three or four girls whose parents owned cars took their friends, who had won the spare seats, home to clean themselves and their clothes. The rest of us endured the filth. It was like being in the summer camp that Mama never visited. I was left hungry, neglected, and desperate. I could not get a glimpse of my future in my exploding head. I was stuck on a single thought, like a car in mud. I revved my mind's engine, but it was in vain.

The only solace I found was in songs. Through times immemorial, there was a practice of keeping Ukrainian field-workers singing. The more we sang, the less we ate. Ukrainian women were always required to sing during the time of forced labor under serfdom rule and after it while the Romanoffs were tsars. Nothing changed under Socialism. The castles belonged to people who had no idea how to run anything, not even the museums or communal apartments they turned the castles into. 250 girls sang and gossiped in the fields and 249 continued singing indoors during the heaviest rain spells.

Inside, I kept mostly to my bed, especially after the girls bought cheap wine and samogon, illegally made homebrew vodka, in the village. When drunk, they all happily exchanged jokes, and the inevitable anti-Semitic rounds followed. Years of summer camps had prepared me for this. At the first sound of the Jewish *r* and invocations of Abram and Sarah, I coiled under my army-brown blanket and pretended to be asleep. I could pretend that sleep so well. My breathing was even; my eyelids did not move. Someone always came to check. That kind of sleep had been my only escape from the vulgar hatred of my peers for many years. Why not endure it one more month? If I remained still, I was unnoticed. They might remember I was there and try to whisper for a while. But usually after someone checked whether I was sleeping, they continued saying one ugly, despicable lie about the Jews after another. Jew bashing was a societal norm and a form of bonding. Jews had been a centuries-long scapegoat of the common people. All non-Jews participated in the Jew-bashing rituals. Some might not say anything vile, but laughing at anti-Semitic jokes or remaining silent during the Jew bashing was, of course, a form of passive participation and approval. Jews, according to a prevalent number of non-Jews, were a source of all evils that befell Soviets. There was nothing new in their hatred. What made this group of girls different was that they were the future teachers of Soviet younglings. These young students, like every elementary school student once upon a time, would worship every word their first teachers said for the first three years of school, like I did, like all children do. These girls were now my commune of peers, my future ... I was no longer sure I belonged in their ranks.

The girls who'd gone home to wash brought back some plastic bags—a very rare commodity—and after the rains stopped, the food gathering included harvesting tomatoes for the next family visitors that might come. In the USSR all property belonged to the people, and no one stopped to think that such illegal harvesting was an act of stealing from the collective farm, of which none of us were members. We all knew, of course; we just did not stop to think about it. Socialism impaled into us a sense of entitlement by depravation. An old USSR adage said, "Show me what you carry, and I will tell you where you work." We worked in the fields. If we could steal a tractor, we would. Everyone stole something. That is what people do when they redistribute. They steal from you to have some of what you have without giving a thought to what you will end up without.

While all the future teachers were stealing hundreds of kilos of vegetables, I regretted that I did not have visitors. Ironically, I always thought myself honest, unbiased, and uncorrupted. My first test at this collective farm proved to me that I was wrong. I wanted to steal something from the fields. I was a true Soviet citizen. No better than the rest.

Am I really no better than the rest? I asked myself when the unyielding hatred of Jews made me distance myself from all the Russians and Ukrainians I knew, even when they did not immediately distance themselves from me. There were some good, honest, decent girls from good homes to whom I owe a great debt for helping me through my dark years. Not letting me lose my sanity or succumb to despair was a demanding pressure I put on my friends. They taught me about hope and shared their precious food, sweets, books, time, and love with me, even though I was probably wilder than I imagined myself and had little or nothing to offer back. I was just looking for a place—any place—to escape Mama.

Mama by then had almost completely abandoned any pretense of most household responsibilities. I can see clearly now that I was not doing well myself, but perhaps I just did not know. I had received no practical housekeeping lessons from a family member since Babushka had died seven years before. Even while she was alive, a sick woman like her was not capable enough to show me by example how to clean, do laundry, iron, and cook.

Since I had no good example, I was lost and confused as to how normal housekeeping happened. I was surrounded by so many dysfunctional examples that I thought such ineptitude was normality. But others knew how to perform such tasks. My friend Natasha Kovalchuk, a Ukrainian neighbor my age, taught me to fry potatoes and clean pots and frying pans. Natasha has three kids last I heard. Lena Osipchuk, my classmate from a mixed Ukrainian-Russian family, showed me how to brush the furry pink bedspread Mama had brought home from her second trip to Poland and how to quickly tidy up our front room every day. Lena died at only thirty years of age from Chernobyl-related cancer. Marina Priahina, a Russian, was in my class only for a short time and became my inseparable friend for the duration. It was such pleasure to build a world that only the two of us inhabited. We played family and ate meals of fried cabbage with bread crumbs and black bread squares with thin slices of lard. We read and discussed books and planned our futures. She disappeared without a trace in the thick of perestroika. All my attempts to locate her failed. Ira Suhozhilina, another half-and-half Ukrainian Russian, had thick and curly brown hair. She taught me what her mama had taught her—to patiently comb my thick hair with my right hand while holding a handful of it tightly nearest to my scalp with my left, so it would not hurt. Ira is on the social network Odnoklassniki.ru. Zhanna Odnoralova, Yura's mother, a Russian, told me to rinse my hair with egg yolk or beer to make it smooth and shiny. I learned to wash my hair leaning over a large metal bowl. I would mix hot water from the metal kettle with some cold water and pour the warm mix over my hair with my right hand while holding and rinsing my hair with my left. Hair conditioner was a science fiction item like cars that could drive without gasoline. The yolk and the beer did wonders. Zhanna survived Yura, who died at fifty.

In those deprived days, I often relied on these and other women and girls when I felt so desperately sorry for myself and needed compassion I could never get at home. They gave me that and more. Would I be abandoning my gratitude to them or blaming them for the USSR's holding me and my kind lower than them and theirs? I now simply understood that I had only one life and if I did not take a major step and go through the door that was opening only for me, some or all of my life would be hopelessly ruined, like Mama's and Grandma's before me. I was very sure that my future did not belong in the Soviet Socialist Republic of Ukraine.

I returned from the monthlong harvesting and washed my hair and scrubbed the rest of me. Not once during our stay there were we taken to the communal bath in the regional center. That period of time is the longest I've ever gone without bathing—an entire month!

Kiev did not realize that my mind was made up: I was not going to spend my life trying to educate a young generation of Ukrainians who would most likely be anti-Semitic no matter what. There were exceptions to the general rule of the land, like random bursts of promise, but not enough to keep me there.

There was no time to contemplate on this decision as classes began, and I attended Kiev Peduchilische, my college, wearing my Polish clothes that I'd saved for this time. I looked so different in them, as if I did not fit into the normal Kiev lifestyle anymore. I would walk back through the familiar streets and wonder why I was still here. People would look at me because I was looking into their faces, as if seeking a reason to reconsider. I imagined myself elsewhere, in places as good and plentiful as Poland or better. I was going through the motions of living. As the days advanced and the fallen yellow and red leaves under my feet turned brown and shriveled, I realized that I'd already resolved to take the reins of my destiny. I wanted to leave the USSR, to become one of the obscure, ostracized people who dared to take a chance and get out.

It was easy to resolve this in my head but not so easy to evade Mama's persistent deliberations: "What if after I register this invitation to Israel, they fire me from my job, and then I will be refused exit? I should kill myself," she asked and answered, repeating herself nightly many times over, obviously cornered by this challenge. We knew people who had been rejected, the *refusniks*, who had spent years without work or were now working illegally. They were now unwanted and discarded members of Soviet society with even fewer rights than the rest. Mama was genuinely concerned and afraid of the worst-case outcome. She also loved to threaten me with her probable suicide. For years preceding this time I'd been afraid she'd go through with her threat, and I was always super obedient for weeks after she spoke of it. I tried to offer her some of my optimism every time she mentioned suicide, but she was unwilling to listen to me. She did not find my optimism valid. To the contrary, my positive outlook irritated her and brought out new fears, but I tried just as hard as she resisted.

"What if I go register the invitation instead of you and everything works out?" I'd inject.

"Yes, yes, we must chance it. The one who doesn't take risks doesn't drink the champagne." That was Mama's then-favorite saying. She'd smile when she'd say this and

for a little while looked pleased with herself. But only momentarily. Very unstable before, she was on the verge of a
breakdown, snapping, yelling, cursing, stuck in her mind
on the unsolvable question: To go or not to go? Someone
had to do something and soon.

Dress 10

The Revolutionary

Was I ever a little girl who knew no trouble?

Wasn't I convincing Yura Odnoralov just a couple of years ago to join the Komsomol so he could fit it?

Now, I refused to accept the dubious pretense of the Marxist-Leninist teachings, which were so imperative to comply with, to embrace, and to follow if I were to move forward with a career as a Soviet teacher. Everything was moving fast, and I was the only one standing still. I was unsure which foot to put forward first in this "let's register the invitation from Israel" dance I was now dancing with Mama.

A month flew by, largely wasted at lectures about the role of a Soviet educator in the formation of young Soviet citizens. The only interludes were during the calligraphy classes and the preparations to put together a show for the October holidays, around November 7, of course. I was not seeking a position of visibility, yet I was chosen to organize our class participation. It was a job nobody would volunteer for. It was as if my days of praepostoring were not over, as if my peers were reading the "good leader" stamp on my face as "put the Jew in charge of what no one else wants to do." Or was I reading too much into it?

By the late 1970s there was a kind of unspoken understanding in the USSR to place Jews in charge so that there would be a Jew to blame should things not work out. Such projects simply did not get turned down; they were made into successes, or else ... they ruined your everything.

A sudden wave of Komsomol nostalgia and euphoria swept over me. I heard the sound of Grandma's caring voice singing to me her favorite revolutionary songs as when she lulled me to sleep all those moons ago. Those songs were from her youth, and she transferred her love of them to me. A romantic idealist, as a young girl of nine, Babushka witnessed the storms of both Russian revolutions of 1917 firsthand, losing her father and surviving pogroms in the revolutions' wake. The Komsomol became her generation's alternative to God. The reverence with which she sang the lyrics to "The Internationale," in Russian, of course, strongly reminded me of the priests shown in the anti-tsarist films—exalted. Grandma was exalted as a youth, and so were her sisters and her children. But not me. My generation was the cynical one.

Besides, hearing this anthem in Ukrainian made even the most devout Communists laugh.

"*Yak u vulkanoviy bezodni, v serdzyah u nas gyrkoche grim.*" The Ukrainian verse translates "the eruption of the end" into a passionate simile: "like in a volcanic abyss, the thunder is rolling in our hearts." The Russian words actually made for a very compelling call to action—arise all the people of the bottom classes and take what the upper classes have; destroy them in the process, and after our final battle, we shall be the ruling class. In a word—redistribution. Still erupting here, there, everywhere.

The English lyrics of this left-wing Socialist anthem, as translated from the Russian, tell the same story, without the volcano spewing the hot lava of contrived sentiments found in the Ukrainian translation.

Stand up, accursed and unwanted
The world of slavery and serfs.
Our mind is boiling with frustration
And wants to enter into lethal bout.
The entire world of tyranny
We will dig through
To its very foundation, and on top of it
We will build our own world.
In it Nobody will become the Almighty Everything.

Russian was the predominant language of the majority of Kievans, and I chose for us to sing this anthem in Russian at the culmination of our presentation. Perhaps, subversively, I chose it as a symbol of my own private revolution. No longer a devoted student, instead of homework, I labored in the evenings to hand sew myself an exquisite revolutionary skirt—slim and slick, a farewell toga, with fine black chiffon lining and bunting used for a wide belt and matching hair ribbons. For this skirt I used a cut of delicate black velour Mama kept in the bed box of my grandparents', now mine, bed. She'd bought this fabric in Leningrad in the 1950s but two decades later was still unsure what to sew from it. The chiffon was stored there too, unclaimed and unused for as many years. I made the decision of what to sew instead of Mama. It was not exactly but sort of payback for selling my graduation fabric out from under me.

Since I was supposed to emcee our class presentation, I wanted to look the part of a legitimate revolutionary, only better, so I used one of those bright-red turtlenecks Mama had imposed upon me in Poland. It looked great with the long, slim velour and my red Poland-bought pantyhose, red fingernails, red lips, red kerchief in my hair, and red-and-black Polish shoes. The day of the concert I looked at myself in the mirror, and, again, I just knew that I was beautiful. Only this time the beauty came from the strange glow of my face—bright red with secret anticipation of the beginning of the end. Perhaps Mama was right and red was my color after all.

Mama could not come to see this presentation even if she wanted. In fact, she did not even have a clue that I'd taken her fabric, made a skirt, and formed all these other plans. I was not sharing my strategy with her. Not yet. I planned to quit school and find a simple job, so that when the time came for me to leave the Komsomol, I could reduce the perceived abomination of the act. Staying in the teachers' college would mean I'd be berated at a public assembly by 250 future eager teachers of Soviet propaganda. For years many accounts had circulated throughout the city about the ugly anti-Semitic assemblies of this or that Jew's exclusion from the ranks of the Komsomol or Communist Party. The smears flung out at these meetings included the mandatory *kike* derogative and the less hurtful array of *traitor, capitalist pig,* and *Israeli aggressor.* Many Jewish men and women had heart attacks at these meetings. Some even were beaten in dark alleys afterward. Women at the nearby textile and milk factories, I heard, were especially ferocious. Furious, loudmouthed Ukrainians screamed abuses until the Jew's tears poured and decent women and men sobbed with him or her. I heard these meetings lasted for hours. I was afraid. If I were to resign voluntarily, I could eliminate that torturous step, I reasoned.

Mama wanted me to stay and complete my education. "We can ask for another invitation, if this one expires," she claimed. My brain refused to accept this proposition. I felt as if my mind had already departed and was waiting on the side of the wide railroad tracks for me to join it, like when we crossed to Poland and smiling people dressed in all shades of well-tailored clothes waved to welcome me.

I brought in my turntable and speaker system to the after-show party at the teachers' college. My uncle Leon had given it to me recently when visiting Kiev. It was a generous present, one I did not think him capable of. In fact, it was the only real gift he ever gave me. As if to reaffirm my surprise, when handing it over, he said, "Got it from work, and I have a much-better one already. So you are one lucky girl!"

The entire all-male class of the nearby pilots' school was invited to Peduchilische. That was the way young people met—at dance parties. Pretty much everyone paired off after a few songs. I was soon the only nondancing girl left unclaimed despite my revolutionary chic. *None of them will ever want me,* I thought, changing records all evening. That sealed my decision. That evening I told Mama that I would be resigning from the school on Monday in preparation for our imminent registration to leave the USSR.

Mama was watching TV on the couch, half-asleep, and did not react right away. When the news sank in, it released the barrage of her what-ifs: "What if I get sick? What if my ulcer starts acting up? What if my boss will not terminate my employment, as required to start the departure process? What if they turn us down?" At all turns of her life, Mama tried to anticipate every possible wrong turn, playacting responses from everyone, using, however, only her own logic.

"I will jump off the Metro Bridge," Mama concluded. She said that often, varying the bridges and methods of ending her life. Such threats always had a disturbing effect on me. She confused and overpowered me, and she won this round.

For a short while I continued to attend classes, indifferent to the teachers and students alike. My only joy was the daily walks from The University stop of the No. 8 streetcar to Shevchenko Boulevard, where my pedagogical college was located in a prewar, even prerevolutionary building. It was a magnificent autumn, the kind that dresses up every city in colors nature has a plentitude of but, like a stingy old maid, saves for only such rare, brief occasions. It was to become my next-to-last autumn in Kiev, but I was already beginning to say my mental goodbyes to my hope of becoming a teacher, to the youth I would not have here, to my beloved city and its many residents I loved with all my heart and would forever miss.

I ended my hesitation one afternoon and visited the director's office, announcing that I would be relocating to Riga to be reunited with my father. That was a lie Mama and I had considered during our nightly negotiations. Since little of my father's family was known in connection with me, the director accepted it—not right away, but after my solemn assurances that I was not planning to escape to Israel. Why they did not check and discover that my father had already left the country, I have no clue. Maybe it did not matter to them after all, and they were just pretending to try to stop me, the ungrateful Jewish citizen, by giving me session after session of interrogation and pretending to convince me to change my mind. I did not waver.

Undergoing expulsion from the Komsomol by the group of women with whom I'd just spent thirty long days harvesting, the women whose anti-Semitic jokes and aggressive intentions I could not tolerate, was out of the question. A week or two later, I asked Darina's sister, Irma, a nurse at Hospital No. 7, which was across from my apartment building, if there were any vacancies. She said yes. Darina and Irma were the only two girls with whom I shared my plans. They were Jews who never seemed to be offended or thrown off their paths when their friends called them or others kikes. In contrast, having that word flung at me by my enemies chiseled away days and months off my life. Irma told me that the doctor in charge of the Komsomol league at Hospital No. 7 was very sympathetic to the Jews and I should have no problem. She was right, and I never forgot just how much she helped me.

There was the huge hurdle of registering the invitation with the OVIR, and that had to happen before any other plans could be made. All Mama was capable of was the daily back-and-forth "to go or not to go" soliloquies. If she could, she would, but every day there was a new "but." An inexplicable sense of urgency did not let me rest. The more I tried to rationalize, the more I knew that we had to hurry. There were many people wanting to leave, and our unpredictable Soviet keepers could slam the narrow exit door on us any day. I was now afraid of being stuck here forever.

My new job at the hospital required no deep thought. I washed and sterilized needles and syringes. I bet I was exposed to at least five debilitating diseases there: hepatitis C, tuberculosis, meningitis, staphylococcus, and malaria. Although we wore rubber gloves, here as everywhere, stealing was prevalent, and most medical supplies were unavailable. The rubber gloves we wore were rinsed at the end of the day, hung to dry, and used until they completely ripped. Countless times I stabbed myself with a needle and continued to wear the punctured glove or just took it off, because only our supervising nurse was able to get us a replacement one. A needle was considered to be "good" if it was under 75 percent rusted. We were not allowed to throw any needle away without first demonstrating to our nurse why we thought the needle was no longer reusable.

There were two other girls besides the nurse. We had fun talking nonsense. They were not going anywhere and saw their futures at Hospital No. 7. I had big plans. This was a perfect exit job for me. I saw no one. No one saw me. I was there for all of three months. By noon, when the syringes and needles were washed, wrapped in brown paper, tied with a cotton string, and placed into a huge sterilization oven, the heat and stench in the room became unbearable, forcing us to scatter. Thus, this job was actually very well compensated, giving a full day's salary for only a half day's work.

That room; the blood-clotted, rusty needles; the smells—all of it resonated of Majdanek to me. I felt that I, too, belonged to the Majdanek generation, only I would somehow be rescued. My salvation was in the fancy blue envelope known as the invitation to reunite with family in Israel.

The Story of Relatives from Poland Becomes the Departing Legend

When the Babiy Yar monument was unveiled in 1976, Jews from everywhere in the Soviet Union descended upon Kiev, even though they were not welcomed and were chased away, detained, and sometimes arrested. A substantial crowd gathered on the wrong side of the Babiy Yar massacre site, actually even on the outside of it, about half a kilometer off. But that was where the authorities who held the power of revisionism decided to erect the monument, which was officially titled *To Soviet Citizens Martyred by the Nazis* despite the well-assessed and equally well-hidden statistic that of the over 100,000 people killed here, at least 33,771 of them were Jews, who died in the first two days of this concentration camp's operations, on September 29 and 30, 1941, shot after having been stripped and lined atop the ravine, into which they fell one by one.

Every Jew of the Soviet Union was reduced to whispering about the Nazi atrocities directed against the Jews—in Ukraine, Lithuania, Belarus, Latvia, Southern Russia, Crimea, and the Caspian and Caucasus regions. Every Jew and plenty of non-Jews knew stories of relatives and friends who perished in Babiy Yar. The USSR, the greatest country of all countries, was deliberately deceiving its citizens into believing that the Nazi actions against the Jews were unimportant or did not really happen in the way the Jews understood they most certainly did. In every former Soviet Jewish settlement, non-Jewish Russian, Ukrainian, Belorussian, Latvian, and Lithuanian neighbors and their children were witnesses to this extermination. Very few of their testimonies were ever made public. Maybe these political attitudes stemmed from the unpleasant reality that many Soviet citizens collaborated with the Nazis, becoming vicious murderers of Jews, whom the Nazis were not always able to identify by sight. Lithuanians and Ukrainians, it was whispered, were the worst, the quickest to identify their Jewish neighbors out of hatred and, most frequently, out of a desire to grab whatever their Jewish neighbors had.

Growing up in the Soviet Union, I was most certainly led to believe that Hitler's war was against the Soviets. The Jewish question was never part of the problem, and the word *Holocaust* was never heard. Then again, I was led to believe that Jews were not a desirable type of Soviet citizens. In fact, I was told that more times than I can innumerate.

My family knew the truth about the Holocaust, even if they did not call it that. My grandfather Avrum, survived captivity in a concentration camp and escaped from both the camp and the Kalinovka ghetto extermination. He witnessed many horrors of that war personally, plenty of them directly in his own family. My grandmother Rivka and her sisters, Raia and Polina, each had a story of escape and survival predating the war. Many of their relatives disappeared in World War II and in Stalin's purges before and after it. In my childhood, the women were bereaved. They gently remembered their perished family and friends and mourned with candles always lit on the anniversaries of their loved ones' deaths—what I now know as yahrzeits.

One of the important Soviet Union holidays was Soviet Constitution Day, December 5. In 1978 Mama and I used that day to evaluate all the pros and cons of leaving the USSR. We did it in between some TV shows we watched. Still, we could not reach a decision. Mama said she needed more time. For all I knew she was going to take as long about this as she did about that black velour. I could not allow that. The very next day I put on my revolutionary look—the red turtleneck and black skirt—walked into our district's passport control office with both of our passports and the invitation, and registered us for departure for Israel. It was an irreversible act of defiance. I, one of the best students from 187, became a traitor of the Soviet motherland, and I was proud for taking this step. If I knew how to pray or understood anything about God, this would have been the best time for prayers. Instead, I pleaded with myself, as I usually do to avert panic in my head, not to fall apart when Mama heard the news.

I thought Mama was going to have a stroke that evening. She always dramatized her illnesses, from heart failure to vegetative-vascular dystonia. She had dozens of pill bottles and elixirs but never followed any treatments beyond the initial visit. She thrived on the attention she received from complaining to doctors, nurses, and family when she was ailing. I despised her for it. She was between phony and fake when she recited her horrible symptoms, escalating the drama with each new listener. The moment she'd get off the phone or a visiting doctor would leave, she would sit up, flip the TV on, and watch it for hours until her troops came home. Then she'd call her roster of girlfriends and talk about the same thing over and over and over, embellishing symptoms, until she herself was properly convinced of her grave situation. She starred in her own little drama without any regard for me. Even though I was used to it, I never understood it. I thought it was very cruel to play upon the emotions of the people who care about you. Mama, evidently, did not.

Why did she have me? I often questioned. She was so unmotherly. She disliked me so much while professing her love of me to everyone but me.

"Why?" she yelled hysterically. "Why?" She blamed and accused me of ruining everything for her now that I'd gotten the nerve to act and had registered the invitation. The names Mama called me were unfair and painful, but I understood her as no one ever understood her—deep under all the hatred she was spewing at me, she really wanted to go and was glad that she did not have to make the decision. If anything ever went wrong, it would be because of me, and she'd have someone to yell at. Confirming my thought, Mama sobbed, "We are lost forever, and it's all your fault." *No one will guide me through this,* I understood then. I was alone. I could tell no friend beyond those I'd already told. I could not even tell my cousins. Mama talked to me about all her fears endlessly. I had to stop paying attention to her, inasmuch as that was possible, because she was driving me nuts.

A miserably cold winter followed. Mama was fired from her work. I could have stayed at mine, even after I was expelled from the Komsomol, but Mama insisted I leave it and be with her. Our household knew no order; she needed me to ward off total chaos. Also Mama was afraid of being recognized by anyone she knew in town, so I had the duty of going twice weekly to the "line markings," roll call at the park nearest our OVIR. Without advancing to the front of this unofficial line, one could not officially enter the OVIR office in regard to the matter of exiting the USSR. Jews were not even allowed to gather in close proximity to the OVIR, so as not to arouse questions from visiting foreigners. Life in the USSR was as "perfect" as ever, and all citizens were happy, right?

This OVIR was the same one where I had taken Pan Zbiegniew and Jadwiga three years before to register as our family. I liked the familiarity of the location and was looking forward to getting to that exciting event that would play an absolutely unanticipated part in our lives. The only reason Soviet Jews were allowed to leave, according to the official line of the USSR, was to reunite with family members already in Israel. The relatives could have been there since the day of the flood or recent arrivals. The USSR and Israel had no diplomatic relations at that time. Soviet family-reunification legends were a source of despair for many of the departing because the story had to be believable and verifiable, or else. Well, how lucky did Mama and I get? The invitation envelope from Israel came from a woman whose last name was Goldstein, my maternal grandmother's maiden name. So our "departing legend" began with the real pogrom my grandmother and her family lived through and with my great-grandmother's nonexistent sister escaping to Poland. Well, actually, my great-grandmother had a sister, who died in childhood, but that was long unverifiable.

The next step was somewhat verifiable: the Polish Goldstein sister, after having some offspring in Poland, made her way to Israel after the war, while some of her offspring stayed in Poland and even came to visit us three years ago on such and such dates, as registered at this OVIR and so verifiable. It was also registered there that we'd subsequently gone to visit our Polish relatives in 1976 and that Mama had gone again in 1977, at which time she and our relatives had discussed the upcoming reunification of the entire family in Israel.

That was our departing legend. It was strong. It was solid. If we only could get through the thousands of people in front of us in this unofficial park queue to submit our case paperwork to the OVIR.

The Departing

In January–February 1979, with so many Jews waiting to submit their cases for exiting the Soviet Union, our OVIR was open for a mere two hours only twice a week. It was most probably a deliberate attempt by the "organs," as the government bureaucracy was called, to reduce the number of exiting persons, or at the very least make them suffer. Many absurd and moronic obstacles were created to discourage and disparage even the bravest and the most patient. For instance, should we be so lucky as to get the permission to go, we'd be required to get a release from the central dry cleaning bureau that we had no debt there and do similarly from the central laundry, central bank, central rental, and so on. Each of the offices dealing with the departing Jews was assigned its own way to manufacture delays, obstacles, mockery, and such other rubbish in the process. The appropriate official was reported to us as being in a meeting, on vacation, away for lunch, out sick, and otherwise unavailable, in the best form of Soviet Socialist impenetrable bureaucratic corruption. All that waste of time was in addition to the initial gathering of a heap of documents required at application time. Only the thick-skinned, the oblivious, and the truly determined were willing to subject themselves to this barrage of everyday institutionalized anti-Semitic abuse.

One after the other, non-Jewish people came in and out of the OVIR with whatever they needed, but it was a given that the Jews needed to be kept waiting. Many would lose their cool, and outbursts followed, but they never ended well. If one wanted to leave the USSR, one had to bite one's tongue and pretend everything was good. The infamous Soviet saying "Address your complaints to the head apothecary's office" was heard hundreds of times at the OVIR, the meaning being equivalent to "Get lost." After all the necessary papers were assembled and the application accepted and approved, a fee of 1,000 rubles per person, an astronomical amount of money, needed to be paid for the official surrender of one's Soviet passport. It was infinitely more of a privilege to be deprived of one's Soviet citizenship than to keep it.

But ahead of all that, the application package needed to get to the clerk at the OVIR with all family members in attendance. After more than three months of registering in the twice-weekly line markings in the park—an absolutely arbitrary way of advancement into the tiny OVIR office, which I am sure was tightly controlled by the KGB, the OVIR being one of the KGB's outposts—our line advancement was dismal. I remember that one of the Jewish keepers of the "departing lists" told all of us in the park not to get too close to the actual OVIR office without good reason. Only those nearest the front of the line-markings list were allowed that. Of course, along with some young people I met during that process, I decided to test the validity of his words.

One early spring afternoon, during document-intake office hours, we walked by the OVIR entrance, where a small crowd of Jews awaited their turn to get inside. The OVIR was located in a street-level office in a five-story residential building, only slightly better than the one I lived in. As soon as we approached the OVIR side of the building, the residents from above tossed some water onto us, just as I'd done in the sixth grade to make the drunks gathered under our kitchen windows scatter or find a new hiding spot to split their vodka bottle. We only got wet but learned later that often bricks and other heavy objects were flung out of that and other windows above the OVIR office. It was very risky to wait right outside, but the throwers also did not dare to aim directly into the line, since a militsiya-man, policeman, was posted at the entrance of the OVIR to guard it from the departing Jews.

Very fortuitous for Mama and me was that our upstairs neighbor Dora was also preparing to leave and was afraid to go the distance alone. She needed us for traveling company. Dora still occupied her very important post as cashier at the Central Kiev Pharmacy. Dora's husband, Mikhail Borisovich, had died a few years before, and her daughter, Nadyusha, had recently gotten married. Dora wanted to join her sisters in Teaneck, New Jersey, and Mama decided that sounded like a good place for us too. Dora always carried herself everywhere with dignity and grace, a manner very becoming for a woman of any age. She had style and class, and her spotless and cozy apartment would be left for her adored, beautiful, intelligent, and kind daughter with all its beautiful china and linens.

Dora knew our OVIR officer personally. In the past, the officer had needed some prescriptions filled, and those were normally not available to the ordinary public. Dora had helped her and formed a good connection, just in case. The woman told Dora that all three of us should wait and come on our scheduled day after advancing through the departing line, which the officer was officially not even allowed to be aware of, because authorities did not acknowledge that so many people wanted to leave the Socialist workers' "paradise." To a passerby, only those few waiting out front—a group of fifteen or twenty, at most—wanted to get into the OVIR, a.k.a. get out of the country. The average passerby did not know about the departing lists. Yet the OVIR officer knew that we could get in only when our turn came among the departing. She gave Dora assurances that she would accept all our papers and not obstruct our process. This promise was undoubtedly a criminal offense, as the instructions from above were to restrict and constrain the departing Jews in every possible manner.

About that time, one of Mama's distant relations, Vova, traded his place in line for ours, as his wife did not want to go anywhere yet. Vova continued in the line, eventually leaving ten years later, after perestroika.

I would not be doing justice to this OVIR story if I did not confess that I loved being among all these departing Jews several hours a week. For the first time ever, I did not need to be afraid of being called offensive anti-Semitic names or to hear stupid remarks by stupid anti-Semitic people. No! Now I heard stupid remarks from seemingly smart Jewish people! I loathed the insistent conversations about what to take or whether to fly or take the train, but by standing in the departing line, waiting for our number to be called, I overheard so much valuable information. My head became filled with knowledge of where to buy this or that and visions of strip searches at the border, complete with the squeezing of toothpaste out of its tube and the tearing up of pillows at container-shipping check-points. I also began to fantasize about our exit visas, the only documents the departing were allowed to bring out of the USSR during this final crossing. I also was getting fast lessons on Jewishness and becoming quite a Jew, even if I did not yet realize it.

A couple of weeks before our turn came, a group of my new young Jewish friends forced their way into the OVIR to help one of them—Leo—turn in his paperwork. Leo had a disabled grandmother, his only living relative. She had to be carried everywhere. Twice already they had come and waited by the OVIR entrance but had not been admitted. This time Leo's friends stood guard and kept the militsiya-man as well as the departing front liners away while Leo carried his grandmother up the four steps into the OVIR officer's room. Leo's friends accomplished this with polite force: young men standing arm in arm with one another on both sides of the entrance.

Some of those scheduled to get in that afternoon protested and yelled, but most of us realized that it was not the end of the world to let the unfortunate invalid in first. Yes, I say most of *us*, because Mother, Dora, and I were among those who were held back that afternoon. I saw this event with my own eyes. Among the departing, everyone realized, there were traitors—Jewish spies planted to observe and report to the authorities any item of potential interest, just like in the wartime ghettos and camps. We all knew that. Leo's documents were accepted that day, but a few months later, Leo and his friends who had helped him in that storm received denials of exit from the USSR. The militsiyaman could not have been the one to identify them, as only those in my friends' group knew all the names of those involved. One of them must have been a spy. But who? I never figured it out.

Dora, Mama, and I were lucky to squeak through the very next time. In March 1979, our papers were duly accepted. We now had to wait for the permission to depart. We tried not to think of the denial option—that is, *I* tried not to think of it. Mama was obsessed with it and anticipated only a doomsday end. The thing that seemed to calm her was to unleash her frustrations onto me. All of it was my fault—the registering of the invitation, the OVIR line, everything. I was the person to blame for the failure of this process. I received my daily dosage of Mama's bitter poison with varying degree of digestion. I was sometimes wise and tolerant, but more frequently, I would yell back at her atop my Kiev lungs, saying things she did not want me to say, throwing back at her words of hurt and deceit I'd gone over in my head for years but only now felt empowered to say aloud. I was, after all, Mama's daughter, an apple that had not fallen far from its tree. I could yell just as well as she, and I could transfer blame just as well too.

When not arguing with me, Mama was bored. For months we had nothing to do except to weed through our possessions, giving away and selling whatever we could. We sold most of our books despite my pleas not to. They were my friends, and I miss them to this day. Mama was obsessed with these sales, as she was obsessed when she discovered Mara's battery plot. But after we'd sold what could be sold, Mama became nearly comatose. Now that the reality of what we were embarking on dawned on her, she acted as if she wanted to stay. She talked about staying for the remainder of the time and threatened to commit suicide by throwing herself on train tracks or jumping off a bridge or under a moving vehicle. It was as if she loved torturing me. Maybe she did. I had to take her threats seriously each time, just in case that should be the time she decided to act out. I did not think she would, but who knew? So I stayed and apologized and begged her to live and not threaten me anymore. She gloated over each of her perceived victories and terrorized me with something small and petty I'd neglected to take care of. But I really did not have time to deal with her.

I had a boyfriend. His name was Felix. I'd met him in the departing line. He was departing with his mother. His papers were accepted shortly after ours. He was very much in love with me. He bought me flowers nearly every day that spring, dedicated poems to me, and held my hand. We did whatever two young people want to do—go to the movies, the theater, museums, parks—whatever. I somewhat reciprocated his feelings while knowing all along he was not the right man for me—not the prince I was waiting for. So, in truth, I just used him for sex.

Back when I still believed in fairy tales, my fairy-tale makers taught me to believe that sex was not good, not clean—evil, in fact. Any sexual impulse was supposed to be rejected and diluted in the guilt my maternal *meshpuchah* (relations) loaded me with, and I obeyed. Mama, all her relatives, the school, and my peers all taught me to be very obedient.

My final spring and summer in Kiev brought out of me a girl I was unfamiliar with. That girl thought there were no boundaries. She believed herself free and acted out, embracing every symbolism of that newly found freedom, including being disobedient and, of course, including sex.

In the USSR, a strong no-sex double standard usually ended with unplanned and unwanted pregnancies terminated by poorly performed abortions. I knew nothing of sex, or at least not as far as my family was aware, but I knew of many abortions and many affairs. Some of the affairs took place under my very eyes, in our apartment, with my mother's facilitation.

The USSR did not condone sex or sexual affairs, so Mama's friends and relatives often used our apartment as a short-stay motel room would be used in the US, as I later learned. In the USSR, hotels asked for passports; we did not. A married person could not register to a hotel room with anyone of the opposite sex but his or her spouse. Most hotel rooms were shared with strangers of the same sex. Some hotel rooms for singles had fifteen or twenty people to a room. A married person caught in the hotel room having extramarital sex—or even just registering with someone other than his or her spouse—risked exposure, public condemnation of his or her actions, forcible denouncement of such anti-Soviet behavior, and a humiliating public apology to the spouse. Hotels got paid. Our apartment was let without payment, even at a great deal of inconvenience to me. On such days, Mama told me in the morning to go to a friend's home after school and not return until the 10:00 p.m. curfew. One of the relatives Mama let our place to frequently was my uncle Haim, Mama's brother, the father of my first cousins. He was then illicitly seeing his next wife. Other people, like Mama's boss and some of her coworkers, used our apartment to have rendezvous with their "extras." By extension, I became a collaborator in these affairs. I especially disliked having to deceive my first cousins, but Mama had completely convinced me for years that my uncle Haim was the injured party in that marriage.

I felt sorry for all these cheating people, some of whom I knew, who were so unhappy in their marriages yet could not divorce, because of the ever-present housing crisis. It was impossible to split or exchange a one-room apartment into two and still remain in Kiev, for example. So instead they stayed in their unwanted marriages and had regular extramarital sex during working hours while their entire organizations covered for them. People were very cynical and very romantic at the same time. And then there were countless stories about abortions. I had already met some women who'd had as many as twenty-eight abortions. Sex in the USSR was very dangerous. There were little or no contraceptives, little or no education about sex and hygiene, and absolutely no protection against sexually transmitted diseases. I never knew of anyone using the existing thick red rubber condoms for their intended purpose.

Regardless of all that, sex, I felt, would be my farewell reward to my Kiev self. A mature way to exile. In the claustrophobic circumstances of our lives at that time, such secrets were impossible to keep secret—or at least not for too long. Felix wanted to marry me. He proposed to me in front of Mama and Grandpa, and I had to say yes, because they thought he was my prince. But I was not ready for this marriage, or any other marriage, in fact. I'm choosing to keep most of this bittersweet memory undisclosed, and I ask that you forgive me for doing so. As I always knew, it was not meant to be, and Felix and I did not part well.

During the last week of October, days before we left, I was riding on the No. 8 streetcar when my friend Yura Odnoralov, whom I had not seen since graduation day, got on. Although the streetcar was not crowded, instead of sitting down, we continued standing and talking, swaying with the car. I was bound by my predeparting awareness not to talk about anything related to our departure to anyone not privy to its details, especially in public. I assumed Yura knew we were leaving—the entire district knew from the building caretakers' grapevine—but he was, as always, sensitive and did not pry. Yura, I noted, had changed in a very sad way since I'd seen him a year and a half before. He looked as if he was drunk, but most probably he was on steroids. He was one of the most promising swimmers in Kiev, and the 1980 Olympics were coming up.

When the streetcar pulled to my stop, I said, *"Poka"* ("See you soon").

We never said goodbye, even though we both knew we would never again meet. Yura was still living with his mother at the time of his death. That is all I know about his life.

Farewell, Kiev

On October 30, 1979, Mama and I left Kiev forever. We took three suitcases and one beach bag, which unfolded into a sheet and pillow, our only pillow for the next several months. The Soviet government strictly controlled what we could bring with us. A true totalitarian regime, it forbade us to take with us anything of real value—for example, no jewelry exceeding 250 rubles. That was an amount less than a PhD's monthly salary but more than Mama's. Mama had purchased a ring with a diamond chip a couple of years before for 253 rubles. This three-ruble difference became a subject of fixation for Mama, who talked about selling or taking this ring incessantly. In the end, she did not sell it.

Unlike other adults, Mama left our packing almost entirely to me, together with surrendering our apartment back to the government and getting rid of the evidence of our three-generation family life in it. I was barely eighteen. What did I really know of anything? What did I really understand about the life we were leaving or the road we were about to embark on? I took on this role because I had to, because no one else in my family would step up to be an adult. I sorted and folded and wrapped and devised ways to preserve in one piece some of the better things left from Grandma, like plates, cups, and the few books we did not sell. We were allowed to ship a container with our stuff, but I was very quickly learning that our stuff as compared to the stuff of some others—with two-earner households, better jobs, better connections, and functioning mothers—was pretty much worthless. In the end, the container we shipped was crammed with lots of junk and sentimental-value items. Those sentimental-value items become more precious to me with each passing year.

In the fall of 1979 I had to make decisions I was not prepared to make. Many of those decisions turned out to be good, but many more were really bad. Mama, true to her character, made even more bad decisions than I, and together, the two of us left the apartment in a complete and utterly disgusting mess for my grandfather to get rid of after we were gone.

Mama was mostly unreachable. She was somewhere inside herself. Her ailments—real and imagined—were her main focus now. She was not as ill as she played herself to be. But she was certainly very scared of the unknown ahead of us. When I look back now, we had virtually no information about the US, and I think that, despite her behavior, Mama was a very brave woman to have agreed to make the journey for me.

What I cannot forget is her torturing me in the process of her self-doubt. During that entire year, it seemed, she took on a habit of controlling me through nearly daily threats to withdraw our applications and then our exit visas. It was one of the darkest periods of my life. The explosive arguments I had with Mama obliterated much of that time from my conscious mind.

Then, about two weeks before our exit visas were going to expire, Mama began complaining about her ulcer acting up. She wanted to stay and ask for an extension because of her illness and check herself into a hospital, but I just knew—with I have no idea what kind of knowledge—that we must leave immediately or we never would. Of course, no one would have agreed to that kind of an extension, and if she'd gone to the hospital, she could have been deliberately injected with something or operated on in such a way that she would be damaged for real. We were no longer citizens of any country. We were now enemies of this one. Mama did not want to grasp that reality.

All this did not stop her preoccupation with endless *chachka* purchases. She had devised and redevised many schemes to buy crafts because she knew that many Russian and Ukrainian craft *chachkas* were needed to sell in transit to make some quick money. Mama bought so many of them that our suitcases eventually had no room for much else. I packed and repacked our suitcases so many times that, in the end, I forgot three or four really important things.

Mama finally conceded and made firm plans and hired a man to accompany us to the border. No relative was willing to undertake this journey, not even Grandfather and certainly not my uncle Haim. The man who accompanied us was named Semeon. He was a part-time driving instructor whom Mama met when she was learning to drive during our last summer in Kiev. She did not succeed in learning to drive then, but Semeon offered to take us to the border. It was his other part-time occupation. He was Mama's full-time "friend" by then.

It snowed the day we left—early Kiev snow flurries. We took a taxi to the Kiev Central Railroad Station. Grandfather, Aunt Zina, Felix, and pregnant Nadyusha were the only people to see us off—not because of the snow, but because it was a dangerous time. Being seen with the departing was a cause for many unpleasant and sometimes tragic events, like job dismissal, a KGB inquest, or worse. People were afraid. Only the unafraid relations and others who were planning to depart dared to come for the farewell. Mama's brother was so afraid he made sure to be out of town on this date, or at least pretended to be and really was hiding out at a friend's place, so that Mama would not guilt-trip him into coming. But his wife, my aunt Zina, came to say goodbye, which was totally contradictory to my family's insistent negative insinuations about her and her character.

To this day, I think Mama doesn't understand the fact that Aunt Zina was our only relative, other than Grandpa, unafraid to see us off. But Mama rarely takes the trouble to truly understand people. People live in her mind as players of her own provincial Shakespearian troupe. She dresses them up for their parts, rehearses their lines in her mind, and punishes them for bad performances—not that they ever find out until it's too late to replay. Mama wrote out Zina's part many years before that day, and only the ultimate tragedy of losing Haim restored Zina somewhat to Mama's mind from a position of archenemy to semifriend.

Zina found words of positive encouragement on our departing day for Mama and for me. She kissed and hugged me, perhaps for the first time in my life. I think Zina, who constantly hid her Jewish side behind her Russian father's last name and patronymic, respected us for doing this much more than she was capable of admitting.

It was snowing very heavily when the train finally moved. Grandfather cried and screamed words I no longer recall, mixing "lyuba moia" ("my beloved") with tears, as he chased after us, his arms stretched toward us, toward me, no longer able to hold on.

I, too, had tears in my eyes, as I do now writing this. I never again saw Kiev quite the same, through a Monetesque brushwork of colors, light, and love. I cried as the city mourned my leaving it by getting beautifully dusted by the falling snow. I cried because we were leaving all of it forever: Kiev, family, friends, Grandfather. Never would I see them again. I stuck my head out the top window and looked at my disappearing grandfather, the station, and the city until I saw nothing but the snow.

I sat down. That part was now over. Farewell, Kiev.

* * *

Semeon shut the window of our train compartment and went to the attendant for tea. It was cold, and I was shivering. I regretted giving away my warmest sweater to my cousin Stella, to whom I also gave my good winter boots and fake-fur coat. Under my Polish overcoat, I wore only a light sweater over my revolutionary turtleneck and the second of the Riga twins. I wore my Monsieur jeans under my dress. My black revolutionary skirt was lightweight and new and came along to be my only dressy garment in my new life. Those were all the clothes I now owned. My Riga dress was just perfect for our long, unpredictable journey; it washed well, dried quickly, and did not wrinkle. It would have to serve as a shirt, a nightgown and a bathrobe until we reached the United States. The rest of my good Polish clothing I gave to my first cousins. My aunt Zina was the only one who acknowledged that I was giving them more than she and her husband, my uncle, had ever given me. None of that mattered now that we were leaving everything and everyone behind.

We spent a night of which I remember nothing riding to the Carpathian Mountains, arriving at our departure point, Chop (pronounced *chope*), in the morning of October 31. Our exit visas were due to expire on November 1 at midnight.

We exited our train at the Chop train station and found ourselves surrounded by people like us. Semeon quickly found out that hundreds of families were already inside the station building, and there was a very strong likelihood we would not even make it out of the USSR on time. I swear that horrible news made Mama happy. She did not want to leave now. She had been so afraid this entire slow, agitated year, and these last few days she'd clung to the most desperate of illusions. She wanted to stay with

Semeon, without an apartment or a job, without citizenship or money. But what was she going to do with me? I was a burden. I wanted to leave. She reminded me that it had been my idea to register the invitation in the first place. Just in case we were unable to exit, she was ready to blame me for ruining everything.

But I was in a different mood. I stood in the center of Chop railroad square. I could smell the air of freedom from over the tall Carpathian hill with streets of homes splattered on it. Beyond it was Bratislava, where we'd change trains for Vienna. In Kiev, we'd bought tickets to Vienna, and we had Austrian visas in out exit IDs that Mama had traveled to Moscow to receive. If we could only get out in time. We *had* to get out in time. The possibility of missing our departure gave me chills, but I took hold of myself, remembering my aunt Zina's new respect for me and Grandfather's desire that I should have a better life.

I will find plenty of strength, I resolved. *I will be strong. I must.*

There, in the central square of Chop, stood I.

Me?! A Jewish girl from school 187 in Kiev?!

I was only a day's ride from Vienna. Life was absolutely amazing.

Dress 11

The Many Layers of Chop

When I was a young girl and believed in fairy tales, they sometimes had ogres and trolls and other nightmare creatures, but I never imagined that I would be wide awake when I'd actually encounter those.

The departing-forever crowd was everywhere inside the Chop train station on October 31, 1979. It was a challenge to find a spot to set down a suitcase or sit. Spread out through the five or six halls that were open to the public at this border station were the departing Jewish families. Small, large, very Jewish, and really Gentile looking. Old, middle-aged, young, childless, and with children of all ages. Finely, neatly, so-so, sloppily, expensively, and poorly dressed. The ailing, the pregnant, the toothless, the gold-toothed. Handsome, ugly, average looking. Fat, skinny, smart, dumb. Well behaved, rude, polite, obnoxious, angry, neurotic, calm. Russian, Ukrainian, and Moldovan. Jews of all kinds were here to cut out of the Soviet Union after months or years of deliberations, preparations, refusals, and humiliation. Here, at the station in Chop, which as I later discovered means "cut" in English, we were gathered together, I thought, like the Jews of Babiy Yar were in September 1941, as if to the slaughter. Chop, chop, chop!

Everyone was dressed in many layers of everything. I had on my revolutionary turtleneck and Monsieur jeans, with the Riga twin dress over them, and over that a sweater of many colors that I knitted myself. Over it all was my Polish coat, the same one that had shielded me against sleet, rain, and snow for the past three years. My brown rabbit-fur hat was on my head, and on my neck, twisted and tucked into my sweater, was my white Orenburg down shawl, like those the heroic Russian women wore during the Great Patriotic War and like those of the Decembrist exiles. I do not remember what I wore on my feet. I just know it was something equally as uncomfortable as all the combined layers of my clothing. I felt like stuffed cabbage, barely able to turn. I was suffocating, itching from the down and wool—completely miserable. *But not as they were,* I kept reminding myself, *not as when they stood naked, waiting to die. I am so much luckier. It will soon end and end well for me.* That quickly became my lifeline mantra at Chop.

The station buzzed in a not-too-happy beehive sort of way. It was as if carnage was actually expected. The sound of it was not yet distinct, but every time a large, dirty, industrial gray door swung open, all heads turned to the boarded-off part of the station, the carnage room. All voices quieted, and a look of fear crossed the adults' faces. This repeated hundreds of times each hour. The fear was also apparent in the children's eyes. It was acute and contagious. It was most probably in mine. I was a scared child who was pretending to be a brave adult.

It was soon the departure-control time for the people of the October 31 morning train. Men in boots from Hungarian, Czechoslovakian, and Soviet customs; border servicemen and servicewomen; medics; and border policemen were everywhere. Cleaning crews with stinky brooms washed the floors with grimy rags out of filthy buckets of dirty floor water. Pretending as if they were doing so by chance, they would deliberately settle their rags among the sandwiches and fried chicken that waiting Jews spread over their suitcases. Sneaking around these makeshift tables and large families, the cleaners were probably spying on the departing. Nobody cared about anyone in Chop. As always in the Soviet culture, a person's problems were that person's problems. Consideration, kindness, comfort, and care are never the attitudes of the oppressed. We were only taught that, never shown that.

To me this grotesque scene was straight out of Goya's *Los Caprichos* etchings. In them he condemned the society in which he lived. I was silently condemning mine. I engraved onto my brain's visual canvas my farewell to the USSR. I wish I could scroll you down the memory in my brain dated October 31, 1979. Maybe technology will allow us someday in the not-too-distant future to exchange our visual brain records as easily as we can now AirDrop between our iPhones or swap pictures through Facebook with relatives all over the world.

I recall this day as a day of anxiety and fear, and at the same time it was a day of anticipation. I was on the brink of freedom. It was real. It peeked through the filthy doors and made the sweaty-itchy discomfort somehow tolerable. Dust, dirt, despair, and darkness were on our side; light, hope, and promise were on the other. The only thing that separated us from freedom was a few people into whose hands our destiny had entrusted our final moments in the USSR.

In whatever towns or cities they were leaving, the departing threw a farewell feast for whomever they were leaving behind. This ritual is called *provody*—a send-off, like those before someone heads to the Soviet Army or jail. Except in our situation, we were heading off as if to a certain death at the battlefield—never to be seen again. Severing all ties was one hell of a price to pay for freedom, and we all paid it, as at the time of our leaving the might of the USSR was impregnable and indestructible.

In my parting nervousness, following the morbid send-off we threw, I could not eat for at least our final two days in Kiev. Yet despite anxious fear and anticipation of imminent slaughter, the sight and especially the garlicky smell of meat *kotletas*, the ground-meat-and-bread patties, our Soviet burgers, made me feel astute hunger. In the post-*provody* final chaos, I'd neglected to pack us any food ... I just couldn't stand the sight of it. Because I was our sole packer, we now had no food.

But we could not eat now anyway, not until we took care of the check-in procedures, which we, like countless other departing families, had secretly received on hand-copied sheets listing every step we were to expect at the crossing. Of course, these were totally illegal papers, and we had to study and remember what we needed to do at what juncture. We were not permitted to take these papers on the road, as, under Soviet rule, the content of these papers was considered a criminal activity. Nothing that could somehow be deemed incriminating could be found on us, not even handwritten addresses of our relatives. One either memorized facts, addresses, and telephone numbers or lost them forever. Chop was the last station tying us, persons without a state, to the USSR, and we had to be extra cautious to not provoke any incidents that would allow the authorities to block our departure, which they occasionally did even without provocation, just to demonstrate their authority and might.

I have no idea which thoughtful émigré took the time to author these departing papers for the rest of us. Since then I found out that there always is a person in every group who takes care of the critical info and its dissemination, even in the most desperate of situations, like the one the departing found themselves in at Chop. I was then simply one of the ungrateful recipients of this invaluable info. These "immigrant's instructions" saved us from many, but of course not all, faux pas.

For example, we knew before leaving home that some rules had been changed and that coral and amber were no longer allowed to be taken out of the USSR. That change happened within weeks of our departure. Uncle Leon came from Riga to say his farewells, and on one of our sentimental Kiev walks, he bought me a very pretty doll, dressed in full Ukrainian dress. She was a large doll, and I shipped her off in the container. We were then considering placing my only thin strand of real coral beads on her, but being scared, we changed our minds. Coral was still relatively inexpensive in Ukraine and abundantly sold in the used-goods stores. All along we were planning to buy some, but sneaking coral and amber out of the country was not something covered in the departing instructions.

I loved my tiny strand of coral beads too much to abandon. Coral necklaces have been an essential element of Ukrainian girls' costumes for several centuries. Called *monistos*, these coral necklaces were probably introduced by the tradesmen bringing ribbons and fabrics from Crimea or other places under the Ottoman rule. Some of the older coral pieces were thick and weighty. They were incredibly beautiful, from unknown seas, bearing witness to unknown misfortunes. Everyone knew the sad stories of Ukrainian girls who were sold into marriage, which entailed slave labor, abuse, no freedom of any kind, and a baby every year. Those left in Ukraine also had similar fates. But when they were young, these daring Ukrainian girls were stately and striking in their coral *monistos*, red leather boots, pure white shirts cross-stitched with red-and-black flower or bird patterns, and heavy fresh flower or silk head wreaths, with red ribbons in their looped honey- and corn-colored, long, thick braids. I never had a full Ukrainian costume, only pieces of it, and I clung to my string of coral, like those Ukrainian slave girls did before me.

The people departing from Ukraine bought pairs of small Ukrainian dolls, a boy and a girl, about nine inches tall. Dressed in full costume, these dolls were known among us as "teeny anti-Semites." I already had a teeny boy anti-Semite. Aleksei Kozyvka had given it to me in fourth grade, when he was still my friend. Mama and I bought a girl to match and another set to sell in transit, in Rome. I knew the dolls' wardrobe and anatomy very intimately. My teeny girl anti-Semite, like all dolls of that thick plastic kind, lost her head with a skillful snap. I tightly wrapped my little coral necklace inside some medical cotton, so that it would not rattle, and stuffed the entire cotton-coral sausage into the teeny girl anti-Semite's hollow plastic body. Mama and I hesitated at home over this contraband. We removed and reinserted the sausage two or three times, snapping the head back on. This contraband was now at Chop. Mama periodically asked me, "Should we take it out?" but I pretended not to understand her meaning.

Where would we do it? Here? In the midst of the departing and spies everywhere? Or in the industrial green, sticky, filthy bathroom on the other side of the station? Without stalls, unshielded from any peering eye? The necklace was going to stay inside the doll and be what may.

We added our names to yet another long departure waiting list maintained by, of course, the departing ones themselves. Next we learned that we were not going to make the early train. There were hundreds of families waiting. We were something like 358. We checked our baggage into the packed-to-the-rim baggage room and crossed the Chop station square to the hotel, the only other large building besides the station house in this entire forsaken settlement.

There was a restaurant in the hotel and hardly any patrons. Semeon ordered our meal most efficiently, with knowledge of this common process in which my family never partook. He quickly substituted menu items that were not available with others that were, as if he'd really studied this greasy menu for hours, not minutes. Most of the menu list was unavailable anyway, but we got something. I thought it very fitting that my final meal in the USSR was at a restaurant. Mama would never have splurged for it, but Semeon did. Or maybe, in the end, that meal was on us, since we were paying him a good sum to be our escort.

The day was long. It stretched into unending minutes that lasted centuries, and hours that became millennia. We counted off the time to the evening train. Perhaps we'd be lucky to make the cut and board it?

No one among the departing knew how the determination process for that cut worked, and so the numbers of people to clear the checkpoint could not be predicted, no matter how many people tried. Everyone agreed, however, that it was best to be processed by a Czech or Hungarian crew shift. The Soviets were particularly vicious toward the departing Jews, ordering strip searches and creating last-minute obstacles. Because Mama had made us wait to the last moment to depart, no obstacle-correction time was left for us, and I was especially scared we'd do something stupid, like the time we went to Poland and Mama had no gold rings on her hands. Panic overtook me. *What if they find my coral string?* But I dismissed the worry with arrogance befitting my age.

We'd converted all the money we had remaining from our Polish ventures into gold to take with us. Mama now had a thick wedding band in addition to her 253-ruble diamond ring. She'd bravely pierced her virgin earlobes just so we could bring out two pairs of earrings. She wore my birthstone (pearl) earrings, her graduation present to me, while I, as the earrings-wearing veteran, wore the heavier pair she'd bought specially. They were deep-green nephrite in a delicately elaborate gold setting, and Mama kept checking my ears every twenty minutes to make sure I did not lose them, even though the locks were just fine. I had to show them to her even from a distance. Mama just had no trust in me.

We'd sold my only good ring, a graduation present from Grandpa that I'd bought for myself, to one of my classmates who wanted to have it. Mama had insisted we should let my classmate have it, because she'd been willing to pay over and above its price. Instead, I was taking out only my "kiss," a very popular ring at the time of very little value—a thin band with two hollow balls that snapped into the "kiss," hence the name. Mama had given it to me when I turned sixteen, and I was not going to leave her present behind. Mama also wore Babushka's gold watch, the only item of value Grandma had left us. I inherited it when I turned sixteen. Mama, as usual, distrusted me so much that when I put the watch on my wrist that very birthday, she kept checking and rechecking the lock. Wouldn't you know it? The clasp unlocked, and I dropped the darn watch, breaking its fragile mechanism.

The watch has never kept time since, but I still have it. I also have my pearl earrings. They seem tiny now. Those are our only valuables that have endured. The 253-ruble ring did not pass the checkpoint. We gave it to Semeon, who returned it to Grandpa. My kiss ring was lost while Mama was wearing it one day in New York. It slipped off her finger into the NYC sewage system as she flushed a toilet. I don't recall what happened to her thick wedding band. We may have sold it in transit, as we did my coral necklace. The nephrite earrings were lost after a wedding Mama and I attended together in New York in 1982. After the wedding, I wanted to go out with friends, and Mama made me take the earrings off. There was ongoing crime at that time, and gold earrings were being ripped out of women's ears. I left the earrings with Mama, who placed them in her raincoat pocket for safety, forgot all about them, and took the coat to the cleaners the very next day. The cleaners said they never saw the earrings. I feel a pang every time I recall those earrings, how beautiful they were and how heavy they felt in my ears at Chop, pulling my earlobes down with their massive weight. I will miss them always, as I miss the many things we lost on our greatest journey—without real regret and with genuine gratitude.

I assume that the total value of all our valuables at the time of our departure could not have exceeded 1,000 rubles. We'd had nothing of value before Poland, except my grandmother's watch, and we'd sold everything else we could to pay for our passage, our Soviet passport surrender, the *chachkas* in our suitcases and the container we shipped, and the gold we wore. Everyone, I thought, was just like us.

I presume the main reason I thought that is that everyone was fully dressed. One could not leave anything unattended for a second. Gypsies were everywhere. Even if not for the Gypsies, the local Carpathians were snooping for the authorities while also looking to mark what was poorly attended. The departing were prey for the many predators. Everyone understood that, without any rights, we were the lowest on the local totem pole, even lower than the professional thieves or the poorest Gypsies who made up the local population.

Since there was nothing else to occupy me, observation and imprinting my surroundings onto my memory was my day's work. There were other observers around. One of them, a girl about my age who was wearing way too much makeup, walked over to me and asked, "How old are you? You have such large earrings." She, too, was dressed in layers and layers, with a Russian floral-print shawl over her head.

"Eighteen. I'm allowed," I answered. I was a legal adult and allowed adult rations of jewelry and money. "You?"

"Sixteen," she replied with disappointment. "I don't think they'll let me have mine—too large." She pulled her colorful shawl away from her head, exposing one of her earlobes, where she wore an earring much more expensive than our nephrite earrings. That instantly united us.

Her name was Nora. She was from Bendery, a town in Moldavia with an odd reputation. With a size somewhere in between a Jewish shtetl (settlement) and a Ukrainian *selo* (village), it had a reputation for being a hideout for Gypsies and thieves. Nora's family was one of those large groups spread out with their food throughout the terminal. There were so very many in her family. I do not recall exactly how many, maybe two or three dozen. Nora and I wandered the station together, discussing the day or just observing the many small injustices. I continued to mentally compare our situation to those in Babiy Yar. Worried and even scared as we were, we had a definite advantage over them. No one was prodding us with a gun to strip before dying. That thought somehow made me feel stronger. I was very grateful to have a companion. Did the girls at Babiy Yar have a friend to share their final moments with? No way to know. No one to ask; no one to tell.

Every time she lost sight of me, Mama boiled over, her anger spilling all over me as soon as I approached. Not even Semeon could stop her.

The early winter evening came. The evening train roll call started from the departing lists. We did not make the cut. The evening crewmen were Soviets and, predictably, a mere fraction of people who could have left actually got processed.

The next problem was curfew. No one was allowed to stay at the station or on the streets between the hours of 10:00 p.m. and 6:00 a.m. We had to find a place to stay overnight, and we had to do it quickly—there was lots of competition there for the available locations. The small hotel across the street was not an option for us. We had no passports to check in even if they had rooms. In the sudden rush of people emptying the station, the untrustworthy-looking Gypsies and Hungarians accosted the departing in what must have been their nightly ritual, offering rooms for a steep fee. Semeon struck a deal with a couple that seemed more or less okay. We followed our "landlords" up the snow-covered hill into the total darkness.

Many years later, in Andorra, I heard a story of an old Gypsy family controlling one of the only two major roads through that country for centuries. Many wealthy Jews perished there on their flight over the Pyrenees as they escaped from Hitler into the hands of their Gypsy guides, who robbed and killed them after the Jews paid hefty fees for passage and shelter. We could have been those Jews. Luckily, we were not.

The only negative thing our Gypsies did was rent the same single-bed room to eight or nine groups of the departing. After they left the four of us, their first customers, they went back for more, again and again. In the end, once they were done, all we could do was sit on the dirty straw mattress, the two hard wood chairs, or the cold dirt floor of this small Carpathian Mountains cabin room. Some of us stood resting our heads on the cold stone walls, some on each other. We took turns sitting, standing, and bringing in snow from outside the door to melt for a drink, with everyone using the same tin cup. An old lightbulb hanging off the ceiling lit the room. Bugs were everywhere. Some clung to us so tightly that, after the end of the night, they left the country illegally, without paying for their passage, on our bodies, inside our clothes, and in our luggage and purses. Whenever I watched films about the war, I wondered how they all tolerated their conditions and one another. I had my answer now. People behave differently once misery unites them without a way out. If people have no human rights left and they know the confinement is temporary, they tolerate the conditions and each other because they have no other options and it will soon be over.

In our overcrowded last point of rest, people were snoring, belching, farting, laughing, playing cards, smoking, crying, telling stories, joking, and napping. We all did our best not to complain. Small children cried intermittently, their moms and dads hushing them to sleep with periodic success. I sat up thinking how this room reminded me of the evacuation from the advancing Nazis in the many stories I heard from Grandma, and I was feeling very fortunate indeed not to have lived then or be bombed now. I shared that bed with eight or nine or ten complete strangers for short rests in between standing. But was it really me, or was it another eighteen-year-old from Majdanek or Kiev who was tolerating such conditions in expectation of ultimate freedom, who endured so much but never got her reward? Maybe I was doing this for her freedom too?

I have no idea how many of us were in that room that night. Too many. The toilet, as in most of Ukraine, was an outhouse. A hole in the ground. No lights, no paper. No heat, of course. Balancing over an outhouse hole without missing a step while freezing your ass is a skill one never loses. I had another skill. I could hold my pee for long periods of time. I had years of practicing that in school. If you don't drink, you don't need to go. I could spend a couple of days without liquids to avoid using the outrageously filthy outhouses, which this one was. Some people had to go, and as the door swung open, we had a brisk change of air in the room and heard the dogs barking. We had an hourslong conversation about the consequences of breaking the curfew. Everyone speculated, and no one knew for sure, adding to my many present fears this new fear of being arrested while on the slippery slopes of Chop.

It was the last night in a chain of too many to recount. Our unifying ordeal, our dreaded Soviet passport line number 5, the nationality line as its description stated, that defined our Soviet inferiority. Our distinct mark of institutionalized discrimination—this short word, *Jew*. Every single one of us crammed into this three-by-eight-meter room had just endured a predeparture series of humiliations, including outright mental and frequently even physical abuse. Government officials of all menial levels put us through our individual hells. From our apartment buildings' *dvorniks* (superintendents doubling as informants) to neighbors, friends, and even family members who simply could not understand why we were leaving—they all loudly condemned us while secretly envying us all along.

Just as every war survivor has a unique story to convey, every one of the departing, too, I'm sure, has a unique story to describe what was done to us, what injustices and degrading words fell upon our departing heads. I am certain that in addition to the USSR scar on our psyches, we also have a Soviet Jewish refugee scar, in part illuminated by the farewell nights like mine of October 31, 1979.

In the morning of November 1, 1979, before light, Mama, Dora, Semeon, and I busted out of that smoke- and sweat-filled room, correctly figuring out that by the time we'd walk into the station square, the curfew would be over.

Some other people immediately followed us. We stepped lightly upon the frosted snow, ripping the crackling sounds from under out feet, moving in the manner of anyone who is hiding—without speaking, motioning with hands and elbows, signaling with nods. During our about half-hour descent in the retreating veil of the night, during which we could have been arrested at any time, we heard distant strong voices, clearly carried to us by the crisp mountain air, and froze in place to avoid discovery. It was bitterly cold. After being inside with so many others, our unwashed, overdressed, sweaty bodies were freezing, and we shivered from fear and chill. Mittens on my hands, with bags to carry, I could not pull up my falling jeans or fold over their leg bottoms, which had unfolded without me noticing. I was tripping and had to wiggle my Monsieurs up. The adrenaline of fear prevailed, and I somehow succeeded without falling. Soon shadows of others appeared as people from other houses merged with our group, and others continued to join in all the way to the bottom station square. We could tell there were more following us without having to look back by the steadily increasing rustling noise, as if we were a part of a live stream. By the time we made it down the hill, hundreds of us had gathered. We reached the station with the dawn's light. The curfew had lifted, and the attendant opened the station's door to let us in. That was my final moment as a Soviet refugee on Soviet soil. *Good riddance,* I thought. *I will not miss anything about you, my union of all the people.*

The departing knew what to do even if something was not covered in the instructions for the departing. I suppose they knew it in the same Russian Jewish osmosis manner of those who had fled from the pogroms in the late 1800s and those who had fled from the Bolshevik Revolution of 1917 and those who had fled from Stalin and the Nazis. It was our turn now, the departing. We used a different legend, took different routes, and were luckier than our predecessors—we actually had some sort of a right to live. They had been totally disposable. We could have been arrested and deprived of our whatever we then called freedom, but at least we would not have been killed—unless, of course, in a staged military accident. I know of a 1973 fatal crash in Lvov and met survivors of a 1979 one from

Minsk. Accidents were only for those who had special enemies with special instructions. But so many hidden traps
awaited us after the curfew was over that nothing was
really certain.

The departing quickly filled the station building, and
with them came the crews, the attendants, and the Gypsies.
The beehive was back to business. First, we checked the
departing lists for the next Bratislava train. There were
other trains passing through this busy border checkpoint.
Those carried tourists, actors, musicians, sport teams, and
officials in and out of the USSR. Somehow, these people did
not go through the same part of the station building, yet
some of them inadvertently witnessed the brutal searches
in the carnage room. Mama and I had heard an account
of such from an actor, a Jew, during the previous summer.
He'd been shocked by what he'd witnessed and tried to
caution us, correctly assessing that we were getting ready
to go. Most Jews were by then. Or did the departing have
a different look in their eyes? A gleam of hope?

Getting as close to the head of the list as possible was
our next bridge to cross. If a family was number one hundred or higher on the list, chances of departure on the next
train were nonexistent. With only two trains remaining
before our exit visas would expire, Mama, Dora, and I
were prisoners of fate. I closed my eyes and prayed to fate,
begged it not to abandon us, because if it did, we would
become prisoners of the USSR at midnight.

The train, customs, and border police crews were in-
jecting their own bureaucratic level of torment for the departing Jews by making sure to board as few of us as possible and to treat us as abominably as their Soviet orders
and Soviet culture demanded. They worked deliberately
slowly, took many people aside for strip searches, closed

for an extra-long lunch, took extra-long toilet and smoke breaks, and did whatever else they could think up to place obstacles in our way.

It was not the first nor the last time I witnessed how a person, who never was able to attain what I call "character," enjoyed exerting pressure over the weak, complete with a broad, sadistic smile. I saw a large number of such amoebas—spineless collaborators of the regime, dishonestly earning their living from doing the dirty jobs decent people would never do. Such people exist everywhere in the world, in every place, every sphere. And I must have a magnet that pulls them in.

Two decades later, in a typically inane twist of fate, I hired a crew of three ex-Soviets, who had left the USSR following perestroika, to install flooring in my large New Jersey house. They included a former customs shift leader at Chop; a militsiya colonel who not only worked at Chop but was also a militia school director in Kiev, the one I'd marched in front of at Uritsky Square; and a tall and dark intellectual of a particular kind, with the distinct posture of a serviceman, most probably KGB. We had some laughs when we matched my departure date to their careers—that is, they, the non-Jews, laughed at the situation, and I, the Jew, laughed at the grim realization that I now had my former enemies in my house, just as my grandfather used German POWs to do the work in his apartment after the war. Life always amuses me with its twists and turns, even the grimmest ones.

At Chop I irreversibly realigned myself against anything Soviet. We, the hated and despised Jews, received a new life. Yet these men, who must have destroyed dozens if not hundreds of hopes while doing their dirty jobs for the USSR, were allowed to follow us on the perestroika bandwagon to all our hard-earned destinations. We bled, sweat, and suffered to be free of them. Yet we were free of them for only a little over a decade. When the Iron Curtain collapsed, they flooded every crevice of the world, bringing with them everything we were escaping from in 1979, spreading and reviving the Soviet principles for the unprincipled or the eager to be deceived everywhere.

The early-morning train of November 1, 1979, left. We did not make it, but the line moved well. Mama and I were now number three on the departing list, and Dora was number four. We were almost guaranteed to leave that night, unless something unpredictable happened. So much was unpredictable in Chop. Anything unanticipated could turn into a disaster. But I was relieved to be at the very head of this long line, especially when the morning trains from the East brought in hundreds of new families. The departing river was full, and I stood with both feet planted firmly at its mouth.

Instead of feeling relief at being third in this critically important line, Mama completely fell apart. She drove me absolutely insane, panicking, chattering endlessly, pulling me, making me do all sorts of things—like taking off and putting back on my coat, my hat, my shawl, my this and that; checking and rechecking the earrings, the ring, the pocketbooks, our suitcases; regretting this and that; commenting on that and this. After the morning train departed, I could no longer leave our spot in the queue, except for a few short moments to use the bathroom when Dora stepped in to hold our place next to Semeon. I ended up standing that entire day from dawn, when we got into the station house, until nearly midnight. Mama and Dora had seats nearby, which Semeon had grabbed as soon as we'd entered the building that morning. There was a lot of purpose to what Semeon did, and we were lucky to have him. Mama directed me from the front row to do this or that. Dora kept her usually dignified cool and only rolled her eyes at Mama's orders and my increasingly snappy reactions to them. Dora's outwardly calm demeanor helped me keep mine, but I was churning inside.

Most of the thoughts preoccupying my mind on that slow-moving day, when undisrupted by Mama's orders, were comparisons to Majdanek, World War II, Babiy Yar, and all Jewish roundups. I kept thinking how fortunate I was to be a child of my era and not one of the 1940s or 1490s or AD 70.

I am now writing these reflections as a mature woman of fifty-something who has invested plenty of thought, self-development, and effort into striving to someday become a Jewish American lady. When I reflect on my very beginnings, I can certainly say a true, heartfelt thank-you to the Soviet Union for the unforgettable day of November 1, 1979. If there was any uncertainty in my eighteen-year-old mind and if my heart pained at leaving Grandfather and some other elders to never see them again, my resolve to better myself was confirmed at Chop. Why? Because the people of the Soviet Union did not want me as an equal citizen among them. And I will always remember that. Always.

The second family in line, right in front of us, was a mom, a dad, and a tall, slightly chubby youth my age, Nick, from Kharkov. Our paths continued to intersect for decades afterward. Nick, Nora, and other teens who did not have to stand in line holding at least one spot for their families formed a fast grouping, as all the departing teens had been doing for these many last months. We were in need of our own shared social purpose and compassion, especially those of us who pretended not to need any compassion at all. I could not rely on that support in Chop. I was the adult in my family and had to stand all day. Semeon went to get sandwiches. I could not eat. There was too much to hear, feel, watch, process, store. It was, except for the fear, discomfort, humiliation, and stress, one the most fascinating days of my life.

Well before our examination time, as the early winter evening approached, the crews changed, and we learned that ours was to be a Hungarian train crew and Soviet customs. I remember a very long and loud argument between the Soviet border patrol chief and our train conductor a step or two to the left of me. There were many families behind me, hundreds of families, in fact. I doubt that the loudness of this argument made the words discernable to the tail of the line, but the departing oral telegraph worked well. Heads turned to whisper the words that would determine destinies.

The Soviet border patrol was telling the Hungarian train crew that they, the Hungarians, were only allowed to process a couple dozen families. The train conductor, one of the most honorable men I ever saw, argued with the Soviet chief for a good thirty minutes for permission to load to capacity. They used some Ukrainian and Polish words I understood. The conductor ultimately said, "I did not come here to pull an empty train, and I will report you. Do what you will, but on my shift my train will be fully loaded. I depart at a quarter to midnight sharp. It's 5 o'clock now. Plenty of time for your guys."

The Soviet patrolman said, smiling maliciously, "Well, if that's your wish, that's exactly how we'll do." They saluted each other and left without a glance at the departing, pulling the mysterious doors in front of us open just wide enough to let them in but not to let us glimpse to the carnage side.

A wave of whispers quickly rustled through the queue. It looked like the wind blowing through a cornfield, forcing the heavy ears of corn to bend down without breaking. One of the countless officials zooming around everywhere made an announcement in Russian. We were to flow through the doors when motioned, quickly. We were to quickly open our bags and suitcases, which would be subjected to an examination. We were to quickly remove our overcoats, hats, scarves, gloves, and shoes. We were repeatedly reminded that we needed to be quick, fast, rapid. I heard these commands as if they were the *"Schneller, schneller!"* commands of the *Appells*, the roll calls of concentration camps. Was there ever going to be any real freedom for Jews?

When the time drew near, we quickly said our goodbyes to Semeon and went through the final doors. They swallowed us into a large, greenish-gray, dirty room with metal tables and customs personnel everywhere. As we opened our suitcases for inspection, our assigned customs man watched our shaking hands with definite enjoyment. He chuckled at our clumsiness and at our obvious fear of him, then motioned to someone. Two women came up and escorted Mama and me behind a dark curtain, where we had to pull down our pants and underwear, so they could finger us between our legs and inside our vaginas for items we may have hidden there.

"You stink," one of these women said to Mama.

"We just spent three days without washing," Mama answered calmly. I was always proudest of her when she held herself with dignity.

My searcher felt inside all my bodily cavities, under my arms, and inside my bra and made me point her to all my pockets. In the smallest jeans pocket, I had my American quarter. I had several foreign coins in Kiev. I was collecting them. But I chanced to take with me only this one—for luck. Except the ninety dollars per person that we'd converted to dollars at a special bank in Kiev, no other currency was permitted. But I thought myself an experienced contrabandist. And it was only a coin.

"Tzo to take?" ("What is it?") she asked her partner in a Western Ukrainian dialect of the Carpathian region.

Her partner took it, examined both sides, holding it up to the overhead electric light, and cringed without recognition. The words "United States of America" were clearly visible on my shiny good luck coin. *"To franzuskie chi niemezkie."* ("It's either French or German.") She stated this with such forceful confidence that my strip searcher returned it to me. My face was motionless as I slowly accepted it from her hand with a "Thank you."

In my other small pocket was a five-ruble bill my grandfather had given me for "just in case" at the Kiev Central Railroad Station two days ago, in the way he always gave me some money without telling Mama whenever I went away. My searcher asked why I had it. I calmly said, "Forgot all about it." Russian currency was absolutely forbidden for departure. She looked at me in a way that left no doubts. I calmly handed it over, and she gladly confiscated it directly into her own pocket, without recording it on the confiscated-items list they had placed between me and Mama.

Throughout our time in that curtained space, we heard similar searches unfolding on all sides of us. Every single person that evening was strip-searched, even babies, pregnant women, and invalids. The Soviets had done just as they'd promised our Hungarian conductor. In the end, 165 families got through Soviet customs that evening, and that was what really mattered. Our middle-aged Hungarian conductor could have been risking demotion, for all I knew, but there was no fear in him. To me, he has always represented all the non-Jews who stood up for Jews at all times when small people of all religions and authorities wanted to make themselves bigger through destroying a Jew.

Our strip search ended. Thoroughly humiliated by the procedure, we were led back to our table, literally buttoning up our shirts and pants on the go. Our customs man was finishing up with our possessions. I observed that dramas were unfolding at all the other tables. The customs workers overturned all the opened suitcases to rummage through them in search of forbidden items. Our suitcases were stuffed to capacity in a neat and efficient way, as our departing instructions had taught us. We'd carefully packed and fitted things everywhere, wasting not a centimeter of suitcase space. Now it was impossible to fit all our possessions back in. But as the instructions had forewarned of this issue, I'd brought a couple Polish-made plastic bags, and they helped. Mama stood helpless as I fumbled through our things trying to fit them back in so they would not have to be discarded. While I was doing that, all our jewelry had to be removed from ears, wrists and fingers for examination. Mama's diamond ring would have probably made it, had she not brought with her the receipt for its purchase and showed the man. "Two hundred fifty-three rubles, *nyet!*" He slid the ring to the side. If we'd had no one accompanying us, it would have become the customs workers' loot. Since we did have someone with us, one of the women took it to Semeon, who waved to us as the door opened to let her back in.

As I was closing the suitcase where my coral necklace hid inside my teeny anti-Semite, a tiny coral bead was left on the otherwise empty metal examination table. Our customs man lifted it up and held it in front of my eyes. "What is it?" he asked, staring right into my eyes. "I don't know," I lied, looking back at him with the most honest of my Soviet-made liar's expressions, as befitted the young Communist I'd once been, not so long ago. He put the coral chip into his pocket and motioned us away to the waiting room through the far exit door. It was over. It had taken no longer than twenty minutes. Twenty very long and very painful minutes, filled with many other unpleasant details I no longer wish to recall. I found it rewarding that my final act and spoken words on Soviet soil were an impenetrable lie.

Mama, Dora, and I were among the first in this final waiting room. It was around six o'clock or so when we entered it. The room was not very large, empty, brightly lit, and very cold. There was no place to sit, except atop suitcases, at the risk of breaking them. As the evening grew older, the crowd grew larger, so that in the end, during the final hour or two, we stood there packed in so tightly that I can only compare it now to the Nazi cattle car transports. If one wanted to fall, one could not. Also, like the deported Jews of those wartime days, we had no rights. We were not allowed to leave this room. There was no bathroom. We were nobodies. And the next piece of land we were to stand on was no-man's-land.

The crowd passed the time, as usual, by joking, crying, coughing, sweating, sighing, reprimanding children, kvetching, biting nails, and smoking—but most ardently complaining about what had just happened to us in hushed voices, in Russian, Ukrainian, and Yiddish. I felt that I was having a day of that other eighteen-year-old Jewish girl's life, except I was sure my experience would end well. I had hope. That other girl had not.

As the departure time neared, the crowd began to boil. Of course, the room was now overstuffed; no air circulated into it, other than from allowing the final departing people inside and squeezing the crowd a little tighter still, forcing us to pile our suitcases and bags higher and higher. The crowd was sizzling with sweat and nerves. "The train will leave at eleven forty five. We will not make it." These words Mama and some others repeated over and over for more than an hour. *What if?* I, too, thought once in a while, but I chased the fear under my humiliation and exhaustion. *There is a purpose to this torture. We will all be okay,* a voice from within me said. *Just a few more minutes, another moment, one more.*

At 11:40 the door to the outside opened, and a loud order was yelled out: "Board, and make it quick! The train will leave on time with or without you!"

One hundred sixty-five families with two suitcases to a person, one in each hand, except for babies and invalids, whose parents or children carried homemade backpacks in back and in front, in addition to the suitcases in their hands, spilled out into the knee-deep, fresh snow.

The first men out in the no-man's-land yelled, "No platform, long way to go—hurry!" Other departing men yelled this out to those behind them and so on.

Our train was far off, maybe three hundred meters, and our pathway toward it was guarded by a double row of Soviet soldiers, most of them as young as me, with Kalashnikovs at ready.

And so we ran—all of us, old, young, sick—to make our train to Bratislava, Vienna, and freedom.

The instructions for the departing had taught us to mobilize our resources as a group should such a situation arise during our departure. These scenes were commonplace. But nothing, not lore, not instructions, not all the other unpleasant experiences we'd just endured, had prepared any of us for that dash to freedom of the 11:45 train on November 1, 1979.

I remember that the snowfall increased as we ran. I was glad I'd prepared well. Before the crowding in the waiting room had made it impossible to stir, I'd tied the strings of my rabbit hat, wrapped my Orenburg shawl over the hat, rolled the bottoms of my jeans legs and pulled the waist up, neatly tucked my Riga twin dress into my jeans, and snapped all the buttons of my coat. I was not tripping over anything. I could not fall now, with the two largest, heaviest suitcases Dora, Mama, and I had banging me on my calves—one of Dora's and one of ours. I mobilized all my resources, all my strength.

I remember that the tracks were poorly lit, maybe only by the moonlight. I remember the young, fresh faces of our Red Army guards, half of them laughing at our despair, half of them crying, tears dripping down their red cheeks onto their uniforms as they helplessly watched the pregnant, the invalids, and the younglings struggle to keep up, pulling behind them bundles and suitcases too heavy to tote. The soldiers were obviously under the strictest orders not to help or show compassion. But they, too, had mental comparisons to make. They, too, were human.

The strongest departing men reached the train first and had to pull themselves up into it. These trains were elevated high up above the ground—too high for women, children, or the elderly to board without a platform and too high for most men as well. But somehow we managed.

The men on the ground formed a chain and quickly loaded all the suitcases and people into the train, pulling and lifting and pushing. Two or three men kept order, as if this was something they'd practiced for all their lives. They knew just what to do, and they did it so well. I thank God for the able-bodied men I traveled with that night and the following day.

I bet our loading took more than five minutes. We later heard stories of trains that pulled out before they were loaded. All the passengers of our train boarded, even the woman on the World War I–type stretcher who was part of Nora's huge family. Nora's numerous uncles were part of the suitcase-identifying group once we were all inside. As the train began to move, everyone was worried about their stuff. But it was all there. Everything was found. Mama, Dora, and I were seated inside a compartment for six with a group of ten or so, but who cared anymore? The train attendant soon began making rounds, offering us sheets, blankets, and hot tea for purchase—with dollars, of course. No one stirred. There was the great unknown ahead, and no convenience was needed on this journey.

The train wheels squeaked as the train rolled slowly by the still-motionless soldiers with Kalashnikovs pointed at us. Then it moved a little bit faster, leaving the station behind and pulling its cargo up the hill into the darkness ahead.

The once-revered and always-feared Iron Curtain now closed tightly behind us.

We were done with the USSR, and it was done with us.

First Day of Freedom, November 2, 1979

I am not sure if I slept or just passed out. It was early light when I came to. We were nearing Bratislava, where we'd need to promptly transfer trains. I barely had time to wait in line to use the long-needed bathroom, and we were in Czechoslovakia. This Bratislava train transfer was, of course, also described in the departing instructions. We were carrying with us a bottle of vodka because Bratislava train station attendants helped carry suitcases for a bottle per family.

Not so on our day! They were forbidden to help us that morning, standing silently on guard to prevent us from going anywhere other than the platform assigned to the departed Soviet Jews, personae non gratae, paperless, confused, scared, and hiding their fear in every possible way.

Our train pulled out, and we found ourselves on a tight platform with the 165 exhausted families, luggage, strollers, and all—probably over 500 people in total. We now needed to climb up a very high staircase to the overhead track crossing and then descend onto a narrow platform, about half the size of the platform we'd just arrived to, where we were to wait outdoors, in the crosswinds of the winter chill, until our train to Vienna. Nick, the young man from Chop, spotted me having trouble with our two largest suitcases and returned to help me, carrying both despite my protests.

We all stood there for a couple of hours or more. Dora, Mama, and I ate the rest of the cheese sandwiches Semeon had bought for us in Chop the day before that had somehow wound up in my overcoat pocket. Some men were now drinking their unclaimed vodka straight from the bottle. They got warmer and louder by the time the train came, and everyone pitched in once again to swiftly board people through the doorways and luggage through the windows.

The Vienna-bound train was like our trip to Poland—from the realm of the unimaginable. We had good, soft seats with white cushions under our filthy heads. There was a water faucet from which we could drink. After a short time, Nick, Nora, and another girl they'd met, Karina, came for me. We were coming to the Austrian border, and we were celebrating by inhaling free air into our polluted-by-the-Soviet-bullshit lungs. As the train was about to stop, the train-car attendants collected our visas. We were stopped at a place without any memorable checkpoints. Austrian patrol was on the ground. They had weapons like the Red Army guards but were not pointing them at us. In fact they looked friendly and grinned widely. Our train-car attendant unfolded special stairs and stepped down to the gravel on the ground.

Just as it should be, I thought, recalling last night's nightmare.

Our group of four was standing on the highest step and leaning over the railings. I stepped down to the bottom step on an impulse: *I'm the oldest—watch me do it.* The Austrian border patrol quickly moved my way, telling me *"Nein, nein"* and waving hands to illustrate.

"Free land," I said in English, pointing down. They understood. They nodded their heads in a welcoming yes and let me set both my feet onto their free land, without taking my hand off the railing.

I stood there only a few very special seconds. Neat winter fields around me, blue sky above. An unforgettable first taste, look, and feel of freedom.

I smiled and said *"Danke"* and climbed back onto the train.

Everything in my life was going to be different now. I was already free. This was my very first act of a free individual. And I was proud.

Karina, Nick, and Nora could not follow me down. Their parents had already screamed nos at them.

I think Mama yelled at me too, but I stopped listening.

Dress 12

My Rabbit-Fur Ears

Not every young girl who believes in fairy tales finds her-self in the middle of one. I did, but I cannot recall it. Well, maybe a little. My fairy tale was not at all what I'd dreamed it would be. That is all I can tell you for sure.

My memory of our arrival to Vienna was hazy, probably because it was a gray day. More likely, I was too busy tuning out Mama's complaints and too overheated under the many layers of clothing I'd been wearing for the last three days. Our suitcase space was occupied by Ukrainian and Russian souvenirs, like *matryoshkas*, towels, wooden plates with roosters and flowers on them, manicure sets, nail files, and such. The only two items of particular value to me in those suitcases were two glass jars of black caviar that Mama intended to sell in Vienna. We'd had many arguments about this caviar. I wanted to eat it; Mama, to make a profit. We'd never had black caviar at home. It had not been within our purchasing means or distribution connections.

Mama loved to tell me the story of her final months of pregnancy when she craved black caviar. In 1960 it was available in every food store, but when Mama craved it in 1961, it disappeared, and no matter how much Garrik was willing to pay to procure it, he just could not satisfy Mama's black caviar desire.

I now wanted our black caviar as badly as if Mama had infected me with the urge in her final months of pregnancy. Aunt Zina had used her connections to get us these two glass jars with the coveted word *"Икра"* (caviar) over their shiny metal lids, one blue, one red. I held these jars in my hands so many times begging Mama to just let me eat it. But my mama did not want to satisfy my craving, because hers was never satisfied. That was my punishment, I thought, my burden, my curse. I was secretly hoping that once we were free and away Mama would become better and maybe let me have the caviar.

Mama showed no signs of improvement. I remember asking her at the Vienna train station if I could take off my rabbit-fur hat, and she told me no, unleashing onto me relentless reminders of how a few months before our final departure I'd accidentally forgotten my head kerchief on the Kiev–Moscow train.

I was so tired and hungry and overheated that I recall nothing from the overall haziness of our arrival to Vienna except wanting to eat that caviar to celebrate our freedom and hearing someone announce in Russian, "America here, Canada this way, Israel over there, all others over there." Throwing her arm in each direction she called out, the greeter repeated this to every bewildered passenger as we stepped down onto the glorious platform. That is how I remember Vienna—crowds of tired Jews being divided to the left, right, and center by her authoritative voice. Yet even through this chaos and turmoil, I admired the striking elegance of the station. The dame was not nearly as elegant as her surroundings. She was likely a former Soviet Jew who had not quite made it to her final destination yet or had already resettled back to Europe from Israel.

That is how I entered my freedom, with the ears of my rabbit-fur hat flopping against my sweaty cheeks, fighting with Mama and oblivious to pretty much else.

Vienna! The city of the Viennese waltz, Viennese cafés and chairs, Viennese pastries, Viennese schnitzels, and a Viennese Jew named Freud. I could hardly catch my breath before life started kicking me.

I had to carry the suitcases to the bus we were led to, all the time fighting off Mama's cussing and attempts to help me lift things. She, being so much shorter than I, actually made it more difficult for me to carry them. I had to exert so much extra force to fight her show-off-in-public efforts to help me. It always seemed to anyone watching us as if I was fighting her for the right to carry and lift. She did this only on certain public occasions. In reality, Mama had an active stomach ulcer, which she could not cease reminding me of or announcing to every new acquaintance. "You see, I carry this even if my stomach ulcer is bleeding." In sum, my arrival to Vienna was oy vey! Good grief!

In Vienna Mama became even unhappier with every passing moment. I could see joy creeping onto her face as the enemy of her frowns, but the negatives in her won every battle on her youthful battlefield of a face.

I was so naive then, constantly saying, "We are free. Why aren't you happy, Mama?"

Mama would reply, "Oh, I will never see my poor father or my poor aunt Polina or my poor brother Haimochka or my poor cousin Lenechka."

She recited the full list of relatives every day. Yet I continued to ask, wanting her to feel some of the elation and excitement that were clearly showing on my own face.

Mama, Dora, and I, along with some others, unloaded off the bus onto the sidewalk across the street from a magnificent building with the sign "Volksoper" on it: the national opera house. The building we were dropped in front of was beautiful too—a large foyer; wide, winding staircase to the second floor; and black-and-white stone floors. We learned later that the first floor displayed red lights in the evenings, the system long used by professional ladies of the night. Madame Bettina, we also later learned, was the apartment building's owner. We heard still much later that she was an aging Jewess who made a ton of profits from the Soviet Jews resettlement program. Soviet Jews brought out of the USSR much more than *matreshkas* and endless attempts to steal something or redistribute the usual. We all suffered from a common handicap—complete ignorance of the West.

Madame Bettina ran a very well coordinated enterprise. These apartments had once been luxurious, and to us they still were. Ours was on the fourth floor. To get to our room we passed through a room full of refugees like us and the only, albeit huge, bathroom of the apartment. One of the many doors of this bathroom led into a very spacious room with several beds and a table. A mother and son already lived there. His name was Misha, and he was in his forties and quite pleasant looking, even too neat for a man. Men I knew dressed this neatly only for weddings. Misha had never been married. He and his mother would be our roommates for the two weeks we stayed in Vienna and the next two in Rome. We were lucky because, after our arrival to Vienna, the inflow of Soviet Jews began to slow down for some reason, and no one else was added to this room. It had a huge window, very low windowsills, a tall ceiling, intricately beautiful decorative ornamentation, and wallpaper throughout. But the best thing about this room was the view onto the Volksoper. I spent hours standing by our giant of a window to admire it. Mama brought up an idea to splurge and go there but then changed her mind. "Next time you are in Vienna," she said, "you'll get to it. Now we must economize."

This apartment had several other rooms, all similarly occupied by refugees like us. There was one kitchen and that one bathroom, located in the center of the apartment. The multiple doors into the bathroom opened into most other rooms, so if one needed to use the bathroom, one was obliged to knock on every door to caution the neighbors not to.

I do not think we cooked in Vienna, because Mama discovered yogurt multipacks. A famous cook of last year's potatoes, frozen pelmeni, and hot dogs, Mama ruled that we would eat only yogurt and bananas now. Both were cheap and plentiful. During the next year or two I ate so much yogurt that I've never enjoyed it since. I do enjoy an occasional banana, but unlike most Soviet Jews, I'd tasted bananas before, so I did not become obsessed by them.

Vienna quickly taught me respect for rules. Prior to that I'd only known fear of them. Mama and I walked everywhere, not daring to spend for transportation. Once, we started to cross an absolutely empty, wide *strasse* at the crosswalk without any regard for the red pedestrian light, just as we would have in Kiev. The only other pedestrian in sight, an older, elegantly dressed woman, startled us by screaming at us. I did not understand the words, but Mama, who had learned German and even spoken with the prisoners who'd come to help Grandpa, did: "Obey the sign! Learn respect!" We retreated and waited. While Mama congratulated herself on her German comprehension, I noted that we must have respect for our host countries. I did not like being yelled at. That was to be a short-lived lesson, as it turned out, since in Italy, and later in New York, pedestrian and driving rules were made to be broken.

I gazed at the statues of Mozart and Strauss in Stadtpark with Mama and then listened to the conversation of other teens, whose parents joined them on explorations of Luna Park, an amusement park on the other bank of the Danube River. Luna Park remained an unfulfilled short-term dream of mine. In a year or two, when I finally got a chance to go to an amusement park, I either outgrew the desire or, rather, learned that I did not find this amusement amusing. But in 1979 Vienna, I wanted it so badly—that and the darn caviar … I can still feel the pain of not being able to afford anything. We walked and penny-pinched always, so that later we could be better off. Only once did we take a streetcar. It must have been either a free-ride day or because we'd walked way too far and could not make it back.

In Vienna, our room, just like all the other rooms, was quickly besieged by Soviet Jews who had left much earlier than we and whose occupation now was to buy goods off the newly arriving refugees at dirt-cheap prices, before they learned anything different. I think it was a gang headed by Madame Bettina herself. Our instructions did not forewarn us about these people. These buyers were very shady men, young and middle-aged, swift on their feet, ready with their fists, and as a rule they had "escaped" from Israel for reasons of their own and trashed it everywhere as being an unsuitable and undesirable destination.

What this actually meant was that going to Israel had been the only choice in Vienna at the time they'd left the USSR. Israel had welcomed them, taught them, employed them, and whatever else. But they did not like Israel, and when the migration routes out of Vienna had expanded to include the United States, Canada, Australia, and other destinations, they'd flown from Israel to some European city, as if for a vacation, and had not returned. Unemployable in Europe as illegals, they were biding time until their paths to other countries cleared, reselling *chachka* and *shmatas*, nick-nacks and clothes. They badmouthed Israel because it did not meet their disproportionate expectations. They sounded generally ungrateful, and ingratitude was a major character trait in them. Many such wanderers eventually made their way to Australia, Canada, and the US, where their unrealistic expectations continued.

Our first unscrupulous, ruthless shyster showed up on the evening of our arrival—must have been tipped off—and promptly persuaded Mama to sell him the two jars of caviar at ten dollars each. All the while this transaction was being negotiated, I pleaded with Mama to keep the darn caviar. "What will twenty dollars buy us in the United States? I have never yet had black caviar from a jar." On three or four memorable occasions I'd had a tiny theater caviar sandwich at the Kiev Opera buffet during entr'acte. That was a thin, round slice of white bread with a thick layer of butter and a skimpy scattering of roe on it, a grain here and there. Mama was deaf to my pleas that first evening in Vienna and coldheartedly chose money over me. The shyster next wanted my rabbit-fur hat, the one I'd worn for the last three years. It was mine, not bought specially to be sold, the same one Mama had been so afraid I'd lose, making me sweat the last few days on this long route.

She sold my rabbit ears to him for another ten dollars while I cried. Dora left the room at this point. My heart crumbled to irreparably small pieces. I wept uncontrollably. It was as if Mama was punishing me for wanting to eat the caviar, for being born, for holding her back, for everything she ever wanted to do and could not, even now, because of me.

I believe that her cruelty of selling my rabbit-fur hat marked a death sentence on our relationship. I never forgot that pain. I also would never again feel the warmth of my rabbit hat, its rabbit ears flapping against my skin, its shoestring ties getting tangled on long, cold walks. In the future I would frequently get sick because I could never find a proper hat for my rather large head. Ever since that night Mama repeatedly chastised me for not protecting my ears and my head. She refused to take responsibility for her tactical error, and I refused to forgive her, as if her cold heart on the first night in Vienna was now mine. We never found a new rhythm, always continuing that clash.

Then, just a couple of years ago, at a time long beyond the point of repair for us, Mama suddenly said, "We should have eaten that caviar." Here we were, thirty-some years after the fact, and she had just come to the realization of that error in judgment. But over the last thirty years, I, too, had gone over that scene countless times and come to the understanding that it was not at all about the rabbit-fur hat or caviar. It was not about me. It was about the fact that Mama was not willing to be a loving and generous parent. Of course, I bear some of the responsibility. I was not an easy child for her to raise. But I still was the child, and she, the parent.

Mama made so many errors during our journey together. I would go insane trying to remember them all, only so that I could tell you about them now. Sometimes I am awakened at night with a thought of these mistakes on my mind, and I am grief-stricken all over again. She made me sell things I loved and buy things that did not matter and were of no appeal to me and that either fell apart or remained unused for years only to be lost or thrown away. This constant buying-selling mode had been happening ever since our first trip to Poland and had already begun disturbing me in Kiev. The pattern continued in Vienna. Mama wanted to constantly buy and sell, neatly writing her sums in columns on the pale-green back cover of our world atlas, a small booklet weighing next to nothing that I'd brought with me to study on the road, knowing that for months I would have no access to other books or entertainment.

On a free day at the Kunsthistorisches Museum, I discovered there were Flemish painters beyond Rembrandt and Rubens, but because I came from the school of thought run by Mama, I had to say that I rejected the Flemish works even though I secretly liked them and was quite moved by their subtlety of colors and their depiction of eyes and smiles. My distant cousin Denis was my art guide that day. A year or two older, he was the son of Grandpa's nephew Myer, Mama's first cousin. I knew Denis's grandparents very well and had attended their funerals just a year or two before.

In Kiev we very rarely got together with Myer and his family, but when it became clear that we were departing for America at the same time, Mama made some steps to reconnect. I don't know and don't care why they parted before. Mama always left a trail of broken connections behind her. All these people were not dislikable; Mama was not easy to please, always punishing others for the same imperfections I found in her.

It was so strange to discover that everything in Vienna was closed on Sundays yet the museums stayed open. We could not figure out why when we all went there together. Denis and his family left for Italy the following week. In this short time Denis and I became good friends. He was intelligent, inquisitive, well read, and pleasant to talk with. We had much free time in Vienna, just waiting to move on. We talked a lot as we walked as lot. He and his family were staying at the Hotel zum Türken, another building just like our red-light apartment building. His parents had met at a sanatorium while recovering from tuberculosis. He was their only child. I'd long ago heard a story that his mother had been advised not to have any more. His parents doted on him, and he loved them. They were actually a very happy family. So unlike mine. I don't remember when they started to show me that they did not want me around. I think it was toward the end of the Vienna leg of their trip or maybe later, in Italy.

Anyway, they left before us, and I was alone again.

It was not easy living in one room with Misha, his mother, and our Kiev neighbor Dora. Mama's and my endless fighting must have been a misery to them. Misha was from Leningrad, and his mother was a Leningrad dame. She would diss us Ukrainians and our incorrect stresses of some Russian multisyllabic words. I was always somewhat intimidated by Dora, our Volgogradskaya building dame, but she was kinder to me on the road then Mama, although she, like all adults of the USSR, showed little respect for children and still considered me a child at eighteen. I tried to escape a lot. Then Mama started up a relationship with Misha, and his mother did not like it.

Some other shysters popped in and out in Vienna all the time. Someone had to stay in the room to guard things. It usually was me. I was there when some Russian sellers of religious items visited. They gave me three books: Jesus's life in pictures, the Hebrew Bible, and the Torah. I had never heard of the Torah at all. All the books were in Russian, of course. For the first time in my life I read religious books. They began to uncover for me the many shady areas of Soviet revisionist history, but still I continued to be under the influence of the superiority facade of the atheistic USSR for a very long time.

Like millions of Soviet citizens, I'd first learned about religion from the forbidden or rarely published works of writers, like Kiev's own Mikhail Bulgakov, a Soviet-era Russian born in my city. He was frequently ridiculed and tormented, especially for his masterpiece *The Master and Margarita*. He started it in the late 1920s and continued it through 1940, the year of his death. The novel was finally published in 1967, after substantial censorship. The plot runs in two parallel lines. One storyline focuses on contemporary characters of the early Soviet Union—bureaucrats, profiteers, skeptics, and deniers of religion and human spirit. The second storyline involves Pontius Pilate, Roman prefect and governor of the Roman province of Judea at the time. This storyline details Pontius Pilate's trial of one Yeshua Ha-Notsri, known as Jesus Christ, and consists of contemplations about the spirit and essence of human beings. It was from this book that I drew my first information about Christianity and religion in principle and the destructive impact of the Soviet revolution on humanity in general. I, like the other millions of Soviet citizens, was quite versatile in reading between the lines, and Bulgakov wrote between them masterfully.

During my second week in Vienna, in our three-family bedroom, squinting to read the very small print while catching the last daylight on the very low granite window-sill overlooking the Volksoper, I studied the life of Jesus through the picture book the Russians had given me. It was written for the very naive and those readers completely unfamiliar with his life, like me. Only much later did I understand that these wandering Russian Baptists had handed me this children's book in hopes of redeeming our wandering ex-Soviet Jewish souls. Anyway, it was perfect for our religion-deficient minds. None of us understood Judaism. None. So we all took turns, read and reread, and learned and discussed all through our journey. Symbolically, it was as if the book of Revelation followed the book of Exodus in our lives.

I also read from my English-Ukrainian dictionary, which Mama had brought so that I would learn English. It was perhaps on this leg of our trip that I invented a method of studying words that worked very well for me. I simply read the entire dictionary, marking every word I knew with a pencil. I restarted it when I finished, again marking the words I knew with a second or first dot, and so on. I used different-colored pens later, to distinguish between my periods of learning. I continued this process until, ultimately, there were no English words left in this dictionary for me to learn. By then it was 1983, and I'd begun to forget Ukrainian.

I had a head cold when we traveled from Vienna to Rome. Most likely, it was because I no longer had my rabbit ears to protect me. I was feverish and barely recall going over the Alps by overnight train.

I do not recall who transferred us or how they got us, luggage and all, to the train station and from it in Rome, but someone did. There was by then an established chain of resettlement of the Soviet Jewry throughout the world.

Vienna, being the first stop in the West, was working very hard for us, but we were too ignorant, self-absorbed, troubled, and confused to recognize and acknowledge this force. The people in the chain of resettlement had to deal with us physically, handing us over to our next caretakers, and they also had to deal with our brainwashed minds. How they did it, I remember not. I can only analyze it from what I subsequently learned.

In the USSR I was a "documented Jew." A documented Jew was any person with Jewish blood in his or her veins whose official birth record, and any subsequent document issued in reliance on such birth record, included the word *Jew*. I was absolutely shocked to learn once out of the USSR that being a Jew did not refer to one's nationality. I'd had a Soviet passport for two years, and in it, on line number 5, which was for nationality, the word *Jewess* appeared underneath my first, last, and patronymic names. It could never be changed. It was a label of shame and dishonor for many who were raised in denial, like me.

Now, after all the denial, abuse, and confusion, I began to understand that religion was not the "opium for the masses," as Lenin taught and as his followers impressed onto me, but a source of pride, self-respect, and determination. The "opium for the masses," in actuality, was Socialism. Only under Socialism could an official serve children a *kotleta* made mostly from bread, stealing most of the meat intended for the children, then make those children sing praises to the regime on empty stomachs. The cities I discovered abroad—Warsaw, Vienna, Rome—had many problems, but compared to what we had inside the Iron Curtain, their problems were no problems.

The USSR took away our rights to religious freedom and made us suffer just because we were Jews, much more than any of the other "nationalities" suffered. I was elated that I had deprived the USSR of me and was free to become anything I wanted.

I think it was in Rome, among the countless daily revelations our resettlement process presented us with, we learned that the label "Soviet refugees" was our immigration status. This would allow us entry to the United States, where we would be called "Russians." In the beginning, after having been hated for being Jewish, my mind and the minds of many others like me refused to accept "Russian" as our new label. We were not Russians. "They" were Russians, not "us," we protested.

But as time passed, we stopped attempting to educate Americans about this technicality. Here, I can openly state for the record that the Americans were wrong. Russia does not mean and never did mean the Soviet Union. The Soviet Union, of course, included Russia. We were so willing to tell our stories then, but the passion of most Americans we encountered was limited only to what happened in the realm of their own pursuits, leaving no time for our long, convoluted stories, told in our inadequate English. So after some attempts, most of us became mute, congregating only with our own "Russian" kind.

Some ethnic Russians also traveled with the Soviet refugee crowd. Their journeys were sponsored by the Tolstoy Fund, known more officially as the Tolstoy Foundation. It was organized and initially funded by Leo Tolstoy's youngest child, Alexandra, who, I later learned, died in the year of my exodus. Her organization was instrumental in helping Russians and some mixed-marriage families during this resettlement process. The Tolstoy Fund took fewer people that Jewish organizations were willing to resettle, and its resettlement process was lengthier. Most mixed families wanted to be wards of the Hebrew Immigrant Aid Society (HIAS), because HIAS was more generous with its stipends. Mama, Dora, and I, as Jews, were on HIAS's lists.

Third Wave of Immigration

To the best of my knowledge, only Baltic Jews left the USSR in the 1960s before the Six-Day War of June 1967, and those were few and far between. I met some later.

During the six days of the war between the twenty-year-old state of Israel and its three Arab neighbors—Egypt, Jordan, and Syria—the Jewish youth of the USSR experienced a surge of patriotism of a Zionistic kind, the kind the USSR especially strongly condemned. Young Jewish men, aged seventeen to thirty, even those who had already served in the Soviet Army and even those who were exempt from serving, were eager to join the fight for the defense of Israel, an unprecedented sentiment from the members of the Komsomol but completely honorable, as the threat to exterminate Israel was as real as the Holocaust.

The entire 1960s generation worldwide had young people rebelling in spurts. The USSR was a totalitarian country and did not tolerate rebels. During the nightly *Vremya* program, with increased frequency, Soviet newscasters delivered anti-Israel statements, condemning only Israel by calling out the "Israeli aggressors" in the escalating conflict that had erupted there. The obvious goal of the Soviet regime was to stir up a new wave of anti-Semitism. The broadcasters' voices, intonation, and pronunciation and the looks they flashed at the viewers were deliberate attacks against people of Jewish nationality presently living in the USSR. I personally felt this libel acutely, because anti-Semitism spiked up everywhere around me—in my preschool, in my building, at summer camps.

I only vaguely recall adult discussions of Israel at some of our family gatherings during the sixties. I was way too young then. And so I resisted being labeled a Jew.

I heard only a whiff of whispers about a Kiev Jew, Boris Kochubievsky, who walked into the OVIR in June 1968, just as I was getting ready to enter first grade, and requested an exit visa. This was a daredevil act of valor, in which he was joined by his non-Jewish wife. Her parents were KGB, and they immediately denounced her, likely out of fear for their own skins, or because of their own hardened Kiev anti-Semitism. In a sad twist of irony, Boris was tried in 1969 in the same room where Mendel Beilis was tried in 1913. None of Boris's friends or relatives were allowed into these closed-door proceedings. All evidence was fabricated. Boris was convicted and sentenced to three years of hard labor in the corrective facility—a horrific sentence, absolutely unbefitting the so-called "crime" of speaking out against anti-Semitism. Although I had to look up his name and the details of the incident, I remember the fear in all adults whenever Israel was discussed in the presence of us children. These were the beginning days of the third wave of Jewish immigration, our exodus, and I remember hiding under the table with my cousin Stella on her birthday so I could hear what the adults were whispering above. My cousin was too young to recall this at all, but later she was the only one of our family destined to resettle to Israel, where she gave birth to our first sabra.

When we finally left, the Hebrew Immigrant Aid Society (HIAS) resettled us to the US. According to a quote from their website from 2015, they list the Jewish emigration from the Soviet Union "in two modern waves," saying "the first wave peaked in 1979."

In 1979 and 1980, while Mama and I were being re-settled, our HIAS handlers called us "the third wave of Jewish immigration."

The following are some HIAS statistics from 1979:

- Jewish emigrants from the USSR: 51,320
- Soviet Jewish immigrants to the United States: 28,794
- Soviet Jewish immigrants to Israel: 17,278

On September 29–30, 1941, 33,771 Jews were murdered in Babiy Yar mostly by Ukrainian collaborators of their Nazi overseers and mostly by bullets. That was a "job" of intense manual labor ... yet performed with precision and efficiency Nazis and Ukrainians would have boasted about for generations, had the war been decided for their side. I compare that efficiency to the painfully slow process we underwent upon exiting the USSR. It took HIAS a year to resettle just 28,794 of us to the United States in 1979. The totalitarian world acted significantly more swiftly when exterminating the Jews than the free world did in absorbing them. It did not make sense.

The Soviet Union covered up the Babiy Yar massacre for fifty years before acknowledging its victims were Jews. To a Jew, freedom is such a temporary and transient state of existence. Survival is a permanent commonplace. Resettlements to a better land always take place during short periods of relative tranquility; the amount one must weather the storms of torrential hatred comes down to the providential luck of the draw. I was such a lucky girl. I always knew I was saved by a higher power of destiny. What exactly was the force that saved me? I had plenty of time during my immigration to discuss its vectors and ponder its sources. But we were so uninformed. All our guessing was miserably ignorant compared to what we later learned. Starting in 1968, the USSR began granting a very small number of Jews permission to exit the country with the idea to reunify with families in Israel. We all witnessed it, wherever we lived in the USSR, without knowing the behind-the-scenes facts. Joint (American Joint Distribution Committee) and HIAS (Hebrew Immigrant Aid Society) led this resettlement process from Vienna on and helped the Soviet Jewish refugees to get to their destinations. The debate of whether Soviet Jews had a right to go to countries other than Israel became a hot point of Western contention. Israel's PM Menahem Begin upheld the freedom of choice for Soviet Jewry. The US agreed and until the late 1980s continued accepting Soviet Jews without them having to prove that they were personally persecuted. Jewish federations of various US cities and towns took in the refugees.

When we arrived to Rome around November 15, 1979, Mama and I sought such acceptance to Teaneck, New Jersey, where Dora was headed. "Just our luck," Mama said as we learned that Teaneck, like most communities, had stopped accepting Jewish refugees without direct relatives already there. Dora's mother and sister were in Teaneck, a town with a population of about forty thousand then. She was a shoo-in. Mama and I were turned down and waited for whatever might come next.

This was the so-called US visa crisis, when HIAS could not process enough of us to complete the allotted visas, but we did not know it then. We arrived to Rome in the midst of a backlog of about ten thousand Soviet Jews. Whatever the excuses, HIAS just did not work as fast as the Nazis did in Kiev in 1941. Finally, the Soviets stopped letting Jews out, and of the twenty-five thousand parole visas given to HIAS, only about half were actually issued.

While we were moved between Chop and Rome, an important meeting of the Jewish Federations of America happened, though we had no way of knowing that at the time. At this meeting it was decided that all Jews who emigrated from the Soviet Union should be strongly encouraged to go only to Israel. That was, they rationalized, what the funding was raised for, after all. Fortuitously, they also agreed that HIAS would continue to aid the Soviet Jews already waiting in Vienna and Rome who did not have relatives in the United States and would, resettle them into the US, if possible

I must go back to 1974, when US senator Henry M. "Scoop" Jackson, a Democrat from Washington who was known for his anti-Communist position and who had been in office for more than thirty years, together with Charles Vanik, a Democrat from Ohio in the House of Representatives since 1955, cosponsored the Jackson-Vanik amendment to US federal trade law, restricting trade relations with countries with nonmarket economies. The Soviet Union and Soviet bloc countries restricted freedom of emigration and other human rights, so they worked on a deal that would ultimately tie Soviet Jewry exodus to grain. This amendment unanimously passed both houses of US Congress and was signed into law by President Gerald Ford on January 3, 1975, snowballing the numbers of Jews wanting to get exit visas. As Mama and I were turning into the departing, my anecdotal understanding of the reason we were allowed to leave was that the Soviet Union had horrible harvest years in 1976, 1977, and maybe 1978 and needed to purchase Argentine grain. The United States, in essence, became the matchmaker, enforcing the

Jackson-Vanik amendment, of which I knew nothing. The Soviet Union was forced to let us out. I have been joking for the longest time now that the price of my head was probably three and a half bushels of wheat. That's my kind of legitimized human trafficking!

Since my own "trade," I've wondered what other powers with vast amounts of government access and money are behind other modern-era legal and illegal human migrations. Desperate people are always running away, and human traffickers of all kinds always use their tragedy for financial and political profiteering. Enslavement by ISIS, ruthless convert-or-die ISIS beheadings, people burned alive in cages, girls stolen in hundreds from their schools ... Compared to these atrocities, my ogres and trolls were not really real.

Dress 13

The Roman Plaid

When I was a little girl and still believed in fairy tales, I could have never envisioned the magical city of Rome. It cannot be understood through stories, photos, or film. Rome can only be felt by stepping into the thick of its monumental history by day and night, breathing its air, looking at its people, drinking its water, and living in its heartbeat.

The day of our arrival from the Vienna train, Mama, Dora, and I were each taken to separate rooms at Pensione Benedetto. I was ecstatically happy to have a room of my own again. Dorming with strangers and being among large crowds of people would forever depress me. Mama was unhappy that I would be alone, on a floor different from hers, but soon she was made to understand that there were not enough rooms for everyone and advised to be happy we got these three tiny rooms with single beds, even if they were on different floors. Mama happy? Sure.

Pensione Benedetto was number 666 on Via Aurelia, one of the oldest roads in Rome. At the time I knew nothing of the significance of this devilish number to appreciate the mark or the defiance of it. I also knew nothing about this road. At the *pensione* we had full room and board, paid for by whoever was paying for everything on our journey. We did not ask; we just took everything for granted then, shell-shocked by everything around and completely unused to charity. After two weeks of our "Roman holiday," providing we made it to all our American embassy appointments, we'd receive 55,000 lire, the Italian currency of the pre-euro days, per person per month. It was soon evident that we'd have to move to a suburban town—most people chose Ostia or Ladispoli, the near-Rome Soviet Jewish ghettos of this in-transit period. There, in rented rooms, we all awaited news on the status of our papers.

At Benedetto I had a room on the second floor. Mama's room was on the first floor, and Dora was above me. Mama meant to guard me all the time, I think, because she was very unhappy to know I was on my own away from her. Or did she just want to vampirize me? I did not yet then understand that some parents fed off their children's energy, but I instinctively, even physically, felt when Mama's energy levels were depleted and she needed to drain some of mine. From very early on, I learned to rejuvenate, to recharge my internal batteries, to restore the powers Mama sucked out of me. At the *pensione*, when I was at last alone for the first time since home, in my small room, I was able to replenish the substantial drainage of the past two weeks. When I entered this room, I was on the verge of the schizophrenia my grandfather always warned me loomed over our family from his side. I kept inside as much as I could, barely interacting with anyone, so that I could heal myself. After a few days I started to come out to be among the rest for more than just meals.

In a large room nearest to mine, there was a Georgian Jewish family of four—mom, dad, and two sons, both slightly younger than me. They were kind, alert, positive, and generally happy people. The sons respected their parents, and all three men respected the beautiful Georgian mother. In the evenings, after supper, when there were many idle hours to kill, while the Odessits (people from Odessa) joked as only Odessits do and the Lenindradzy (people from Leningrad) made the snooty comments they are known for, the Georgians quietly kept to themselves and taught me the game of backgammon—*nardy,* they called it. They had a large, intricate inlaid wood set. Mama resented all table games. She preferred to discuss prices and complain to everyone about me. I suddenly realized that I loved the company of the quiet, dignified Georgians because they were so unlike the rest. They did not pry, did not bring into the common social rooms their for-sale inventory or discuss best strategies and prices. They, very much like me, forced to playact in the *balagan,* an oldtime Russian fair show with primitive scenery and players, and were patiently waiting for this stupidity to be over.

Via Aurelia is long. It is actually the road leading through most of northern Italy, dating to the ancients, when Aurelia, the town on the road's northern end, was the summer residence of one or the other of the country's countless Caesars.

By day Mama and I wandered through Rome on foot. We took the bus from across the hotel to get us closer to the center, where the Vatican, Fontana di Trevi, and Colosseum were walking distance. In a word—*fantastico!* Every girl of eighteen should have a tiny room in Rome and take daily walks though this eternal city. Even with cold rains and winds, the experience was an eye-opener.

But Rome was also an array of challenges to our worldly inexperience. And then, oddly, there was the inexplicable. On our walks we almost immediately discovered that what Italy wanted and was fighting to bring to power was Socialism. Demonstrations happened daily. Socialist five-pointed stars, hammers, and sickles were painted on the walls of most apartment buildings, bus stops, and the roads themselves. Lenin's profile decorated the banners and T-shirts of protesters, staring at us from the protesters' posters and, sometimes, even their facemasks. Imagine that—those strange, loud, wonderful Italians wanted what we'd just escaped from! People are always blinded by idealistic promises and become easily misled by politicians catering to mass idealism without any intent to feed the masses after the starvation of Socialist realism sets in. No one keeps a tally of how many idealists have started revolutions wanting to improve the world's or just a specific country's social conditions only to end up dying of starvation, torture, disease, or some other form of prolonged demise and deprivation of liberty at the hands of their former comrades or intended beneficiaries. Power, like all addictions, is easy to get hooked on, and only a few are able to kick the habit before it engulfs them.

Unlike the Italians, we were learning for the first time what wealth and abundance of uninterrupted capitalism were able to create, produce, and steadily deliver to a capitalist nation. The storefronts and variety of passersby were striking with their understated elegance. Pages from the Russian classics, referencing those who wintered in Italy before the October Revolution, arose in my mind when first I saw people of all ages and body shapes simply dressed in solid-colored, well-tailored clothes. The openly friendly Italian faces on the streets of Rome were a smiling sight previously unseen to us. We were used to the angry Soviets, ready to bitterly bicker over anything, anytime, and never looking anyone in the face. Here, even the quick purse-snatching Italian motorcyclists, whom the residents of the *pensione* were cautioned to beware, elegantly wore their denims and leather jackets and smiled and made passes at pretty women. Of course, compared to our in-transit *balagan*, even the Gypsies at the Roma Termini railway station were elegantly dressed in their Gypsy rags. My opinions of behavior, style, elegance, fashion, and tastes were, as the rest of me, fresh from behind the Iron Curtain. What did I really understand? *"No capito niente"* ("I do not understand anything") was one of the first Italian sentences I started using.

The large market in the center of Rome was called the Rotondo Mercato (Round Market) and was somewhere near Roma Termini. In Kiev, the produce, meat, and other consumables were more plentiful and of better quality and condition at the markets than in the Soviet stores but also significantly more expensive. Lots of things were very cheap and hundreds of time more plentiful at the Rotondo Mercato than at the small convenience stores. Besides, not even in Poland had we seen mounds of oranges, mandarins, bananas, figs, and dates. And that was just in the fruit aisles. We took a long time to make simple, commonplace decisions. Unused to choosing, we did not know how to handle abundance of choices. All we knew was we wanted the best for our money. But who knew what was better than the next? We were afraid of missing out, of making the wrong decision, of not getting a fair price. We still did not understand that there was always tomorrow and everything would still be there. As long as you had money, you could buy anything you wanted. I believe that my inextinguishable love and loyalty to Italy was born some-where in those food aisles.

"Mandarini! Buoni mandarini!" ("Mandarins! Beautiful mandarins!") screamed some round Roman female pur-veyor in a rich, melodic voice, while a skinny one seconded in high squeaks, *"Tre kile una mille lire!"* ("Three kilograms for one thousand lire!") I loved Italy. None of the "You'll chow what I throw you" arrogance of the markets and stores I was used to. Italian vendors tenderly sliced an or-ange and let me try it before buying, laughing, prodding, and teasing all the way through my shopping experience in the friendliest of ways.

Rome had electric energy and vitality. Like the Italians I watched going about their lives, I, too, was thrilled to live and be free and not be ashamed to be me. Soon I could have screamed about it from that market square: *"Viva l'Italia! Viva Roma!"* ("Long live Italy! Long live Rome!") These words could have been the ones I learned right after *grazie* (thanks) and *prego* (you're welcome). Italian lan-guage came surprisingly easy and naturally to me, as if I had been there before. Everything was familiar. "Why am I feeling like this?" I wanted to shout. But of course, I did not dare to scream or shout. My eyes were sad, and my face bore a frown. I, like most of the departing, had been transformed into an in-transit refugee. I was in a state of semipermanent shock befitting a refugee, dealing with daily uncertainty, unfairness of our birthplace, and fear that our status in the world would always be as pitiful as that. Our Roman holiday was not truly a holiday. But if it sometimes did feel like it and I felt and acted happy, Mama reminded me of our deprived circumstances.

I loved Rome and returned to the market often to hear the calls of *"Tre mille! Tre mille lire, signora! Tre pezzi una mille, signorina!*" ("Three thousand! Three thousand lira, lady! Three pieces for a thousand, miss!") and the Italian phrases "*Quanto costa?*" ("How much is it?") and "*Quanto dare?*" ("How much do you give?") Those two questions ensured our basic survival needs were met for the Italian leg of our journey. Perhaps I felt exactly what many other Jews, who have transitioned through Italy for centuries, felt. Too quickly, the orange peels settled, the first two weeks ended, and we were very roughly told we were now sufficiently exposed to Rome and had to move on.

I do not know what I was expecting at that point. A parade? An unending welcome with wide-open arms? Probably. At least a pat on my idealistic head. Instead, I was constantly shocked by the condescending, even demeaning, treatment we were subjected to, en masse, coming from the people of little authority who were in charge of our baby steps as freed people. I cannot say that I blame them for making it so hard on us, because, en masse, we were a huge collection of problems. We were not easy to deal with. We had so many disproportionate expectations, and our demands were likely seen as aggressive and arrogant, such were our Soviet survivalist behavioral patterns. But we were also confused, scared, poor, needy, inept, unprepared, passportless, unhappy, unwell, depressed, and angry. Maybe there were some relatively easy souls among us, like the Georgian family, but most were bitter, vulgar, exhausted by the departing processes, and suffering from the anxieties of endless what-ifs and the torture of endless faux pas.

Shortly before we were to vacate our *pensione*, a funny thing happened. Someone from our batch of refugees, clueless even more than the rest, bought a lot of cucumbers at the market, no doubt the "*tre kile una mille lire*" sort, and started pickling them in the bathroom. The cleaning woman, whose daily chores included washing the bidet, discovered the pickling enterprise, and the entire *pensione* gathered to watch the argument that ensued—cheap refugee entertainment.

"How was I supposed to know this tub is for pussy washing?" the hairy Moldovan grandfather yelled in Russian, after the Georgian father tactfully explained to all of us the bidet's intended purpose. "Nobody is using it here. Our women don't need your fancy washings. What am I to do? My pickles will be ready in a day or two." His good wife stood guard in the entryway of the common bathroom on their floor, periodically enumerating in Russian just how many lire had been spent on cucumbers, vinegar, bay leaves, dill, and salt.

"*Mamma mia, che pazzo!*" ("Crazy!") screamed the cleaning woman, twisting her index finger by her temple.

This argument went on for hours, the circus eventually ending with the pickling liquid going down the drain, pissing off Grandpa and Grandma for good.

In the decades since, I have heard many former refugees reminisce about those hard days of complete ignorance, when some people even used bidets for pickling. In those moments I always wished that I could pull out my mental Polaroid to show them our picklers.

Around the first of December, Mama and I moved to Ladispoli, a Mediterranean seaside resort town, halfway to the ancient Italian port of Civitavecchia, where Mama rented a room for us. Mama originally planned to take Misha with her on her initial visit there, not me, but she miscalculated. Misha's mother did not like mine, and so she and Misha quietly and discreetly rented in Ostia.

So did Dora. I knew they were all escaping Mama and our constant bickering. So Mama and I had to split our rented room in Ladispoli with another mother and daughter, whom we'd never met before. Just like in Vienna, the refugee shysters were there to educate the new arrivals about what was what and who was who. An operator or two "matched" families and "showed" rentals for a fee, sort of like when we would go to Crimea in summers. The rental matchmakers were refugees like us, who met fresh refugees at the Ladispoli train station, so that no others could intercept or educate them. Once settled, we would no longer have a reason to visit Pensione Benedetto, and soon everyone we'd met on the road had moved out. This separation was very sad to me. Not as sad, of course, as being parted from Grandpa forever, but I felt helpless and unshielded, especially after Dora went her separate way. Nothing now connected us to home. We were truly alone against the unknown.

"We can't afford" became Mama's most used phrase again. Our half a room was in a three-room ground-floor apartment on Via Del Mare (Sea Street) in a quaint Italian seaside resort town, then completely infested with the in-transit ex-USSR *balagan.*

Before leaving Rome, Mama and I went to the clothes aisle on the outer perimeter of the Rotondo Mercato. We bought our first ever nonstick frying pan, so we could start making our own meals in Ladispoli, and two skirts.

"A young girl needs warm fabric to protect her body from winter chill," Mama insisted.

"But I'll itch all over from the wool," I protested, to no avail.

"Even if she must be itchy all day long," Mama concluded in a tone disallowing further discussion. "That's all we can afford."

I admired the Italian mothers in solid-color dresses and coats of bottle green, gray, beige, and blue and wanted to buy a dress like that—plain. Mama would not have any of that. Plaids were also everywhere in Rome, on Italian school uniforms and Italian schoolkids' mothers' skirts. These mothers looked stylish and nonthreatening even as they yelled at their kids to keep up. I felt a significant gap in my education—fashion! I noted fine and durable fabrics and happily elegant patterns and learned from making a mental list of likes and dislikes.

Our two skirts were plaid. Mama's was beige, cream, and blue; mine, off-white, black, and burgundy. Hers was the one I originally chose for myself, but Mama redistributed it, and hers became mine. I spoke ample Italian by then and bargained with the vendor, so Mama and I actually bought two for the price of one. Mama felt that haggling was beneath her Soviet engineer's dignity, and from then on it was my responsibility. We paid 5,000 lire for two. I wore that skirt for five years, retiring it only after college. One of the best bargains I ever got!

As I fell asleep in the unheated, marble-floored room in Ladispoli, using the folding beach bag we'd brought from Kiev for a pillow, layered in my Polish turtleneck, second Riga twin dress, and jeans, covered with a sheet and with my Orenburg down shawl, and overcoat instead of a blanket, I dreamed that when we sold all our *chachkas*, we'd have a chance to buy a really well-made garment of solid color for me. Mama disagreed whenever I spoke up of my likes: "Plain? Why, you should be wearing something orange or yellow if not your usual red. A young girl should wear only bright, strong colors. We can't afford your dreams, so stop dreaming." It was useless to remind Mama that when she'd been young and living alone in Leningrad, she'd chosen elegant patterns and fabrics and had been, once upon a long-forgotten time, as stylish as some of these Italian mothers.

In Ladispoli I soon began to note how weird the former departing were acting after just a few weeks of freedom. It suddenly became important to brag about what you'd been able to procure back there, in the USSR, and how your connections had delivered that whatever to you. This "I was a distribution king/queen" routine worked best within a circle of people from one's original city, who were most impressed by the corruptive inventiveness of various channels and schemes. It was a type of nostalgia that was working its way through our ranks. Or maybe it was cultural, because it stayed with many people for decades to come. Likely, it was our "classless" Soviet class system that bred a new kind of superiority-driven layer in its people, who hadn't been taught how to handle the world this side of the Iron Curtain. Those who had formerly lived well on well-oiled procurement connections suffered the worst. One look at the plentiful markets made them realize how futile their skills would be in their new lives. They were completely lost. They endlessly smoked and ate and drank and fantasized about their futures.

Ordinary professionals, like Mama, or those with doctorates, like many we knew, were busy studying English faithfully. They formed classes and discussion groups. There were also religious studies circles in Ladispoli to get the departed up to speed with Judaism. Mama kept me from joining, after I tried once and became interested. Like our aunt Polina in Riga, Mama wanted to tie me to her skirt, and the more she persisted, the more I rebelled. Our feud was now beyond repair. Mama denounced me to all our new neighbors as the source of her constant misery and misfortune. She shamed me for any independent move, thought, word, desire. She controlled all our money and would not give me an allowance. I watched other teens enjoy life a lot on 1,000 or 2,000 lire, and I became even more depressed, uncertain of myself and my abilities. I felt wounded, injured, while understanding all the time that I should be as joyous as the day I'd planted both my feet onto Austrian soil victoriously. But Mama somehow insisted I should continue to feel inadequate, like she did. And it worked.

We were all in different stages of "inadequate." Yet every one of us, brought up under Socialist doctrine, obnoxiously pretended oneself better than the rest. It was a ridiculous pretense, and many of us assumed that role long-term. In reality, we were all ignorant of so many commonplace things, and our unfounded superiority often caused funny mishaps.

We were told of some early Soviet Jewish refugees, who, at the very beginning of the Soviet exodus out of Rome to Ostia and Ladispoli, tried to rent apartments by knocking on doors and asking *"Appartamento?"* only to hear *"Adesso no,"* meaning "Not now." Because our refugee superiority caused those early refugees to imagine themselves quite fluent in Italian, they heard this refusal as "Odessa no," meaning "Not if you are from Odessa." This refugee story spread fast, and all Odessits became Moscovites, just in case they'd be told that apartments were not being rented to Odessits. *Adesso* then became an important word to me. Our past was lost, our future very murky. We lived for today. Each *adesso* became a discovery.

Ever since I'd read the books on Jesus Christ in Vienna, something fundamentally significant was perplexing me. We were all atheists. I'd been taught thus far that the entire universe should be atheistic. Except for a Sunday-morning church service Mama and I had attended with the Molases in Skierbieszów, I'd never assigned any importance to religion. Even though the church bells always rang on Sundays in Kiev, we were told, and accepted it axiomatically, that prayer was prerevolutionary atavism, restricted to the disabled, the very aged, and the dull witted. So I'd simply dismissed the Molases' religious observances as a demonstration of their despair under the Soviet boot. All of a sudden, when the bells rang on our first Sunday in Italy, I realized that the world prayed, went to church, and believed in God, regardless of what the Soviet regime wanted us to think. Rome was the center of the world, and the world wanted prayers, even if some of it wanted Socialism at the same time.

Soviet atheistic Kiev was extremely proud of its famous churches. Forbidden to practice their religions, punished for secret observances, jailed, deported to Siberia and worse, people continued to search for their religious identity in secret. I knew it even though I never learned it from anything other than obscure references and rare glimpses. Communist Party membership, love of Lenin and his teachings, and every Socialist pursuit, from education and collectivization to sending Gagarin into the cosmos, could not completely eradicate a Soviet citizen's quest for religious identity. Almost all my non-Jewish classmates had been secretly baptized. If found out, my classmates explained it by saying, "My grandmother made my parents do it." This deception, the need to cover up by stressing that the baptism was a superstitious old woman's idea, crazy and useless and not to be taken seriously, was one of the prime Soviet pretenses. A woman from my childhood was old at a mere fifty-five. I think there were rare exceptions among the non-Jews of true believers in Communism who adhered to the prohibition of religion on every score. The majority of Jews, on the other hand, had completely and irrevocably abandoned religion. For one, persecution against Jews under the Soviet system got increasingly worse with every decade. But so many Jews thought that through denial they will gain acceptance. They were wrong.

Mama and I returned to Rome often and visited our favorite sites. They were mostly churches and cathedrals. In conversations with Mama on these long walks, I realized that Easter eggs in Kiev were colored in every household, but I'd never known they were for Easter. My grandmother and grandfather, who were under Mama's strictest orders not to expose me to anything Jewish, colored the eggs with me, to keep me uninformed of this tradition not being part of Jewish heritage for as long as possible. We boiled them with beets or onions, so they'd become pink or yellow. Of course, I had no idea about synagogues or any other Jewish religious observances. I knew how to color eggs and did it well! My Soviet-made religious curiosity gravitated only toward the church. Some teens I knew tried to attend an Easter mass once by crushing through the militsiya border posted around Saint Vladimir's Cathedral, a magnificent functional Russian Orthodox church. It was open to the public except for holy days, about which, by age sixteen or so, I knew a little from reading prerevolutionary classics and studying the art of painting through my older cousin Lora. Hordes of tourists from the USSR and abroad flocked to Saint Vladimir's to see the artwork of Vrubel and the elaborate traditional icons. The scent of candles and incense permeated the otherwise stale church air. It was a marvel to be inside the church on hot days. The high stone walls and cold stone floors kept the church cool and made it a desired repose for many passersby on long walks to their destinations. Whenever I ventured inside, a priest or two would always be visible observing but would never approach. It was generally accepted knowledge by that time that all clergy were KGB.

When we unsealed our apartment windows after the winter, we could hear the bells calling to midday and midnight mass even on Batyeva Gora. As summers grew hot and humid, the church bells reminded me of the cool repose during my errands to the center of town.

In my sixteenth year I sometimes hung out at the adjacent apartment building in the evenings with my playground buddies. There was an obligatory playground next to every Soviet residential edifice, but I'd given up on the one abutting mine. My building was way too anti-Semitic in the daytime, and in the evening too many drunks and thugs occupied the designated children's space. Our building had the supermarket, and the entire collection of derelicts gathered on our playground to split the spirits they could purchase until nine o'clock each night. They'd stay there in good weather through all hours of the night, cursing viciously and torturing stray animals, and were either beaten into leaving by their mighty wives or taken into alcoholic detox by militsiyamen.

My neighborhood circle, a group of no more than ten teens, included various vocational school students. We gathered on the playground of the adjacent building from nine to ten each night, when our parents were glued to the evening news program *Vremya*. These buddies of mine formed their plan to crash the church there. I would have gone too, but someone said that Jews were not allowed in church because they'd killed Christ, so I ran home crying. Some of my buddies were arrested, their parents notified. Worse still, a couple of these boys were prevented from pursuing higher education, which meant that on the first draft day following their eighteenth birthdays, in May or October, it was their turn to join the Soviet Armed Forces. All because young people were prohibited from entering a church during services.

All of that seemed so far away and fantastic as I stood in Vatican's St. Peter's Square in late December 1979. Mama and I stood in the happiest and best behaved of crowds I'd ever seen, probably the only two standing there who had no idea that it was Christmas. The Pope spoke in Polish during some of his sermon and said some important things that rang true. Why, these people had no intention to be enlightened by atheism! It was us, the duped Soviets, who were deprived, deceived, and cheated. They gathered in front of St. Peter's in an act of free will. All mass gatherings in the USSR were mandatory. Or else! It was in St. Peter's that I first realized why Lenin taught us that religion was "opium for the masses." The USSR got high on Socialism, wanting to make it like religion is, and all of us were forced to become addicted!

"We are here to watch their rituals and see Michelangelo's works," Mama said dismissively once we made it inside St. Peter's, "'Religion is opium for the masses,' just like Marx said. Look at the crowd of them; see how exalted they act. It's because they are brainwashed by religion."

Mama may have been better informed about the sources of Soviet opioid addiction, but I understood that she was still continuing with her preprogrammed role of making her child into a Soviet.

My mama did, is doing, and, God willing, will do many mean things to me, but she is my mama, and I reserve the exclusive privilege of criticizing her. I will defend her whenever anyone says anything negative about her, because she is *my* mama, and I love her in a way neither you nor she will ever understand. Mama has my loyalty no matter what just for giving birth to me. She may be my personal saint. Fallible, human, yet saintly, and I love her.

Dress 14

The Ladispoli Beige

When I was a little girl and still believed in fairy tales, I already knew that most of them ended before I was ready.

I never did get a glimpse of Ostia, the ancient Roman port I heard so much about and where most people we knew went. At that time it was completely and most absurdly filled with Soviet Jews. Ostia had cheaper rents, and we could have had better conditions there.

As it was, our half-room Ladispoli rental was in a three-room apartment. We had a communal kitchen and bathroom, inconveniences I abhorred. But how long does it take to boil a hot dog or eggs? So I tolerated the kitchen. At least it did not smell nearly as foul as the bathroom. I hated our cleaning rotation. In Ladispoli we lived totally detached from the rest of the world, unwelcomed, unwanted, unemployed, unengaged. All of us together and each of us individually had just survived a year or two—or, in some cases, ten—of a nerve-racking, health-depleting experience, and together we wandered the cold winter streets of Ladispoli, bravely staring toward the unknown.

I was happy to live on a street bearing my name—Via del Mare. All my life I'd known, of course, that my first name meant "sea" in Italian. Now I was learning to love my name, which I hadn't been too happy with before. I was named with an *M* after Garrik's father, Misha, from the side of the family that never bothered about me. I, Marina, belonged to Italy. It was actually a great first name, I finally acknowledged, because it transcended all cultures and languages. It was infinitely easier than Yelena, Lyudmila, Anastasia, Svetlana, Elizaveta, Ekaterina, and many other multisyllabic names, which I'd been so sorry not to have while I was a child. I realized suddenly that many other things that I'd so desired as a child would become trifles as I matured.

Our roommate Irina was a tiny Jewish mother with long gray hair and small bone structure. She seemed frail and too old to have a daughter like Tatiana, a tall and stout picture of Siberian health. Secrets were not kept long in our new life, devoid of TV, newspapers, and books. In a day or two they told us that Irina had adopted Tatiana in 1952, after the Kurilskie Ostrova (Kuril Islands) were hit by a tsunami, in which they'd each lost all their family. Tatiana was a non-Jew by birth, just like Nadyusha, Dora's adopted daughter. Irina had raised Tatiana since she was a toddler.

Maybe I am not Mama's daughter either, I questioned silently. I did not look like her at all. *That could explain so many things,* I thought. It was actually an old recurring idea of mine, a secret wish, to one day find out that I was adopted and that was why Mama could never find compassion for me in her heart.

Being a refugee without anyone's moral support through the process does many disturbing things to a young woman. I was emotionally vulnerable. Mama did not ease up on me for a moment, imposing her own disturbing behavior onto me and transferring to me all the guilt she felt at leaving her father, because I'd gone to register the invitation. Most of the time she made few attempts to have conversation with me when we were indoors alone, but in front of others, she underscored her role as a mother and moral superior. She chastised, lectured, and corrected, making fun of my errors, missteps, mix-ups, moods, emotions, appearance. In short, she made fun of me. She was relentlessly driving me insane, and at times, when the confines of our situation were too much to endure, I broke down and ran off to wander the streets, as I so frequently did in Kiev.

It seems to me that in Ladispoli I broke down from her ridicule nearly daily.

I soon discovered that Denis and his parents were also in Ladispoli, so he and I spent lots of time together. The formerly departing, presently in-transit Jews congregated at the town square to share news and gossip. The news from the USSR was not too happy. It was three weeks before the Soviet invasion of Afghanistan on December 24, 1979, but we still did not know that invasion was coming. What we did hear and witness was a decreasing number of newly arriving Soviet Jews. We didn't notice the decrease immediately but after a couple of weeks or so. Then we began hearing from the freshly arrived refugees that border strip searches had become more frequent and the lawless treatment had escalated at Chop and Brest, two major departure points. Ultimately, we heard how people who had already cleared customs were being yanked off their trains—all because of Afghanistan.

I will never understand why a country like Afghanistan, so mountainous and difficult to traverse, with hidden dangers, without a great deal of natural resources, and with a population Westerners can never comprehend, would be a desired conquest for any nation considering itself "civilized." The mighty leaders of this world must know something I don't.

The first sign I had of the coming war was in July 1979, way back in Kiev, and I only understood it in retrospect. One of our Batyeva Gora neighbors was killed on the Afghan border and was brought home in a closed military casket. He'd been drafted a couple of months before, in May. The Soviet draft happened twice a year and was a dreaded affair, frequently with funeral-like singing. I'd heard such singing from this neighbor's windows. Now he had a real funeral. His huge funeral procession had the most mournful singing I'd ever heard. It was the second-largest funeral I'd seen, the first one being my homeroom teacher's. I think nearly everyone on Batyeva Gora came to escort this young soldier, who had been a bully while he was among us, terrorizing little kids, animals, young girls, and seniors on our playground and beyond. The funeral procession filed down Volgogradskaya toward the end of the streetcar line, then descended Batiy Mountain to the same cemetery where Olga Porfirievna, my most favorite teacher ever, had been brought to rest when I was twelve on that unforgettable, bitterly cold February day. I think the entire city of Kiev came to bid her farewell. She was loved and respected by so many. She inspired many and was extinguished too soon.

Vitalik, the bully, did not have my respect, even if his death was a tragedy. Besides, it was not advisable for the departing to participate in mass gatherings. I returned home to safety to hear all night long singing, crying, mourning, and drunken arguments.

All the boys I grew up with, I thought when the news of the war with Afghanistan broke, *what a waste of life.* I was sorry for all of them—Yura and all the boys I knew, even those two who had wanted to rape me. They would all be drafted now, even those with deferments. *If they survive this war,* I wondered, *what will be their real damage? An arm, an eye, a lifetime of nightmares?*

But we were too busy with our own daily survival and our real and petty gripes. Ladispoli's station square had a small store with gum, newspapers, dry soup, milk, fresh fruit, and ice cream. Mama never allowed me to buy anything there. We did our grocery shopping at the supermarket, a few streets farther, where things were a little cheaper. I would usually meet Denis at this square. Together we wandered around in the chilly seaside town imagining the American future for each of us. I was always on the verge of tears, was always complaining about Mama. I felt more alone than ever. Denis was now the only relative I trusted in my entire world.

It was, therefore, a complete shock to me when one evening, as we sat on a park bench, after I'd cried, complained, and cried some more, Denis kissed me so very softly. It felt good. It was a sign of hope, and I loved being kissed that way. His parents, however, soon insisted that he stop spending so much time with me. Maybe someone saw us kiss. I'll never know. Shortly after, he and his family left for Rochester, New York, disappearing from my life.

Some years later I heard about them from someone who knew them. I followed the lead, locating my uncle and aunt in a small city near where I now live in Florida. They were not too happy to hear from me and did not even inquire about my mother. When I called Denis's home, his wife was the only person happy to hear from me. We talked and talked. It beats me to this day why his parents thought I was such a threat. Marrying him would not have occurred to me. He was always safe from me. I just wanted a friend and a caring relative. And he kissed me. Big deal!

My next Ladispoli friend was Lucy. Her family was waiting for visas to Australia. They'd already been in Italy a few months and were expected to be there for at least ten more. Lucy worked and so did her parents, helping Italian owners in their shops and cafés.

We teens in transit loved getting to know people we otherwise would have had no exposure to. Once or twice we gathered at some apartments, where all residents were friendly and welcoming—not like in my apartment, where everyone was afraid a neighbor would take the crust of their stale bread.

At those gatherings, some Russian-speaking religious Jews explained about such unfathomable matters as Talmud, Kabala, Torah, Moses, Abraham, the Red Sea, King David. What did we know? Nothing. I knew some Russian poetry and literature, geometry, and trigonometry. I'd studied useless subjects like Soviet Society and Beginnings of Military Education. King David was a complete stranger to me. Yet I was suspicious of the looks on the faces around me, of zealots eager to replace the Soviet mentality with religious fervor. Perhaps Mama had a point, after all, and atheism was best.

Another place I recall in Ladispoli's center was its cinema. It was right next to a café, where other refugees had coffee and ice cream. I never sat down in a Ladispoli café. Mama just would not have it.

Everywhere in Ladispoli—on the beach, on the building walls, at the train station painted with improvised hammers and sickles—were pro-Socialist demonstrations.

Why did they want this so, this horrible regime called Socialism, when we wanted to distance ourselves from it and were experiencing so many hardships because of it? I'll never understand.

Mama and I had brought from Kiev one small enamel bowl to cook in and eat out of, a knife, a spoon, and a fork. Lucky for all the occupants of our apartment, some of our predecessors had left some other kitchen necessities. Mama and I, however, left nothing of ours when we moved on into our next nothingness.

Whenever Mama and I returned to Rome to wander its streets, we brought back the usual three-kilos fare—*tre kile* of chicken wings and *tre kile* of mandarins or sometimes dates. We ate lots of hot dogs, as always, but hot dogs tasted better in Italy. We always had yogurt for breakfast, and we always drank Orangina and instant coffee. Nutella became one of our favorites too. We would spread it over some very cheap, fluffy, tasteless bread. We had no clue that this bread needed toasting. Chicken wings were everyone's dinner, because of their affordability. We continued to return to Rome and shop at the Rotondo Mercato. Perishables spoiled quickly. I think we did not pay for the fridge rights. After these trips to Rome, a chicken wings feast it was, until we were so winged we could fly. The refugee joke of that time was to call them Soviet wings, which was the name of a very well known and popular Soviet hockey club, team, and arena—Krylya Sovetov. This was a name all of us knew, thanks to Stalin's prewar Soviet sports propaganda efforts.

Mama, who to this day is not famous for her cooking, bought carrots and onions to continue the tradition of chicken soups. While I like chicken, as nearly all Jews do, and love chicken soup, I never liked Mama's way of boiling

a halved onion in the broth and leaving it in the pot to split
and float. Chicken soup is so much better when the onion
is boiled whole and removed immediately after the soup is
done. Mama also overboiled the carrots and any parsley or
dill she used. I always insisted on fishing these things out
to have just a clear broth and maybe some boiled chicken,
incurring her wrath for wasting precious "vitamins." As
always, she would end with "You waste so much money."

Since my early childhood Mama called me *barynya*, a
matron of wealth in tsarist Russia who could dictate her
rules to others. I was like that about my food. Yet I remember myself always being hungry because food in our home
was never taken care of properly. Raw and prepared food
was kept uncovered in our little refrigerator, causing both
the food and the refrigerator to stink. Any such unappetizing smell, in turn, caused me to gag or vomit. I always ate
selectively of the food Mama prepared, even though I was
always hungry, and looked for alternative tables at other
people's homes. To boot, our kitchen in Kiev—in fact, our
entire apartment—was never clean, but as always in such
circumstances, it was our own "dirty" secret.

Now, during our in-transit immigration, we were bringing that secret out of the dark. I compared Mama's Soviet
wings creative processes to those of other mothers, to the
right and left, picking up important tips here and there to
carry forward. Other mothers' food always looked more
appetizing. I had to eat Mama's wings. To save money
and preparation time, she boiled them to make soup first,
and then we ate the wings as our main course. The only
condiments Mama used were mayonnaise and ketchup.
She would usually boil spaghetti, which we all used as
noodles. Boiled spaghetti with mayonnaise—yummy! On
occasion we'd eat fried potatoes with ketchup and some

sliced tomatoes with sour cream. Anyway, our meals were almost the same as in Kiev, without pelmeni, and improved by Orangina and Nutella, of course, and great-looking, fat *krylya Sovetov.*

It took us years, decades even, to abandon most of those horrible eating habits, which our former poverty refused to let us relinquish, causing us to suffer various digestive problems. I wish I could say we are 100 percent cured.

Mama and I debated several times the possibility of exploring Italy on the Russian tour bus. A trip to the north cost around 40,000 lire per person; to the south, 35,000. Mama pondered these amounts several times daily, adding minute expenses on a sheet of paper out of the little notebook we had. That was her occupation in Italy: adding long columns of numbers together. And then re-adding them. How much we'd made so far after selling some of our *chachkas*, how much we could make if we sold all our *chachkas*, and so on. I pleaded, volunteering to go hungry for a week, so that I could see Milan and Florence or at least Naples and Pompeii. Mama was taking so much time on this issue, so I pressured her and at last heard a firm "No, we can't spend any of our savings. We'll need all the money in America." It broke my heart to know how close we were and that we'd never see those cities.

At Pensione Benedetto, I'd become friends with an Italian boy, a young man, really, who showed up one day in Ladispoli, found me, and invited me to spend a weekend with his family in Cosenza, all the way down in the south of the boot. Enrico was a table waiter at the *pensione.* He drove an old Fiat, listened to wonderful songs of then-popular Italian singers Lucio Dalla and Francesco De Gregori, and drove fast on the scariest of roads, periodically pulling me closer and planting unexpected kisses on my face and hands. I experienced so many firsts with Enrico, like riding in the passenger seat of a car, traveling the highways, eating real spaghetti and pizza, drinking cappuccinos, stopping in Naples for a very brief look ... He did not want to leave the car in Naples; robbers were everywhere, he explained. True, no sooner than we opened the door to exit, a would-be thief was ready to steal something from the backseat. Enrico screamed *"Pazo!"* ("Lunatic!") and *"Cornuto!"* ("Horned!") atop his lungs, scaring the thief and many pedestrians around us. We got back into the car and drove on. I saw a sign for Pompeii as we drove past the mountain and understood, as if I did not before, that Enrico's plans did not include visiting historical sites.

His family—parents, grandparents, and a younger brother—lived in a multistory house, cold with marble floors and warm with hospitality. The family gathered to look at me—a wild creature from the red USSR—participating one and all in dinnertime preparations. I was awkward and socially numb, not understanding how to behave.

Everyone in Enrico's household had chores. There was a huge wood table, like a butcher block, in the kitchen, where Sunday's meal of sauce and spaghetti was being made. Thin, long spaghetti stuck out over the edge of an enormous metal cooking pot, and once in while, a boy in charge pushed them down with a wooden spoon. Still as much of a bewildered child as I was in 1976 in Poland, I suggested, showing with my hands just how to do it, "Why don't you break them in half?" causing the entire family to laugh. I can just imagine what they said then: "Mamma mia! Who does this nobody in our kitchen think she is! How dare she tell us, the people of spaghetti, how to cook our pasta!"

All I meant to do was to offer a good suggestion, as a proper Soviet overachiever was taught to do, as I so often did in my childhood when I'd observed my relatives' kitchen or other household inadequacies. I did not understand but was about to learn that spaghetti need to soften slowly and then will ease into the pot in their unbroken lengths. We used spoons and forks to reel them to eat—like Charlie Chaplin, but with much less fun.

I was bombarded by unknowns of many kinds. I felt helpless, useless, unwanted, unclaimed.

When I announced to Mama that I'd accepted Enrico's invitation and would travel with him to see his family, Mama became very angry. I could handle angry, but this time she called me "prostitute," "whore," and "slut," using these words together and repeating them over and over till I had to turn myself off. Tears and frustration blocked my comprehension of anything. Then she went off to tell anyone she could find. The first one she told, probably, was the Italian man she'd met in the central square, whom she'd been sort of dating these last few weeks.

Mama never understood that I was really a good girl, because she did not believe in me. Because I was so eager to get out from under my mama, I actually started listening quite seriously to Enrico's suggestions that I marry him and stay in Italy. I'd known him only a few weeks, but that was eons compared to Romeo and Juliet. *Do I love him?* I kept asking myself. The answer was veiled by Mama's hatred of me and my desire to put a quick end to her insanity.

When we returned from visiting his family, Enrico came to ask Mama if he could marry me, and Mama said, "Absolutely no! My daughter will go to America, like we planned. Then she will write you, and you can come there, if you want."

To my shock, Enrico really liked that idea. From that day he started planning how he would come to America, we'd marry, and all his family would join us.

"You don't need him," Mama said. "You will forget him as soon as he's out of your sight."

Now, as I am writing these words more than thirty-five years later, I still do not know if I loved Enrico. I had no idea then what love is, because I did not know myself. But I've always missed him.

I wonder what his life was like. He never came to the United States to follow me. We wrote to each other for a year or more. Then my immigrant's life took hold of me with silly priorities like assimilation and education, and I wrote to him that I no longer wished him to come, or he wrote to me first that he was not coming. And that was it.

Mama's Smelly Feet

There was something essential that I did not learn from my mother—cleanliness. Yes, the same trait I now know is next to godliness. For whatever reasons, Mama never liked anything clean: her home, her language, her clothing, her child, herself.

As a child I shared Mama's bed. We slept "valet style," which meant my head was next to her feet. Mama's feet stank. The skin of her feet was coarse and crackled. Pedicures were something she never did, so I did not even realize such a thing existed until much later in my life. Sometimes Mama asked me to burn the hair off her legs. She never bathed the way clean people bathe. Her bathing was a rushed shower, never scrubbing, never allowing herself to enjoy the splendor of creams and lotions, scrubs and potions, which she could have procured somewhere even under the watchful and restricted Soviet rule. She was the epitome of a Soviet Socialist woman, depriving herself of womanhood and its privileges in all possible and improbable ways. She knew very well what to do as a Soviet Socialist student and a Soviet Socialist worker. But she knew nothing of keeping herself, her home, and her child clean and appealing to outsiders.

Before I learned otherwise, I, too, had very smelly feet. I remember very well that they were coarse and cracked, and when I pulled the skin off my heels, it peeled in thick, long strips, exposing a new flesh layer underneath and often causing a lot of pain.

And that is how I remember my mama's treatment of me: to discover who I really was, I had to peel away the old, thick, dirty layers in order to reveal the fresh and fragile one underneath, the one yet undisturbed by the dirt of my mama's motherhood. The pain was inevitable, but it, too, peeled off in long, thick strips.

After I understood that Mama's feet smelled bad and that I wanted to be clean, I began learning, finding a way out of the unclean mess my home life was. I wanted to educate Mama as I was learning from others the things I never learned at home. But Mama never wanted me to become better than her. And then I was. I was cleaner and had more practical skills, and I was liked and I liked to be liked, gathering boys and girls around me. It all came together in Ladispoli.

Mama must have been desperate, losing her grip on me completely, as I reveled in my freedom, cleanliness, and womanhood. So she soiled me as only my mama knew how. She called me a whore. She told people she knew about her daughter, the whore, and she wrote to my grandfather and all the other people we'd left behind, telling them that I'd become a whore. It mattered little to her that the truth was not as she saw it. She was, I now understand, envious of my freedom of mind and behavior, as completely foreign to her as clean feet, clean underwear, or clean sheets.

In time, after all the years of unwillingness to accept Mama as an unfriendly entity, I learned to stop sharing with her my emotions and facts about my life. It took a long time to understand that my mama was unsupportive, not a well-wisher, and a user of all my good intentions. That did not mean that I stopped loving her. I'll love her always—the way I saw her before I understood how badly her feet smelled and how unlike me she would always stay.

* * *

In the last days of 1979 an announcement came that Mama and I were to fly to the United States on January 10, 1980, a Thursday. It was a painful goodbye to everything I loved about Italy, and I stretched that pain carefully. Over my two months there, I'd fallen in love with Italy in a way I will never again be able to love another country, not Poland or the US or Israel. Italy liberated me from Mama's influence on my mind and my affairs. It did not completely free me from Mama or her ways or the shared baggage of our relationship, but it was there that I understood that with time, hard work, and money, I would become a worthy human being. That is why it pained me to go, but I knew that go I must.

New Year's Eve 1980. I spent almost the entire night walking from home to home of the Soviet refugees with kids as a sort of "helper" to a sixteen-year-old boy who was playing the Soviet Santa, Ded Moroz. We had no understanding of Christmas. Our Soviet souls were New

Year's worshipers of Ded Moroz and Snegurochka, his helper snow girl, who melted if brought into the warmth.

On our last Sunday in Rome, January 6, 1980, we woke up early to join a small group of others like us at the Ladispoli train station for a trip to Americano, a humongous weekend market in Rome. Everything that we'd schlepped over from Kiev and still not sold had to be disposed of now. The linens, the *chachkas*, the spoons, the nail files, the Ukrainian plates with *pivnyki* (roosters painted by Soviet-era Ukrainian artisans on plates, cups, and jewelry boxes), the whatever—all the USSR items made for export that the departing were permitted to take out of the country while leaving their meager possessions behind.

On the train, during the half-hour ride, a man and a woman from Kiev, whom we knew by sight since Chop, shared with us the details of their strip search of November 1. She was a very large woman with at least a DD cup, and her husband was tiny but not skinny. She showed us her string of coral beads, finger-thick and dark, the expensive kind. While every one of us on the train admired them, she said, "I pasted them under my boobs, like so, and they felt me up all over but never found them. I have so many fat folds." Everyone laughed.

Then her husband pointed to the large diamond ring on her finger. "See that?" Yes, we saw it without having to be told. Rings like that were forbidden, just as coral necklaces were. The husband continued, "She worked in Kashtan, the store for foreigners, so there is a mark in our exit visas to search us even more than the rest of you. I hid this ring up my ass." He was shining with pride. "That's right! Up my ass! And they stuck their fingers up my hole and never found it. There!" The few Italians riding to Rome that morning looked dumbfounded at the sight and sound of the gypsylike wanderers roaring with laughter.

It was raining that day in Rome, and Oleg, a young man who made the trip from Ladispoli in our pack, offered to buy me a cup of coffee after we set up. I was shocked when Mama agreed to let me go for a few moments. It seemed impossible that other people were splurging for coffee and that a complete stranger would offer me a cup. In my world of every lira being saved for the hardships ahead in the unknown land of plenty, it seemed an act of chivalrous proportion.

Maybe it was this coffee, but I became very flirty with the customers after, using whatever Italian I knew, selling everything quite well, including the suitcase out of which I was selling my stuff. Mama stood aside and told me numerous times how shamed she was by this entire ordeal. "Who would have thought that I, an engineer who has worked for twenty-five years, would be reduced to selling at the market, like *bydlo*?" Mama loved using the Ukrainian word for "cattle" to mean "nobody" like all her fellow members of the Kiev intelligentsia class.

In vain, I reminded her that many who had gone before us—the first wave running away from pogroms and revolution and the second wave running away from the terrors of war—did not even have *chachkas* to sell. Standing at Americano selling my *chachkas* did not shame me. My mother's constant shaming did.

My reward came in the form of a plain-colored dress— my beige dress, the kind I'd dreamed of when passing by Italian women in solid colors and by the storefronts displaying their best. We bought the dress right there at the market. It was cheaper that way. It was loose fitting, made of very light wool, with a pale square pattern on its cuffs and collar. Mama did not want me to buy this one, but I was the one who had sold all our *chachkas*, and I insisted I choose the dress I want.

My plain Italian dress made me at last look like the locals more than the rest of the immigrants, who looked clown-like and grotesque to me in their bright reds, purple paisleys, and similar *balagan* garb. There was no elegance about us. It made my fighting for the beginnings of my own elegance even more difficult. I wanted to be different. I wanted to be like the Italian women in plain green, navy, or gray overcoats, leading their plainly and neatly dressed children to cafés after school. It was an expensive, down-played kind of elegance I was observing for the first time in my experience. It made me yearn to stay in Italy for good and be like them. I was afraid of America, like Little Red Riding Hood is afraid of the Big Bad Wolf—afraid yet drawn.

Our last days were saved for shopping. We bought a brown sheepskin coat for Mama and a navy sheepskin coat for me. I wore mine for several years after. I think Mama still has hers. I think mine cost 30,000 or 40,000 lire—a fortune equivalent to a trip to the north of Italy. Mama insisted I buy black suede boots, which I cherished and refused to wear until almost two years later. I then wore them once and ruined them the very first day by my own inability to choose between vanity and common sense. They were gorgeous. I can still feel their soft suede under my fingers.

Mama insisted I buy strap sandals too. I do believe she felt a sort of delayed guilt for those other graduation shoes I had to give up. Well, the beautiful white leather sandals I bought in Rome I also got to wear only once, two years later, to a wedding, which turned out to be in someone's grassy backyard. By the end of the night, the leather had peeled off the heels completely. Before they were ruined, they were gorgeous and *so* comfortable. I've never had a pair like that again.

I do not exactly remember what Mama bought for herself—similar clothes, I am sure, which made us both feel good about buying Italian. Later, as I learned a little about fashion and even when I could afford some very pricey garments, I always remembered how wonderful my inexpensive Italian clothing felt, just like my Latvian and Polish clothing before it, so I was rarely tempted to spend my hard-earned money on designer labels. Over time, I may have developed some inconsistent sense of style. But I've disliked shopping ever since those last days in Italy. And I finally stopped comparing our journey to those of the Jews during the Holocaust. We were the fortunately ungrateful ones.

* * *

And then, goodbye Soviet wings. Hello, Alitalia!

Of course I had layers of clothing on again on January 10, 1980. Mama insisted that the suitcase would be lighter and I would be warmer that way. I would have preferred to leave our bowl and some other Kiev stuff behind, but Mama won, and I layered up to make room for these items. I was hot, angry, and confused again. A whole busload of us were escorted to board the flight from Rome to New York. The sight of an airplane made me ill right away. I was always nauseated at airports. We thought it was a direct flight. Even if I'd learned enough Italian to carry a simple conversation, I was unable to comprehended, neither in Italian nor in English, what the pilot announced.

Since very early that morning, we'd been among the former departing, who would now proudly be known under the label of "new Americans." The others were visibly better dressed, just like us, in newly purchased, made-in-Italy clothing, and they acted just as irritated, confused, intolerant, and scared as we did.

The airplane was huge. We sat in a far-off section near a smoking area. It was hot. I was nearly suffocating under my clothing. Mama was wrong again; the plane was not cold. They fed us well, but she made me eat the cheese sandwiches and oranges we'd brought for the trip. She knew that no food would be admitted into the States, but I could not eat. My stomach was not handling the air pockets well. I was overcome by Mama's agitated urgency of minutiae, the totality of the flight itself, the heat, and the many arrogant and unimportant conversations of other ex-Soviets around us.

A short time after we took off, we landed in Milan. To this day I do not know if it was a planned landing. The word I caught the pilot saying aloud was *bomba*, a word that sounds universally the same, no matter the language. We were held on the ground for a significant amount of time but were not asked to leave the plane. Something was being checked and rechecked; even if there was no *bomba*, there must have been some sort of a technical problem with the plane.

No one else seemed as scared or worried as me, except maybe Mama. Smokers smoked. Everyone ordered extra Orangina and Coca-Cola. Stewardesses unhappily squeezed through crowded aisles blocked by ex-Soviet men, women, and children, dressed in wool clothing, sweaty and smelly, as no personal hygiene lessons had yet been impressed onto us. Smoke and sweat dominated the aisles as we resumed the flight.

The wild herd that we were was as oblivious to the customs of the natives as, perhaps, Captain Cook was or Magellan before him. Our herd, despite the tragic circumstances of our complete ineptness in the Western world, thought itself a carrier of superior Soviet traditions and culture. Thank God by then the "savages" had stopped killing the would-be invaders. In fact, we were headed to the United States as welcomed newcomers, the recipients of the most fortuitously amazing hospitality, which we then completely misunderstood.

A charming old couple had settled in back of us as we were boarding. She sat in a chair. He was immediately helped to lie down across the remaining seats in the center of their row. His niece and her husband told the rest of the passengers a wonderful story. This couple were her uncle, ninety-nine years of age, a war veteran, and his young wife, only eighty-six. They'd lost their children in the war, and the niece had not wanted to leave these wonderful family members behind. Their family was going west as one, united and whole. The passengers fell silent when she finished, most likely thinking of their own family members left behind, as I was thinking of my uncle, who had practically condemned our decision, and my grandfather, who had not wanted to leave the graves of his family. Some time later, over the ocean, in a moment of complete silence, the feeble but clear voice of the ninety-nine-year-old man, the oldest human being I'd ever encountered then, asked, "Niece, where are you taking me?"

The niece, who stood in the aisle, leaned over so he could hear her better and yelled, "To America, Uncle. We are flying to America over the Atlantic Ocean."

"*Weizmir*, oh my God, open the door," he called out with all his might, rising from his position. "I'd like to get off."

Everyone around us exploded in laughter, for a moment dulling the annoying hum of the plane engine. It was the best moment of the flight and, in fact, of our entire journey thus far.

A rare thing is ever better than laughter.

I have never forgotten that old man, who most likely did not live long after arriving to America. I remembered the lesson: real families stick together. I never forgot it. Old man's niece, I know nothing about you, but I never forgot you or your uncle's pale-haired, fragile wife. Her face is etched in my mind. Her presence kept me sane on that crossing, especially as Mama began to harass me the way she always did—and does till this day—in order to stabilize herself.

At the end, Mama drove me so completely out of balance that I needed to vomit as we were landing, causing a crunch among the stewards, who screamed, "*Idiota!*" while pointing to a vomit bag—as if I knew there was such a thing! In the USSR, I'd never seen one. Anyway, after we landed, I felt better almost immediately. I needed water, but there was none. I was overwrought with the heat, the motion sickness, the layers, Mama, the time warp, and the many people questioning us. One asked if we had any fruit. Mama said yes and showed him the remaining package of clementine oranges. He said no and showed her where to toss them. Instead, Mama started peeling the oranges and forcing me to eat them right there, at customs.

These were my first moments in the United States, combatting motion sickness and fighting Mama's force-feeding through tears of humiliation. Throughout my childhood, when we flew on planes, I always threw up either during the flight or the landing. I was used to it. I had not flown for three or four years immediately before this flight because I refused to fly. Now, to all my stress, Mama added eating. I was crying as I chewed the *mandarini*, gagging and begging her to stop. Finally, Mama threw away the remaining clementines.

Processing us was taking a long time, and we had nowhere to sit. I had not slept a wink on our crossing, and now all I wanted was to lie down. But I had the duty of carrying everything I could, because of Mama's active ulcer. I had to pull our suitcases off the carousel and drag them to where they would be checked, all while making sure that Mama was situated somewhere, not pacing, which she had been doing. By the time they were finished processing us, I was completely drained.

If there was a greeting sign "Welcome to New York," I was too upset to notice. I arrived to America with tears in my eyes and orange scent obscuring my sweat.

It was not at all a beginning I would cherish.

Epilogue

Mama and I arrived to the US in the late hours of January 10, 1980 and set our feet on the US soil for the very first time outside of the International Terminal at JFK. We were confused and scared. No wonder – our journey and future were full of uncertainty and danger. Of course, it was not nearly as dangerous as that of our predecessor generations of Jewish refugees from Eastern Europe, but we were not thinking about anyone but us. Our place in line, our seat on the bus, our room, our destination. It took a long time before I understood just how unprepared I was for life outside of the USSR. Mama never fully realized it.

Assimilation is a never-ending process. One is free to make it a daily joy, or turn it into a daily regret and succumb to nostalgia and depression. The essential point is that one is free in the US to make this choice for oneself. Mama and I still differ on that.

A Journey of a Recovering Idealist continues with *In The Land Of The Freed*, which spans the next several years of Marina's life after arrival to USA to earning US citizenship and embarking on a successful career path.

Will Marina know how to make life choices now that she is free to choose?